Normandy Lifeline

by
Val Gascoyne

£0.50

SURVIVAL BOOKS • LONDON • ENGLAND

First published 2005

Survival Books Limited, 1st Floor,
60 St James's Street, London SW1A 1ZN, United Kingdom
☎ +44 (0)20-7493 4244, 🖨 +44 (0)20-7491 0605
✉ info@survivalbooks.net
🖳 www.survivalbooks.net
To order books, please refer to page 379.

British Library Cataloguing in Publication Data.
A CIP record for this book is available
from the British Library.
ISBN 1 901130 63 0

Printed and bound in Finland by WS Bookwell Ltd.

ACKNOWLEDGEMENTS

I would like to thank the hoteliers in Normandy who made my many nights away from home so much more bearable and Peter Elias for his specialist advice. Another thank-you to my editor, Joe Laredo, who continues to stay calm – I think – when faced with my manuscripts and for his photographs that have been used in this book. Thanks also to his wife and colleague, Kerry, for designing and laying out the pages, producing the index and checking the proofs. A final thank-you to Jim Watson for his superb illustrations, maps and cover design.

TITLES BY SURVIVAL BOOKS

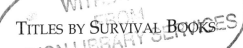

Alien's Guides
Britain; France

The Best Places To Buy A Home
France; Spain

Buying A Home
Abroad; Cyprus; Florida;
France; Greece; Ireland; Italy;
Portugal; South Africa; Spain;
Buying, Selling & Letting
Property (UK)

Foreigners Abroad: Triumphs & Disasters
France; Spain

Lifeline Regional Guides
Costa Blanca; Costa del Sol;
Dordogne/Lot; Normandy;
Poitou-Charentes

Living And Working
Abroad; America;
Australia; Britain; Canada;
The European Union;
The Far East; France; Germany;
The Gulf States & Saudi Arabia;
Holland, Belgium & Luxembourg;
Ireland; Italy; London;
New Zealand; Spain;
Switzerland

Making A Living
France; Spain

Other Titles
Renovating & Maintaining
Your French Home;
Retiring Abroad

Order forms are on page 379.

WHAT READERS & REVIEWERS HAVE SAID

If you need to find out how France works, this book is indispensable. Native French people probably have a less thorough understanding of how their country functions.

LIVING FRANCE

This book is a Godsend – a practical guide to all things French and the famous French administration – a book I am sure I will used time and time again during my stay in France.

READER

I would recommend this book to anyone considering the purchase of a French property – get it early so you do it right!

READER

Let's say it at once: David Hampshire's *Living and Working in France* is the best handbook ever produced for visitors and foreign residents in this country. It is Hampshire's meticulous detail which lifts his work way beyond the range of other books with similar titles. *Living and Working in France* is absolutely indispensable.

RIVIERA REPORTER

I found this a wonderful book crammed with facts and figures, with a straightforward approach to the problems and pitfalls you are likely to encounter. It is laced with humour and a thorough understanding of what's involved. Gets my vote!

READER

I was born in France and spent countless years there. I bought this book when I had to go back after a few years away, and this is far and away the best book on the subject. The amount of information covered is nothing short of incredible. I thought I knew enough about my native country. This book has proved me wrong. Don't go to France without it. Big mistake if you do. Absolutely priceless!

READER

If you're thinking about buying a property in France, Hampshire is totally on target. I read this book before going through the buying process and couldn't believe how perfectly his advice dovetailed with my actual experience.

READER

ABOUT OTHER SURVIVAL BOOKS ON FRANCE

In answer to the desert island question about the one how-to book on France, this book would be it.

THE RECORDER

It's just what I needed! Everything I wanted to know and even things I didn't know I wanted to know but was glad I discovered!

READER

There are now several books on this subject, but I've found that this book is definitely the best one. It's crammed with up-to-date information and seems to cover absolutely everything.

READER

Covers every conceivable question concerning everyday life – I know of no other book that could take the place of this one.

FRANCE IN PRINT

An excellent reference book for anyone thinking of taking the first steps towards buying a new or old property in France.

READER

Thankfully, with several very helpful pieces of information from this book, I am now the proud owner of a beautiful house in France. Thank God for David Hampshire!

READER

I saw this book advertised and thought I had better read it. It was definitely money well spent.

READER

We bought an apartment in Paris using this book as a daily reference. It helped us immensely, giving us confidence in many procedures from looking for a place initially to the closing, including great information on insurance and utilities. Definitely a great source!

READER

A comprehensive guide to all things French, written in a highly readable and amusing style, for anyone planning to live, work or retire in France.

THE TIMES

THE AUTHOR

Originally from Hertfordshire, Val Gascoyne worked as a retail manager before returning to college to qualify as an administrator and going on to run her own secretarial business for five years. Having spent most of her earnings on travelling, she eventually moved to France for fresh challenges, a calmer life and French neighbours. There she set up Purple Pages (see below). This book and its companions, *Poitou-Charentes Lifeline* and *Dordogne/Lot Lifeline*, are a development of that activity in collaboration with Survival Books.

Purple Pages
Grosbout, 16240 La Forêt de Tessé, France
☎ 05 45 29 59 74, UK ☎ 0871-900 8305
🖳 www.purplepages.info

This company produces tailored directories, unique to each family, which are the result of exhaustive research and contain everything you could possibly need to know about an area – from when the dustmen call and where the nearest English-speaking doctor is to be found to facilities and services for specific medical needs or sporting passions.

CONTENTS

IMPORTANT NOTE

Every effort has been made to ensure that the information contained in this book is accurate and up to date. Note, however, that businesses and organisations can be quite transient, particularly those operated by expatriates (French businesses tend to go on 'for ever'), and therefore information can quickly change or become outdated.

It's advisable to check with an official and reliable source before making major decisions or undertaking an irreversible course of action. If you're planning to travel long-distance to visit somewhere, always phone beforehand to check the opening times, availability of goods, prices and other relevant information.

Unless specifically stated, a reference to any company, organisation or product doesn't constitute an endorsement or recommendation.

Author's Notes

- Normandy is officially two regions, Upper Normandy and Lower Normandy; the term 'Normandy' in this book refers to both.

- Times are shown using the 12-hour clock, e.g. ten o'clock in the morning is written 10am and ten in the evening 10pm.

- Costs and prices are shown in euros (€) where appropriate. They should be taken as guides only, although they were accurate at the time of publication.

- Unless otherwise stated, all telephone numbers have been given as if dialling from France. To dial from abroad, use your local international access code (e.g. 00 from the UK) followed by 33 for France and omit the initial 0 of the French number.

- His/he/him/man/men (etc.) also mean her/she/her/woman/women (no offence ladies!). This is done simply to make life easier for both the reader and, in particular, the author, and isn't intended to be sexist.

- Warnings and important points are shown in **bold** type.

- The following symbols are used in this book: ☎ (telephone), 🗏 (fax), 🖳 (internet) and ✉ (email).

- British English is used throughout. French words and phrases are given in italics in brackets where appropriate and are used in preference to English where no exact equivalents exist.

- If there isn't a listing for a particular town under a given heading, this facility or service wasn't available in or near that town at the time of publication. For facilities and services that are available in most towns or are provided on a regional basis and are therefore not listed individually in the department chapters, see **Chapters 1 & 2**.

INTRODUCTION

If you're thinking of living, working, buying a home or spending an extended holiday in Normandy, this is **the book** for you. *Normandy Lifeline* has been written to answer all those important questions about life in this region that aren't answered in other books. Whether you're planning to spend a few months or a lifetime there, to work, retire or buy a holiday home, this book is essential reading.

An abundance of tourist guides and information about these departments is available, but until now it has been difficult to find comprehensive details of local costs, facilities and services, particularly in one book. *Normandy Lifeline* fills this gap and contains accurate, up-to-date, practical information about the most important aspects of daily life in the Normandy regions. If you've ever sought a restaurant that's open after 10pm, a 24-hour petrol station or something to do with your children on a wet day, this book will become your 'bible'.

Information is derived from a variety of sources, both official and unofficial, not least the hard-won experiences of the author, her friends, family and colleagues. *Normandy Lifeline* is a comprehensive handbook and is designed to make your stay in the region – however long or short – easier and less stressful. **It will also help you save valuable time, trouble and money, and will repay your investment many times over!** (For comprehensive information about living and working in France in general and buying a home in France, this book's sister publications, *Living and Working in France* and *Buying a Home in France*, written by David Hampshire, are highly recommended reading.)

Normandy is a popular holiday destination and has long been a magnet for discerning holiday homeowners; the relaxed lifestyle and quality of life attract an increasing number of foreign residents. Its countryside is lush and varied, its beaches are extensive, its cultural heritage (including the Mont Saint Michel, Bayeux Tapestry and Monet's garden) is rich, its architechture is unique and its cuisine – using seafood, apples and lashings of cream, accompanied by *pommeau*, cider and calvados – is second to none. I trust this book will help make your life easier and more enjoyable, and smooth the way to a happy and rewarding time in Normandy.

Bienvenue en Normandie!

Val Gascoyne
April 2005

Manor house, Beuvron-en-Auge

1

Introducing Normandy

This chapter is divided into two sections: Section 1, below, provides a general introduction to the area covered by this book and a brief description of each of its five departments and their main towns; Section 2, beginning on page 25, contains information about getting to (and from) the area and getting around by public transport once you're there.

OVERVIEW

The term Normandy as used here covers two regions, Upper Normandy (*Haute Normandie*) with two departments – Eure (27) and Seine-Maritime (76) – and Lower Normandy (*Basse Normandie*) with three – Calvados (14), Manche (50) and Orne (61). The location of Normandy in relation to France is shown on the map below, which includes relevant airports outside Normandy; those within Normandy are shown on the map opposite.

The map below shows the area as a whole; detailed maps of each department are included in **Chapters 3**, **4**, **5**, **6** and **7**.

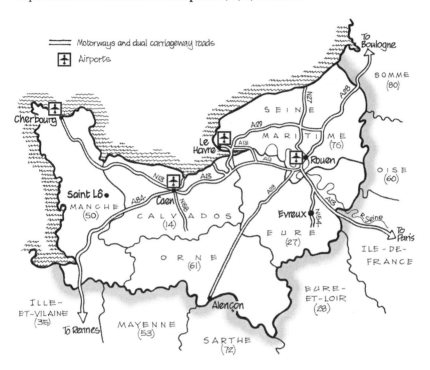

In each department, a selection of main towns has been made and facilities and services in these towns are given, although others are included where appropriate. The selected towns are geographically spread, so at least one of them should be reasonably close wherever you choose to stay or live, although not necessarily in your department. The selected towns are as follows:

Calvados (14)	Eure (27)
● **Bayeux**	● **Les Andelys**
● **Caen**	● **Bernay**
● **Falaise**	● **Evreux**
● **Lisieux**	● **Pont Audemer**
● **Vire**	

Manche (50)

- Avranches
- Barneville Carteret*
- Cherbourg Octeville*
- Coutances
- Saint Lô

Orne (61)

- L'Aigle
- Alençon
- Argentan
- Domfront
- Mortagne au Perche*

Seine-Maritime (76)

- Dieppe
- Le Havre
- Neufchâtel en Bray*
- Rouen
- Yvetot

*   Hereafter, these town names and are referred to as Barneville, Cherbourg, Mortagne and Neufchâtel.

Calvados

This department has a long coastline with numerous marinas and a wealth of watersports. Calvados boasts 120km (75mi) of beaches, ideal for bracing walks and wind sports (sand sailing is particularly popular). The beaches of Calvados are also an area of remembrance, being the landing beaches of the Allied troops in 1944, and there are many museums, cemeteries and sites in the department to commemorate D-Day (*Jour J*) and the liberation of Normandy.

Inland the fertile countryside of Calvados produces many regional products, including, of course, the spirit of the same name, plus cider and a wide variety of cheeses.

Bayeux

This town is famous for the Bayeux Tapestry, a 70m (225ft) long embroidery depicting the conquest of England by William in 1066. There's also the magnificent cathedral with its Romanesque crypt and gothic choir. Bayeux isn't far from the coastal town of Arromanches, where the remains of the artificial port that was built to assist the landing of the troops in the Second World War can be seen offshore.

Caen

The capital of Calvados, this city has trams, 'bendy' buses and a large pedestrian area overlooked by a chateau. The two abbeys, Abbaye aux Dames and Abbaye aux Hommes, were built at the instruction of William the Conqueror and his wife Mathilde, who had married against the Pope's wishes and were seeking forgiveness. Today these buildings are the city hall and the administrative offices of the regional government. On the south-eastern outskirts of Caen is Mondeville, which is one of the largest retail parks in Normandy.

Falaise

Dominated by an austere, fortress-style chateau that was the birthplace of William the Conqueror, this town straddles the valley of the Ante.

Lisieux

A large, bustling town with a cathedral and large square in the centre. There's a long pedestrian street and a little 'train' that give tours of the town. To the south of Lisieux is the Basilique Sainte Thérèse, which attracts thousands of pilgrims each year.

Vire

In the centre of Vire is the Porte Horloge de Vire – twin towers with a clock tower rising up between them – along with small side streets containing unusual shops. On the outskirts of the town is a disused railway line, now popular with cyclists and walkers.

Eure

Only an hour from Paris, this department offers forests and waterways full of wildlife, towns steeped in history, and cultural attractions, such as the house and gardens of Monet, as well as the largest market in Normandy at L'Aigle.

Les Andelys

A linear town with three distinct areas; the east with schools, apartment blocks and industry; the town centre with shops and businesses; and the old town of Le Petit Andely to the west. Le Petit Andely lies alongside the river Seine with picturesque, timbered houses in small quiet streets, watched over by the ruins of historic Château Gaillard.

Bernay

This town has one main street of shops that tends to get congested with both cars and pedestrians, whilst in the old quarter there are many second-hand and antique shops, restaurants and half-timbered houses. There's a signposted route around the town referred to as *l'eau, la pierre, le bois* (water, stone and wood) for you to explore at your own pace.

Evreux

The capital of the department, Evreux lies on the Iton river. The city centre has a harmonious mix of old and new, with the modern library tucked away by the side of the old town hall. The large Saturday market spreads out across place du Marché of this former Gallo-Roman city with its many monuments, parks and riverside walks.

Pont Audemer

A beautiful town best visited at night to appreciate the plentiful and artistic lighting of fountains, streets and little alleyways. Canals running between the houses and small bridges over the waterways give a distinct Venetian feeling. Formerly a major centre for leather tanning, the medieval side streets and half-timbered houses can be explored via a signposted route or guided tours in July and August.

Manche

The north of this department is a peninsular with Cherbourg at the top and a large regional park in the centre, surrounded by ports and beaches. Further south is the spectacular monastery of Mont St Michel overlooking the bay on which you can walk, play or horse ride. The south-east of Manche is more undulating with hills, lakes and waterfalls, a haven for fishermen and ramblers.

Avranches

With origins that go back as far as 9AD, this town is east of Mont St Michel and has vantage points across the bay. During the Second World War Avranches was the location for the break-out, led by General Patton, that caught the Germans by surprise; it's commemorated by a monument in the town at Place Patton.

Barneville

The towns of Barneville and Carteret became one in 1965, and Barneville-Carteret now has three parts; the main town centre with shops and the town hall (Le Bourg); the original town of Carteret Le Cap, including the marina (Carteret); and the small peninsula of Barneville Plage (La Plage). The peninsula is almost entirely edged with beaches and is a traditional seaside resort, the buildings dating from the time when sea bathing first became fashionable.

Cherbourg

More than just a ferry port, this town has a casino, ice rink and a road full of nightclubs overlooking the marina, right in the centre of town. With many beaches and a pleasure port offering numerous activities there's also plenty to do here, including La Cité de la Mer, where you can discover the underwater world.

Coutances

A town dominated by churches, with the 13th century cathedral in the centre flanked by the two churches of St Pierre and St Nicolas. The maze of paths in the *Jardin des Plantes* take you among Italian-style terraces and exotic trees, while the restaurants and bars offer a contrast for the evening.

Saint Lô

The capital of the department, Saint Lô has a bustling centre and an array of restaurants and cultural events. There's a replica of the Second World War parachutist who was caught on the spire of the church of Sainte Mère, and the world famous national stud (*Haras National*) is open to visitors from June to September.

Orne

One of the two departments in Normandy with no coastline, Orne has a large national park in the centre with a host of sporting activities, concerts and festivals throughout the year. Local producers in the department include organic farms, cider making, cheese and honey, plus forges and pottery and ceramic craftsmen who welcome visitors wanting to discover their trades.

L'Aigle

L'Aigle is home to one of the largest markets in France, and it's easy to get lost in the maze of streets when they're lined with market stalls. A truly international community lives in and around L'Aigle and with details from the tourist office you can take a tourist trail by car or bike across the town and surrounding areas.

Alençon

The capital of the department, Alençon has a picturesque Hôtel de Ville and other buildings. The glass domed *Halle aux Grains* is quite a landmark as you enter the town centre, which has cobbled streets leading to the detailed facade of the Église Notre Dame.

Argentan

In the heart of the Orne, this town was once a railway junction and shunting yard and has grown to be a strong industrial town with three weekly markets, a race track and an aquatic centre.

Domfront

Overlooking the valley of the river Varenne are the ruins of the 12th century chateau built by the youngest son of William the Conqueror that was later destroyed by Henri IV. The town spreads out to the east from the chateau and has several walks around the outskirts and alongside the river. A town that was once an impregnable fortress with ramparts and numerous towers is now picturesque, having maintained its narrow streets and half-timbered houses, set off with an abundance of flowers.

Mortagne

A compact town on the edge of the regional park, Mortagne has spectacular views over the surrounding countryside to the south-west and ornate gardens off rue Montacune.

Seine-Maritime

A coastal department, Seine-Maritime not only has many beaches and watersports facilities to offer but is also worth exploring further inland. The capital, Rouen, is the largest city in Normandy. The *Avenue Verte* is a 40km (25mi) route dedicated to walkers and cyclists stretching from Forges les Eaux to Dieppe.

Dieppe

The seafront at Dieppe is dominated by large bourgeois houses separated from the sea by a wide grass area and promenade, ideal for rollerblading and walking. It's a pebble beach with an outdoor pool alongside the promenade. Further along towards the marina there are numerous restaurants with seafood an obvious speciality.

Le Havre

A bustling commercial area with beautiful formal gardens and fountains in front of the town hall in the centre. In fact there are 700ha (1,750 acres) of parks, gardens and forest within the perimeters of Le Havre and four different walks linking just some of them.

Neufchâtel

A small town close to the *Avenue Verte*. Once situated on the crossroads of two major routes, it was a popular staging post and now produces one of the rarest cheeses in France.

Rouen

Rouen is a large, historic city with links to famous Impressionist painters and to Joan of Arc, who was martyred there. A busy city to drive through, it's best explored on foot, with individual shops and restaurants tucked away in small side streets. Rouen is known for its amazing lighting and is home to the oldest *auberge* in France, La Couronne, which has been serving customers since 1345.

Yvetot

A network of streets centred around the distinctive round, pink church built in 1956. Yvetot has suffered several major fires in its history that have on each occasion nearly destroyed the entire town. As a result of the last fires, in 1944, the town was re-designed, rebuilt and modernised with streets and squares carefully spaced and houses made of stone with tiled roofs, instead of timber and thatch.

GETTING THERE & GETTING AROUND

Getting There by Air

Flybe is currently the only UK airline that flies direct to Normandy (Southampton-Cherbourg), but there are numerous flights to Paris from a variety of UK airports. From Paris you can fly to Cherbourg or Rennes, hire a car (or a helicopter, if money is no object) or complete your journey by rail. Details of all three options are given in this section.

Although budget airlines can offer cheap fares, the scheduled airlines also offer some good prices and are sometimes cheaper. In late 2004, the majority of the flights listed below were under £100 return, plus airport taxes.

Air France	🖳 *www.airfrance.com*	UK	☎ 0845-084 5111
		France	☎ 08 20 82 08 20
BMI	🖳 *www.flybmi.com*	UK	☎ 0870-607 0555
		UK from abroad	☎ +44 1332-854854
British Airways	🖳 *www.britishairways.com*	UK	☎ 0870-850 9850
		France	☎ 08 25 82 50 40
Easyjet	🖳 *www.easyjet.com*	UK	☎ 0877-750 0100
		France	☎ 08 25 08 25 08
Flybe	🖳 *www.flybe.com*	UK	☎ 0871-700 0535
		UK from abroad	☎ +44 1392-268529
KLM	🖳 *www.klm.com*	UK	☎ 0870-507 4074
		France	☎ 08 90 71 07 10
Ryanair	🖳 *www.ryanair.com*	UK	☎ 0871-246 0000
		France	☎ 08 92 55 56 66
		from Ireland	☎ 0818-303030
Thomson Fly	🖳 *www.thomsonfly.com*	UK	☎ 0870-190 0737
		France	☎ 01 70 70 81 36

The following websites may help you to find low-cost flights with scheduled airlines:

- 🖳 *www.cheapflights.co.uk*
- 🖳 *www.ebookers.com*
- 🖳 *www.expedia.co.uk*
- 🖳 *www.flightline.co.uk*
- 🖳 *www.travelocity.co.uk*

Ryanair is planning to charge up to £50 for all checked-in luggage, although the limit for hand luggage has been increased to 10kg from 7kg. Easyjet allows hand luggage of any weight provided it doesn't exceed certain dimensions and you can lift it into the overhead lockers unaided.

First Luggage (☎ 0845-2700670, 🖳 *www.firstluggage.com*) is a new company offering a luggage transfer service. Your belongings are transported to your destination in conjunction with FedEx, and you're kept up-to-date with its progress. Prices start at around £25 one way and cover items such as prams, suitcases and sports equipment such as golf clubs or skis.

International Airports

There's one small international airport in Normandy and several others nearby, as listed below (department numbers are given in brackets). Note that, although Beauvais, Charles de Gaulle, Orly are called 'Paris' airports, none is in Paris!

Cherbourg (50)   Cherbourg Maupertus   ☎ 02 33 88 57 60
💻 www.aeroport-cherbourg.com

Beauvais (60)   Paris Beauvais   *Information* ☎ 08 92 68 20 64
💻 www.aeroportbeauvais.com   ☎ 03 44 11 46 90
Although called 'Paris Beauvais', this airport is in the department of Oise in Picardy, well over an hour from the centre of Paris.

Val d'Oise (95)   Charles de Gaulle   ☎ 01 43 35 70 00
💻 www.paris-cdg.com
This airport is sometimes known as Roissy, which is the name of the nearby town.

Val de Marne (94)   Orly   ☎ 01 43 35 70 00
💻 www.paris-ory.com (*sic*)

Rennes (35)   Rennes   ☎ 02 99 29 60 00
💻 www.rennes.aeroport.fr

The following tables list direct routes from England, Ireland and Scotland that were in service at the end of 2004. These are intended only as a guide, as airline services are constantly changing, and you should check with the relevant airports or airlines (see below) for the latest information.

England

From	To	Airline
Birmingham	Paris CDG	Air France, British Airways, KLM
Bournemouth	Paris CDG	Thomson Fly
Bristol	Paris CDG	British Airways, KLM
Coventry	Paris CDG	Thomson Fly
Doncaster/Sheffield	Paris CDG	Thomson Fly
Durham Tees Valley	Paris CDG	BMI

Exeter	Paris CDG	Flybe
Leeds	Paris CDG	BMI
Liverpool	Paris CDG	Easyjet
London Gatwick	Paris CDG	BMI
London Heathrow	Paris CDG	Air France, BMI, British Airways
Luton	Paris CDG	Easyjet
Manchester	Paris CDG	Air France, BMI, British Airways
Newcastle	Paris CDG	Air France, Easyjet
Southampton	Cherbourg	Flybe
	Rennes	Flybe

Ireland

From	To	Airline
Belfast	Paris CDG	BMI, Easyjet
Cork	Paris CDG	BMI
Dublin	Beauvais	Ryanair
	Paris CDG	BMI
Shannon	Beauvais	Ryanair

Scotland

From	To	Airline
Aberdeen	Paris CDG	Air France and BMI
Edinburgh	Paris CDG	Air France, BMI, British Airways
Glasgow	Beauvais	Ryanair
	Paris CDG	Air France, BMI, British Airways

Flights from Paris to Normandy include the following:

From	To	Airline
Paris Orly	Cherbourg	Air France
	Rennes	Air France

National Airports

Caen (14) Caen Carpiquet ☎ 02 31 71 20 10
www.caen.aeroport.fr
Air France flights to Lyon, with national and international connections.

Cherbourg (50) Cherbourg Maupertus ☎ 02 33 88 57 60
www.aeroport-cherbourg.com
Flights to Paris Orly with connections to the UK.

Le Havre (76) Le Havre Octeville ☎ 02 35 54 65 00
www.havre.aeroport.fr
Air France flights to Lyon, with national and international connections.

Rennes (35) Rennes ☎ 02 99 29 60 00
www.rennes.aeroport.fr
Flights to Paris Orly with connections to the UK.

Rouen (76) Rouen Vallée de Seine ☎ 02 35 79 41 00
www.rouen.aeroport.fr
Air France flights to Lyon, with national and international connections. (Rouen airport is at Boos, around 20km south-east of the city.)

Plane & Helicopter Hire

Air CB Hélicoptère Aérodrome Dieppe St Aubin ☎ 06 14 22 15 93

Air Taxi & Charter Aéroport Bourget, Le Bourget ☎ 01 49 34 10 71

Chalair Aéroport Caen Carpiquet ☎ 02 31 71 26 26
www.chalair.fr

Phénix Aviation Le Havre ☎ 02 32 85 00 81
www.phenix-aviation.biz
Flights on request and air taxi.

Car Hire

The larger towns have several car hire companies; listed below is just one company for each town. The websites of the 'big five' companies are as follows:

Avis *www.avis.fr*
Budget *www.budget.fr*
Car'Go *www.cargo.fr*

| Europcar | 🖳 *www.europcar.com* |
| Hertz | 🖳 *www.hertz.com* |

Airport-based

Beauvais	Avis	☎ 03 44 05 22 50
	Europcar	☎ 03 44 15 05 03
	Hertz	☎ 03 44 45 01 28
	National Citer	☎ 03 44 11 46 71
Cherbourg	ADA	☎ 02 33 20 65 65
	Budget	☎ 02 33 94 32 77
	Europcar	☎ 02 33 44 53 85
	Rent A Car	☎ 02 33 20 14 06
Le Havre	Avis	☎ 02 35 53 17 20
	Budget	☎ 02 32 72 70 80
	Renault Rent	☎ 02 35 53 42 49
	Rent A Car	☎ 02 35 41 76 76
Le Havre	Avis	☎ 02 35 53 17 20
	Europcar	☎ 02 35 25 21 95
	Hertz	☎ 02 35 19 01 19
	National Citer	☎ 02 35 21 30 81
Paris CDG	Avis	☎ 01 48 62 34 34
	Budget	☎ 01 48 62 70 21
	Hertz	☎ 01 48 62 29 00
	Euro Rent	☎ 01 48 62 40 77
	Europcar	☎ 01 48 62 33 33
Paris Orly	Avis	☎ 0820 61 16 19
	Budget	☎ 01 49 75 56 05
Rennes	National Citer	☎ 02 99 29 60 22
	ADA Location	☎ 02 99 27 22 22
Rouen	Europcar	☎ 02 32 08 39 09
	Hertz	☎ 02 35 70 70 71
	National Citer	☎ 02 32 10 01 22

Calvados

| Bayeux | Lefebvre Location, Station Esso, boulevard d'Eindhoven | ☎ 02 31 92 05 96 |

Open 8am to 8pm, cars, people-carriers and minibuses.

Caen	Budget, 54 place de la Gare	☎ 02 31 83 70 47

Open Mondays to Fridays 8am to noon and 2 to 7pm,
Saturdays 9am to noon and 2 to 6pm.

Falaise	ADA, Garage Collet, L'Attache	☎ 02 31 90 11 81

(opposite Super U supermarket)

Lisieux	Renault Rent, Garage MSA, rue Paul Cornu	☎ 02 31 32 44 37
Vire	Budget, Garage Renault, route de Caen	☎ 02 31 66 19 70

Eure

Les Andelys	ADA, Garage Bignon, 26 route Paix	☎ 02 32 54 35 35
Bernay	ADA, 32 rue Maurice Lemoing	☎ 02 32 44 53 27
Evreux	Rent-a-Car, 36 rue Faubourg St Léger	☎ 02 32 62 27 40

💻 *www.rentacar.fr*

Pont Audemer	Europcar, ZI rue Général Koenig	☎ 02 32 41 01 56

Manche

Avranches	ADA, 25 rue de la Liberté	☎ 02 33 58 38 00
Barneville	Budget, Carteret Yacht Club, Carteret	☎ 02 33 53 60 73
Cherbourg	Rent-a-Car, 48 quai Alexandre III	☎ 02 33 20 14 06

(facing the marina, just along from the tourist office)

Coutances	ADA, 72 rue Gambetta	☎ 02 33 07 52 52

Open Mondays to Saturdays 8am to noon and 2.30 to 7pm.

Saint Lô	Europcar Salva, 41 rue Alsace Lorraine	☎ 02 33 05 56 57

Orne

L'Aigle	ADA, ZI No. 1, route de Crulai	☎ 02 33 24 30 92
Alençon	ADA, 71 avenue de Basingstoke	☎ 02 33 80 33 90
Argentan	Renault Rent, 2 boulevard Victor Hugo	☎ 02 33 39 86 00

Domfront	Carrosserie GT, 20 rue Pressoir	☎ 02 33 38 51 43
Mortagne	Location U, Super U, route d'Alençon, St Langis lès Mortagne	☎ 02 33 25 42 44

Seine-Maritime

Dieppe	Avis, Hall de la Gare	☎ 02 32 90 94 23
Le Havre	National Citer, 91 quai de Southampton	☎ 02 35 21 30 81
Rouen	Budget, 14 avenue Jean Rondeaux	☎ 02 32 81 95 00
Yvetot	Avis Location, place de la Gare	☎ 02 35 56 82 14

Taxis

Calvados

Bayeux	Taxis du Bessin, Clos St Nicholas	☎ 02 31 92 92 40
	Taxi Station, place de la Gare	☎ 02 31 92 04 10
Caen	Abbeilles Taxis, 52 place de la Gare ✉ *taxis.abbeilles.caen@wanadoo.fr*	☎ 02 31 52 17 89
	Basourdy Taxis, 39 rue Auguste Lechesne	☎ 02 31 84 25 82
	Caen Radio Taxis, place de la Gare	☎ 02 31 94 15 15
	Costa Taxis, 22 rue du Thibet	☎ 02 31 44 48 91
	Lecacheur Taxi, 60 rue des Luthiers	☎ 02 31 47 63 19
	Station Taxis, place de la Gare	☎ 02 31 52 17 73
Falaise	Jacques Bouquend, 26 place Belle Croix	☎ 02 31 90 14 10
	Patrick Schreck, 8 rue Léonie Macary	☎ 02 31 20 39 77
Lisieux	Abbeilles Taxis, place Pierre Semard	☎ 02 31 31 23 23
	Allais Taxis, 3 bis rue Duhamel	☎ 02 31 31 02 02
	Station de Taxis, place Pierre Semard	☎ 02 31 62 00 69

	Taxi Augerons, 47 chemin du Sap	☎ 02 31 31 35 00
Vire	Taxis du Bocage, 14 place de la Gare	☎ 02 31 68 01 97
	Taxis du Centre, route des Vaux	☎ 02 31 68 02 44

Eure

Les Andelys	Taxi Accord, 1 rue Brossard de Ruville	☎ 02 32 54 06 71
Bernay	Alliance Taxis Vert, 14 rue Guy Pépin	☎ 02 32 44 59 59
	Taxi Jacky Noeyau, 52 route du Chanoine Porée	☎ 02 32 44 14 27
	Taxi Pierre Desprez, Hameau de Champeaux	☎ 02 32 43 07 24
Evreux	Taxi Alexandre Schibiness	☎ 06 07 81 85 97
	Artisans Radio Taxi d'Evreux, boulevard Gambetta	☎ 02 32 33 44 33
	Taxi Bocquet, 23 rue Val Fleuri	☎ 06 08 23 31 46
	Taxi Mainier, 66 rue Vernon	☎ 02 32 39 54 52
	Taxi Serée, place Gare	☎ 06 07 44 17 20
	Taxi Station, place de la Gare place Grand Carrefour	☎ 02 32 33 29 89 ☎ 02 32 33 29 85
Pont Audemer	Taxi de la Poste, route de St Paul	☎ 02 32 57 44 33
	Taxi Romain, 12 rue Aristide Briand	☎ 02 32 41 04 07

Manche

Avranches	Abeille Taxi, place Littré	☎ 02 33 58 77 21
	Taxi de la Baie, Précy	☎ 02 33 48 65 62
	Taxi Garnier, 26 avenue de Baffé	☎ 02 33 58 01 89
	Taxi Leblalier, Ponts sous Avranche	☎ 02 33 79 08 88
	Taxi Prime, 71 bis rue Commandant Bindel	☎ 02 33 68 32 70

Barneville	De la Côte des Isles, place Docteur Auvret, Le Bourg	☎ 02 33 04 61 02
	Taxi Davodet, 2 rue Franklin Bouillon, Carteret	☎ 02 33 53 05 30
Cherbourg	Allô Taxi Hague, 39 rue Val de Saire	☎ 02 33 43 01 01
	Cherbourg Octeville Taxis, 52 boulevard Schuman	☎ 02 33 53 36 38
	Cherbourg Taxis Communauté, 4 rue Louis Lumière	☎ 02 33 53 17 04
	JP Barrafort, 52 boulevard Robert Schumann	☎ 02 33 93 16 16
Coutances	Allô Taxi, 2 impasse Bord de Soulles	☎ 02 33 45 01 41
	Taxi la Croix Bleue, ZI du Château de la Mare	☎ 02 33 19 42 42
	Taxi Lemonnier, 41 boulevard Alsace Lorraine	☎ 02 33 07 11 11
Saint Lô	Allô Taxis, Le Petit Candol	☎ 02 33 05 07 55
	Taxi du Centre, 5 rue Fontaine Venise	☎ 02 33 55 83 92
	Taxi Guérin, 325 rue St Ghislain	☎ 02 33 05 62 48
	Taxi Lerivager, 1 rue Houssin du Manoir	☎ 02 33 05 52 43

Orne

L'Aigle	Taxi Rassant, 36 rue Clémenceau	☎ 02 33 24 00 45
	Taxi Viron, 18 bis rue Horloge	☎ 02 33 24 59 59
	Alençon Alençon Boismal Taxi, place de la Gare	☎ 06 87 68 19 85
	Alençon Cuchet Taxis, rue Gré du Moulin, St Germain du Corbéis	☎ 02 33 32 21 20

	Taxi le Roch, 48 boulevard 1er Chasseurs	☎ 02 33 28 82 28
	Taxi Ricordeau, 34 bis rue de l'Église	☎ 06 30 12 80 87
	Taxi Vesque, la Cour, Lonrai	☎ 02 33 31 09 66
Argentan	Beaudoire, 20 rue des Eperviers	☎ 02 33 67 62 98
	Durand Ruffray, 28 boulevard Carnot	☎ 02 33 36 05 62
	Pelchat, 5 rue des Roitelets	☎ 02 33 36 90 00
	Station Taxi, place Pierre Semard	☎ 02 33 36 67 67
	Taxi Loubé, 22 rue du 6 Juin	☎ 02 33 36 86 34
	Mobile	☎ 06 08 71 95 84
	Taxi Nicole Brard, 12 quater rue des Moulins	☎ 02 33 35 85 85
Domfront	Taxi Marcel Ponchon, Maison Neuve, Perrou	☎ 02 33 30 49 88
Mortagne	Taxi Mariette, ZI la Grippe	☎ 02 33 25 07 08
	Taxi Meeuwes, 4 rue Ferdinand Boyères	☎ 02 33 25 45 88

Seine-Maritime

Dieppe	Allô Arnaud Taxi, 8 rue Victor Hugo	☎ 02 35 84 80 83
	Radio Taxi Dieppoise, Pont Jehan-Ango	☎ 02 35 84 20 02
	Taxi Boivin, 19 rue de Strasbourg	☎ 06 09 31 27 98
Le Havre	Taxis du Havre	☎ 02 35 25 81 81
	This phone number is for all taxis in the town.	
Neufchâtel	Bray Taxi, 8 rue Tremblante, Esclavelles	☎ 02 35 94 28 43
	Francine Trousse, 38 Grande Rue St Jacques	☎ 02 35 93 48 63

	Taxi Duhoux, 19 rue Denoyelle	☎ 02 35 94 55 30
Rouen	Radio Taxis, 67 rue Jean Lecanuet This phone number is for all taxis in the city.	☎ 02 35 88 50 50
Yvetot	Taxi Dubigny, 31 rue Clos des Parts	☎ 02 35 95 36 46
	Taxi François, 14 rue du Clos des Parts	☎ 02 35 95 15 71
	Taxi A. Lavenu, 5 rue Clos du Manoir	☎ 02 35 95 16 74
	Taxi R. Lavenu, 43 rue du Docteur Richard	☎ 06 09 75 11 56
	Taxi Yvon, place de la Gare	☎ 06 09 39 49 59

Trains

There are trains direct from Paris Charles de Gaulle airport to Le Mans, from where you can connect to Alençon. For other destinations take the underground, bus or a taxi to the relevant station in Paris for westbound trains (see **Getting There by Rail** on page 46). For details, contact the SNCF:

SNCF   ☎ 3635
💻 *www.voyages-sncf.com*
The website has an English option and enables you to look up and book train travel both to and within France.

Getting There by Road

Channel Crossings

The ferry ports within Normandy are (from west to east) Cherbourg, Caen, Le Havre and Dieppe; Boulogne and Calais are to the north-east and St Malo to the west. The Channel Tunnel runs from Coquelles near Calais. The main carriers are detailed below.

As an alternative to booking direct with a ferry company or Eurotunnel, you can use one of several companies that will help you to obtain the cheapest fare. These include:

💻 *www.ferrycrossings-uk.co.uk*   UK ☎ 0871-222 8642
💻 *www.cheap4ferries.co.uk*   UK ☎ 0870-700 0138
💻 *www.ferry-crossings-online.co.uk*

Route	Method	Crossing Time	Company
Dover/Calais	Tunnel	35 minutes	Eurotunnel
	Fast ferry	1hour	Hoverspeed
	Ferry	1 hour 15 minutes	P&O, Seafrance
Dover/Boulogne	Fast ferry	50 minutes	Speed Ferries
Newhaven/Dieppe	Ferry	4 hours	Transmanche
Plymouth/Cherbourg*	Ferry	8 hours overnight	Brittany Ferries
Plymouth/St Malo*	Ferry	9 hours 30 minutes overnight	Brittany Ferries
Poole/Cherbourg	Ferry	2 hours 15 minutes	Condor Ferries
Poole/St Malo	Fast ferry	4 hours 35 minutes	Condor Ferries
Portsmouth/Caen	Ferry	5 hours 45 minutes	Brittany Ferries
Portsmouth/Cherbourg	Ferry	4 hours 45 minutes	Brittany Ferries/Condor Ferries
Portsmouth/St Malo	Ferry	8 hours 45 m inutes	Brittany Ferries
Rosslare/Cherbourg	Cruiser	18 hours 30 minutes	Irish Ferries
Weymouth/St Malo	Fast ferry	5 hours 15 minutes	Condor Ferries

*   Routes from Plymouth to Cherbourg and St Malo haven't yet been confirmed for 2005.

Brittany Ferries   🖳 *www.brittany-ferries.co.uk*   *UK*   ☎ 0870-366 5333
                                                        France ☎ 08 25 82 88 28
Ferries from Portsmouth to St Malo, Caen and Cherbourg, Poole to Cherbourg, and provisionally Portsmouth to Le Havre.

Property Owners' Travel Club UK   ☎ 0870-514 3555
Brittany Ferries' Property Owners' Travel Club offers savings of up to 33 per cent on passenger and vehicle fares and three guest vouchers for friends, providing up to 15 per cent savings on standard fares. There's a one-off registration fee of £35 and a £45 annual membership fee.

Condor Ferries   🖥 *www.condorferries.co.uk*   *UK*   ☎ 0845-345 2000

Fast ferries operate on most routes from February to the end of December. Crossings from Poole to Cherbourg and from Poole or Weymouth to St Malo are via the Channel Islands. A Portsmouth to Cherbourg ferry operates on Sundays from mid-July to the second week in September.

Frequent Traveller Membership entitles you to a 20 per cent discount on all Channel crossings and a 10 per cent discount between the Channel Islands and France. Annual membership costs £66 for an individual plus £20 for a spouse.

Eurotunnel   🖥 *www.eurotunnel.co.uk*   *UK*   ☎ 0870-535 3535
   France ☎ 0810 63 03 04
UK lines are open Mondays to Fridays 8am to 7pm, Saturdays and bank holidays 8am to 5.30pm, Sundays 9am to 5.30pm. French lines open Mondays to Saturdays 9am to 5.30pm. There are two or three crossings per hour during the day and less frequent crossings during the night.

Note: Eurotunnel doesn't allow vehicles that use LPG or are dual-powered. Campervans and caravans that have bottled gas for appliances, are accepted provided bottles are switched off and disconnected.

As from 2005 Eurotunnel have withdrawn all loyalty schemes, intending to make all fares more competitive.

Hoverspeed   🖥 *www.hoverspeed.com*   *UK*   ☎ 0870-240 8070
   France   ☎ 03 21 46 14 54
The fast ferry operates from mid-March to mid-December, up to eight crossings a day in high season.

Note: There's a Frequent User loyalty scheme which offers a 20 per cent discount with free membership, but you need three booking references of crossings taken within the last six months to qualify.

Irish Ferries   🖥 *www.irishferries.com*   Irish Rep. ☎ 0818-300400
   N. Ireland ☎ 08705-171717
   France   ☎ 02 33 23 44 44
Ferries from Rosslare to Cherbourg daily.

Note: There's a Business Travellers' Scheme that credits you 10 per cent of your total expenditure to use against future travel if you cross six times or more in any 12-month period.

P&O Ferries   🖥 *www.poferries.com*   *UK*   ☎ 0871-2002 444
   France ☎ 08 25 12 01 56

P&O has cut many routes recently and the future of the Portsmouth/Le Havre route is still undecided; it may be taken over by Brittany Ferries. The Dover/Calais route has crossings every day except Christmas day.

Homeowner Traveller   *UK*   ☎ 0870-6000 613
This loyalty scheme gives up to 30 per cent discount for the member, friends and family.

Season Ticket   *UK*   ☎ 0870-600 0613
If you travel to France five times or more per year, you can save money by block booking five return crossings for £120 each, which are fully flexible up to 24 hours before travel. Up to five tickets per year can be assigned to friends and family. Free registration.

Sea France   🖳 *www.seafrance.co.uk*   *UK*   ☎ 08705-711711
                                               France ☎ 08 03 04 40 45
Ferry crossings all year, up to fifteen each day in high season, crossing times vary between 70 and 90 minutes depending on the vessel.

Speed Ferries   🖳 *www.speedferries.com*   *UK*   ☎ 0870-220 0570
                                               France ☎ 03 21 10 50 00
This is a 50-minute fast ferry service that operates between Dover and Boulogne. One way fares start from £25 for a car and passengers. Suitable for cars, motorbikes, small camper vans and small trailers. There are three crossings a day throughout the year with five from mid-March to September. UK lines open Mondays to Fridays 9am to 7pm, Saturdays and Sundays from 10am to 5pm. There's a £10 charge for bookings made through the call centre.

Transmanche Ferries 🖳 *www.transmancheferries.com* *UK*   ☎ 0800-917 1201
                                               France ☎ 08 00 65 01 00
Three crossings daily from Newhaven to Dieppe Mondays to Thursdays, two a day Fridays to Sundays.

Suggested Routes

Suggested routes from each port to the main town in each department (in numerical order of department) are given below. These are based on an average driving speed of 120kph (75mph) on motorways and 80kph (50mph) on other roads. Costs are based on fuel at €1.15 per litre and fuel consumption of 30mpg in towns and 40mpg on main roads.

Note: If you're travelling in a GPL-powered vehicle to Rouen from the north-east on the A28, you must leave the motorway just before entering the city to avoid a tunnel that doesn't allow GPL vehicles.

From Calais

● Calais ➔ Caen

Suggested Route
A16 down the coast to Abbeville
A28/A29 towards Le Havre
Stay on A29 to the A13
A13 to Caen

Summary
Distance: 346km (213mi)
Time: 3 hours, 5 minutes
Cost: €33 plus tolls (€21)

● Calais ➔ Evreux

Suggested Route
A16 down the coast to Abbeville
A28 to Rouen
D18 down through Rouen
Join the A13 at junction 21 towards Paris
At junction 19 take the A154 to Evreux

Summary
Distance: 266km (167mi)
Time: 2 hours, 50 minutes
Cost: €29 plus tolls (€8)

● Calais ➔ Saint Lô

Suggested Route
A16 down the coast to Abbeville
A28/A29 towards Le Havre
Stay on A29 to the A13
A13 to Caen
N184 north around Caen, direction Bayeux
N13 to junction 37
D572 & D972 to Saint Lô

Summary
Distance: 406km (252mi)
Time: 3 hours, 55 minutes
Cost: €45 plus tolls (€21)

● Calais ➔ Argentan

Suggested Route
A16 down the coast to Abbeville
A28 to Rouen
A28/N138 towards Alençon
At Gacé, D14 & N26 to Argentan

Summary
Distance: 348km (216mi)
Time: 3 hours, 45 minutes
Cost: €38 plus tolls (€6.30)

● Calais ➔ Rouen

Suggested Route
A16 down the coast to Abbeville
A28 to Rouen

Summary
Distance: 214km (132mi)
Time: 2 hours
Cost: €22 plus tolls (€6.30)

From Boulogne

● Calais ➔ Boulogne

Suggested Route
A16 down the coast to Abbeville
A28/A29 towards Le Havre
Stay on A29 to the A13
A13 to Caen

Summary
Distance: 310km (191mi)
Time: 2 hours, 35 minutes
Cost: €30 plus tolls (€21)

● Boulogne ➔ Evreux

Suggested Route
A16 down the coast to Abbeville
A28 to Rouen
D18 down through Rouen
Join the A13 at junction 21 towards Paris
At junction 19 take the A154 to Evreux

Summary
Distance: 230km (145mi)
Time: 2 hours, 20 minutes
Cost: €26 plus tolls (€8)

● Boulogne ➔ Saint Lô

Suggested Route
A16 down the coast to Abbeville
A28/A29 towards Le Havre
Stay on A29 to the A13
A13 to Caen
N184 north around Caen, direction Bayeux
N13 to junction 37
D572 & D972 to Saint Lô

Summary
Distance: 370km (230mi)
Time: 3 hours, 25 minutes
Cost: €42 plus tolls (€21)

● Boulogne ➔ Argentan

Suggested Route
A 16 down the coast to Abbeville
A28 to Rouen
A28/N138 direction Alençon
At Gacé, D14 & N26 to Argentan

Summary
Distance: 312km (194mi)
Time: 3 hours, 15 minutes
Cost: €35 plus tolls (€6.30)

● Boulogne ➔ Rouen

Suggested Route
A16 down the coast to Abbeville
A28 to Rouen

Summary
Distance: 178km (110mi)
Time: 1 hour 30 minutes
Cost: €19 plus tolls (€6.30)

From Dieppe

● Dieppe ➔ Caen

Suggested Route
N27 to the A29 towards Caen
Stay on A29 to the A13
A13 to Caen

Summary
Distance: 186km (114mi)
Time: 1 hour, 50 minutes
Cost: €19 plus tolls (€13)

● Dieppe ➔ Evreux

Suggested Route
N27 south
After Tôtes it becomes the A151 to Rouen
Join the A150 into Rouen
N138 through Rouen
A13 towards Paris
At junction 19 take the A154 to Evreux

Summary
Distance: 118km (73mi)
Time: 1 hour, 25 minutes
Time: 1 hour, 25 minutes
Cost: €15 plus tolls (€1.80)

● Dieppe ➔ Saint Lô

Suggested Route
N27 south to join the A29
Stay on A29 to the A13
A13 to Caen
N184 north around Caen, direction Bayeux
N13 to junction 37
D572 & D972 to Saint Lô

Summary
Distance: 246km (152mi)
Time: 2 hours, 40 minutes
Cost: €27 plus tolls (€13.50)

● Dieppe ➔ Argentan

Suggested Route
N27 south
After Tôtes it becomes the A151 to Rouen
Join the A150 into Rouen
N138 through Rouen
A28/N138 towards Alençon
At Gacé, D14 & N26 to Argentan

Summary
Distance: 194km (120mi)
Time: 2 hours, 30 minutes
Cost: €24 (no tolls)

● Dieppe ➔ Rouen

Suggested Route
N27 south
After Tôtes it becomes the A151
Join the A150 to Rouen

Summary
Distance: 65km (39mi)
Time: 50 minutes
Cost: €5.50 (no tolls)

From Caen

● Caen ➜ Evreux

Suggested Route
D514 towards Caen
N814 north around Caen towards Rouen
N13 past Lisieux to Evreux

Summary
Distance: 124 km (77mi)
Time: 1 hour, 45 minutes
Cost: €15 (no tolls)

● Caen ➜ Saint Lô

Suggested Route
D514 towards Caen
N184 north around Caen towards Bayeux
N13 to junction 37
D572 & D972 to Saint Lô

Summary
Distance: 73km (45mi)
Time: 1 hour, 5 minutes
Cost: €6 (no tolls)

● Caen ➜ Argentan

Suggested Route
D514 towards Caen
N158 to Argentan

Summary
Distance: 69km (41mi)
Time: 1 hour
Cost: €5 (no tolls)

● Caen ➜ Rouen

Suggested Route
D514 towards Caen
A13 towards Rouen
Exit at junction 23
N138 into Rouen

Summary
Distance: 136km (84mi)
Time: 1 hour, 20 minutes
Cost: €8 plus tolls (€7)

From Cherbourg

● Cherbourg ➜ Caen

Suggested Route
N13 to Caen

Summary
Distance: 124km (76mi)
Time: 1 hour, 30 minutes
Cost: €10 (no tolls)

● Cherbourg ➜ Evreux

Suggested Route
N13 to Caen
N814 north around Caen towards Rouen

Summary
Distance: 247km (153mi)
Time: 3 hours, 10 minutes

Continue past the junction to the A13
N13 past Lisieux to Evreux

Cost: €24 (no tolls)

● Cherbourg ➔ Saint Lô

Suggested Route
N13 to Carentan
Take the third exit, the N174 to Carentan
N174 into Saint Lô

Summary
Distance: 78km (48mi)
Time: 1 hour, 10 minutes
Cost: €7 (no tolls)

● Cherbourg ➔ Argentan

Suggested Route
N13 to Caen
N814 south around Caen towards Le Mans
N158 to Argentan

Summary
Distance: 182km (113mi)
Time: 2 hours, 10 minutes
Cost: €16 (no tolls)

● Cherbourg ➔ Rouen

Suggested Route
N13 to Caen
N814 around the north of Caen
A13 to Rouen
Exit at junction 23
N138 into Rouen

Summary
Distance: 248km (154mi)
Time: 2 hours, 55 minutes
Cost: €21 plus tolls (€7)

From St Malo

● St Malo ➔ Caen

Suggested Route
N176 to Pontorson
N175 to Avranches
A84 to Caen

Summary
Distance: 172km (106mi)
Time: 1 hour, 55 minutes
Cost: €16 (no tolls)

● St Malo ➔ Evreux

Suggested Route
N176 to Pontorson
N175 to Avranches
A84 to Caen
N814 south around Caen towards Le Mans
N13 past Lisieux to Evreux

Summary
Distance: 295km (183mi)
Time: 3 hours, 25 minutes
Cost: €27 (no tolls)

● St Malo ➔ Saint Lô

Suggested Route
N176 to Pontorson
N175 to Avranches
A84 to junction 38
D999 to Saint Lô

Summary
Distance:128km (79mi)
Time: 1 hours, 40 minutes
Cost: €9 (no tolls)

● St Malo ➜ Argentan

Suggested Route
N176 to Pontorson
N175 to Ducey
N176 to St Hilaire du Harcouët
D977 to Mortain
D157 & D25 to Flers
D924 to Argentan

Summary
Distance: 175km (108mi)
Time: 2 hours, 45 minutes
Cost: €15 (no tolls)

● St Malo ➜ Rouen

Suggested Route
N176 to Pontorson
N175 to Avranches
A84 to Caen
N814 south around Caen towards Le Mans
A13 to Rouen
Exit at junction 23
N138 into Rouen

Summary
Distance: 297km (184mi)
Time: 3 hours, 20 minutes
Cost: €25 plus tolls (€7)

Tolls & Télépéage

At toll booths (*péage*) there are lanes marked '*CB*' (for *carte bancaire*), which accept British credit cards and are a usually a faster option than a manned kiosk. No signature or PIN are required.

If you travel regularly on French motorways, it's worth considering Télépéage to avoid queuing at toll booths and, in some cases, qualify for discounts. With the standard contract there's no discount on the price per kilometre but the advantage is that you no longer have to queue up to pay, as you can use a dedicated lane. There are various other contracts that give discounts of up to 40 per cent on your journey, but these are primarily for commuters. An invoice is sent out monthly. If you use this system and your average speed between tolls exceeds the limit, you may receive a speeding penalty soon after your monthly bill!

You must pay a deposit of €30 for a disc that fits to your windscreen, then an annual subscription of €20. To sign up you must visit a Télépéage office, which are usually to one side of the toll booths. You will be given an application form and an authorisation request for a direct debit from a French bank account to complete and must provide your bank account details (*relevé d'identité bancaire/RIB*). The disc will be available within around 20 minutes. Alternatively, go to the website (🖳 *www.cofiroute.fr*) and click on 'Liber-t & Subscription'. The same disc can be used at all *péages* across France.

Motorway Information

🖳 *www.autoroutes.fr* – This is a comprehensive site giving weather and traffic conditions and it even has webcams showing the level of traffic on various sections of the motorway network.

Getting There by Rail

| Eurostar | 🖳 *www.eurostar.co.uk* | *UK* ☎ 08705-186186 |
| | | *France* ☎ 08 92 35 35 39 |

The Eurostar travels from Waterloo (London) and Ashford to both Lille and Paris. However, there are no direct routes from Lille to this region, so it's better to travel to Paris, from where you can connect to Normandy. There are one or two trains per hour and the journey time to Paris Gare du Nord is around two-and-a-half hours. Once in Paris you then take the underground, a bus or a taxi to the relevant station for a westbound train, as shown below.

Destination	Paris Station	Route
Calvados		
Bayeux	St Lazare	Direct
Caen	St Lazare	Direct
Lisieux	St Lazare	Direct
Vire	Vaugirard	Direct
Eure		
Bernay	St Lazare	Direct
Evreux	St Lazare	Direct
Manche		
Avranches	St Lazare	Change at Caen
Cherbourg	St Lazare	Direct

Coutances	St Lazare	Change at Lison
Saint Lô	St Lazare	Change at Lison
Orne		
L'Aigle	Vaugirard	Direct
Alençon	Vaugirard & Montparnasse	Change at Le Mans
Argentan	Vaugirard	Direct
Seine-Maritime		
Dieppe	St Lazare	Change at Rouen
Le Havre	Massy Palaiseau	Direct
Rouen	Massy Palaiseau	Direct
Yvetot	Massy Palaiseau	Direct

There are no railway stations at Les Andelys, Barneville, Domfront, Falaise, Mortagne, Neufchâtel or Pont Audemer.

For details of mainline train services, contact the SNCF:

SNCF   ☎ 3635
🖳 *www.voyages-sncf.com*
The website has an English option and enables you to look up and book train travel both to and within France.

Station telephone numbers are no longer published and you must dial the number above, which provides details of trains, timetables, tickets and all other train-related information.

Getting Around

Buses in the region are primarily to serve the schools and colleges and so the routes pass not only the schools but in many cases railway stations as well. Unfortunately, this also means that there's a drastic reduction (if not a total cessation) in services on some routes during school holidays. Timetables are usually displayed at bus stops and can be obtained from tourist offices or the relevant transport company's offices. For details of taxi services, see page 32.

Local Trains

Ter Basse Normandie operates a local rail network in conjunction with the SNCF.

Ter Basse Normandie   ☎ 3635
🖳 *www.ter-sncf.com/Basse_normandie*
🖳 *www.ter-sncf.com/Haute_normandie*

Two comprehensive regional transport guides (one for Lower Normandy and one for Upper Normandy), called *Guide Régional des Transports*, which include details of local transport services and timetables for trains and buses, are available from railway and bus stations.

Buses & Trams

Calvados

General   Bus Verts du Calvados, ZI Sud-Est,
               rue des Frères Lumière, Mondeville   ☎ 08 10 21 42 14
               🖳 *www.busverts14.fr*
               This bus service covers the whole department and has depots
               in Bayeux, Caen, Deauville and Lisieux.

Bayeux   Bybus, place de la Gare   ☎ 02 31 92 02 92
               Local bus with routes across the town.

               Bus Verts, Gare Routière, place de
               la Gare   ☎ 08 10 21 42 14
               (next to the railway station)

Caen   Bus Verts, Gare Routière, rue
               R. Bastion   ☎ 08 10 21 42 14
               (next to the railway station, south-east of the city centre)

               Twisto, 15 rue de Geôle   ☎ 02 31 15 55 55
               🖳 *www.twisto.fr*
               🖳 *www.caen.fr/infos_pratiques*
               A tram service that runs across the city. The websites have
               details of timetables, route planners and special offers. The
               office is open Mondays to Fridays 7.15am to 6.45pm,
               Saturdays 10am to 5.45pm.

Lisieux   Bus Verts, Gare Routière, place François
               Mitterrand   ☎ 08 10 21 42 14

Vire   Amibus   ☎ 02 31 68 00 50
               Local bus service with three routes through and around the town.

Eure

Les Andelys   Cars Jacquemard   ☎ 02 32 14 09 09
Local buses. Timetable available from the tourist office.

Bernay   Bernay Bus   ☎ 02 32 46 63 00
Service operated by the town, using minibus-size vehicles.

Evreux   Trans Urban, 1 rue Jean Jaurès   ☎ 02 32 31 34 36
Local bus service in and around the town.

Manche

General   Autocars   ☎ 02 33 44 32 22
Various routes across the department, including Barneville and Cherbourg.

Cherbourg   Zéphir Bus, 40 boulevard Schumann   ☎ 08 10 81 00 50
🖥 www.zephirbus.com
Local bus service that covers Cherbourg and the surrounding areas.

Orne

General   CapOrne, STAO, 13 rue Lazare Carnot, Alençon   ☎ 02 33 80 09 09
🖥 www.cg61.fr
Bus service that covers the whole department.

Alençon   Alto Buses, Espace Alto, Maison d'Ozé   ☎ 02 33 26 03 00
🖥 www.altobus.com
Local bus service that covers Alençon and the surrounding area.

Argentan   Argentan Bus, Hôtel de Ville   ☎ 02 33 36 07 11
🖥 www.argentan.fr
Local bus service with four routes around the town.

Seine-Maritime

General   Airplus, 16, rue Manchon Frères, Rouen   ☎ 08 20 90 23 80
🖥 www.airplus76.com
Shuttle service between Rouen, Dieppe, Le Havre and the railway stations and airports of Paris.

Dieppe   Stradibus, 56 quai Duquesne   ☎ 02 32 14 03 03
Local bus service in and around Dieppe.

Créabus, 56 quai Duquesne   ☎ 02 32 14 09 09
Bus service that you call to arrange your transport Mondays to Saturdays.

| Le Havre | Bus Océane, Hôtel de Ville | ☎ 02 35 22 34 00 |

Local bus service in and around the town.

| Rouen | Métrobus, 9 rue Jeanne d'Arc | ☎ 02 32 08 30 57 |

🖳 *www.tcar.fr*
Local bus service in and around the city.

Bus de Minuit, avenue de Bretagne,
St Sever ☎ 02 35 52 52 52
🖳 *www.tcar.fr*
Night bus service that runs from 11pm to 1am with a route
through the centre of the city.

2

General Information

This chapter lists useful general information in alphabetical order – detailed information relating to each department is contained, under similar headings, in **Chapters 3** to **7**.

Accommodation

Chateaux

Bienvenue au Château
💻 *www.bienvenue-au-chateau.com*
This website is available in English and gives details of château accommodation in the north and western areas of France.

Gîtes and Bed & Breakfast

Tourist offices have details of bed and breakfast facilities (B&B) in the area and may display information in their window. Many tourist office websites have details of *gîtes* and B&B (see page 99). Some communes have *gîtes* available for renting via the *mairie*.

The following websites list both *gîte* and B&B accommodation, the majority of which you can book online.

💻 *www.clevacances.fr*
💻 *www.frenchconnections.co.uk*
💻 *www.gites-de-france.com*
💻 *www.holidayhomes-france.co.uk*
💻 *www.ouestfrance-vacances.com*
💻 *www.pour-les-vacances.com*

Hotels

Most French hotels charge per room rather than per person. All prices given in the following chapters are therefore per room unless otherwise stated.

National Chains

Formule 1   ☎ 08 92 68 56 85
💻 *www.hotelformule1.com*

Hôtel de France   ☎ 01 41 39 22 23
💻 *www.hotel-france.com*

Hôtel Première Classe   ☎ 08 25 00 30 03
💻 *www.envergure.fr*

Ibis Hotels ☎ www.ibishotel.com	☎ 08 92 68 66 86
Mercure ☎ www.mercure.com	☎ 08 25 88 33 33 From UK ☎ 0870-609 0965
Novotel ☎ www.novotel.com	☎ 08 25 88 44 44 From UK ☎ 0870-609 0962

Long-term Rentals

If you're coming to France house-hunting and have already sold up in your home country, you may be looking for a property to rent long term. There are many *gîtes* (see above) that are empty for long periods, and you may be able to arrange a long let with the owners, even across the summer period, as they may prefer to have a guaranteed income for a long period than unpredictable short-term rentals. Prices are higher near the coast than in the large inland towns, a two-bedroom house near Dieppe costing around €600 per month, a similar property in Rouen only €450.

Most large estate agents have properties to rent with contacts from six months upwards. There's a small monthly charge, generally less than 10 per cent of the rent, plus a one-off fee to the estate agent.

Local classified newspapers such as *le 14, le 50, le 61, le 76, le Caen Poche, Le Havre en Poche, Eure Inter Annonces* and *Paru Vendu* have advertisements for properties to rent.

Properties can be found on notice boards in *mairies* or shop windows. *Mairies* may also handle *gîte* accommodation that can be let on a long-term basis.

Villages de vacances are either mobile homes or chalet-type accommodation, often alongside campsite facilities, which can provide inexpensive long-term accommodation. These can be found in the yellow pages or via tourist offices. The larger complexes, with indoor pools and comprehensive facilities, accommodate holiday makers all year round, so it's usually the smaller, more basic sites that offer good rates out of season.

Administration

Regional Capitals

Caen	Conseil Régional de Basse Normandie, Abbaye aux Dames, place Reine Mathilde ☎ 02 31 06 98 98

 ☐ *www.cr-basse-normandie.fr*

Rouen

Conseil Régional de Haute Normandie, 5 rue
Robert Schumann,   ☎ 02 35 52 56 00
☐ *www.cr-haute-normandie.fr*

Préfectures

The *préfecture* is the administrative centre for each department and is
located in the department's main city. You may need to contact or visit the
préfecture or *sous-préfecture* (see below) to register ownership of a new car
or apply for planning permission.

Calvados

rue Daniel Huet, Caen   ☎ 02 31 30 64 00
☐ *www.calvados.pref.gouv.fr*

Eure

boulevard Georges Chauvin, Evreux ☎ 02 32 78 27 27
☐ *www.eure.pref.gouv.fr*

Manche

3 place de la Préfecture, Saint Lô   ☎ 02 33 75 49 50
☐ *www.manche.pref.gouv.fr*

Orne

39 rue St Blaise, Alençon   ☎ 02 33 80 61 61
☐ *www.orne.pref.gouv.fr*

Seine-Maritime

7 place Madeleine, Rouen   ☎ 02 32 76 50 00
☐ *www.seine-maritime.pref.gouv.fr*

Sous-préfectures

Calvados

Bayeux	7 place Charles de Gaulle	☎ 02 31 51 40 50
Lisieux	24 boulevard Carnot	☎ 02 31 31 66 00
Vire	rue des Cordeliers	☎ 02 31 66 37 00

Eure

Les Andelys	rue de la Sous-Préfecture	☎ 02 32 54 74 87
Bernay	2 rue Alexandre	☎ 02 32 46 76 87

Manche

Avranches	place Daniel Huet	☎ 02 33 79 04 40
Cherbourg	106 rue Emmanuel Liais	☎ 02 33 87 81 81
Coutances	rue Palais de Justice	☎ 02 33 19 08 80

Orne

| Argentan | 8 rue du Point du Jour | ☎ 02 33 12 22 00 |
| Mortagne | 1 rue du Faubourg St Eloi | ☎ 02 33 85 20 70 |

Seine-Maritime

| Dieppe | 5 rue 8 Mai 1945 | ☎ 02 35 06 30 00 |
| Le Havre | 95 boulevard de Strasbourg | ☎ 02 35 13 34 56 |

Town Halls (Mairies)

All French towns have a *hôtel de ville*, which is the equivalent of a town hall, and most villages have a *mairie*, which has no equivalent in the UK (and certainly isn't a 'village hall'!). To avoid confusion, we have used the French word *mairie* to apply to both town hall and *mairie* unless otherwise specified. The 'mayor' of a town or village is *Monsieur* or *Madame le Maire* (yes, even a female mayor is '*le Maire*'!).

Although *mairies* are usually open Mondays to Fridays, the opening hours vary greatly and in small communes they may be open only two or three times a week. There's usually a function room (*une salle des fêtes* or *salle polyvalente*), attached to the town hall/*mairie* or close by. Notice boards at *mairies* are used for formal notices, while local shops usually display a variety of posters for local events.

The *Maire* is the equivalent of a British mayor but is usually more accessible and has more immediate authority in the community. If you buy or rent a property in a small community, you should visit the *mairie* at the earliest opportunity to introduce yourselves to the *Maire*.

Local rules and regulations can be surprising strict; some communes can even stipulate the colour you paint your front door. So if you're considering making any alterations to your house or boundaries, it's essential to contact the *mairie* before undertaking any work or even drawing up plans. Full details of the required procedures are described in **Renovating & Maintaining Your French Home** (see page 379). The *mairie* should also be your first port of call if you need any advice, as they're a mine of useful information and, if they haven't got what you need, will either get it for you or point you in the right direction.

Embassies & Consulates

| British Embassy | 35 rue du Faubourg St Honoré, Paris | ☎ 01 44 51 31 00 |
| | 🖳 *www.britishembassy.gov.uk* | |

Banks

The majority of French banks close for lunch and are open on Saturday mornings. Banks are rarely open on Mondays and in small towns may be open only in the mornings or even for just a few sessions a week. Below are the names of the most commonly found banks, with a web address and a central contact number (if available) to allow you to find the branch closest to you.

Banque Populaire   🖳 *www.banquepopulaire.fr*
To find your local branch click on '*Nos Agences*' and then on the map.

BNP Paribas   🖳 *www.bnpparibas.net*   ☎ 08 20 82 00 01
To find your nearest branch click on '*trouver une agence*'.

Banque Tarneaud   🖳 *www.tarneaud.fr*   ☎ 08 10 63 28 28
To find your nearest branch click on '*recherche d'agence*'.

Caisse d'Epargne   🖳 *www.caissedepargne.com*

Crédit Agricole   🖳 *www.creditagricole.fr*
To find your nearest branch, on the front page of the site use the box in the top right corner with the map of France.

Crédit Lyonnais   🖳 *www.creditlyonnais.fr*   ☎ 08 21 80 90 90

Crédit Mutuel   🖳 *www.cmso.com*   ☎ 08 21 01 10 12

Société Générale   🖳 *www.societegenerale.fr*   ☎ 01 53 30 79 17

English-language Banks

Britline   15 esplanade Brillaud de Laujardière,
14050 Caen   ☎ 02 31 55 67 89
🖳 *www.britline.com*

Britline is a branch of Crédit Agricole and is located in Caen. It's an English-language bank with some of its forms in English, although most forms and its newsletter are in French. However, an English-speaking teller always answers the telephone.

Note that apart from those in Calvados, branches of Crédit Agricole aren't always familiar with dealing with Britline and, unless you live in the department of Calvados, you cannot pay in cheques at your local branch. To pay a cheque into your Britline account you need to post it to Britline at the above address. Withdrawals, however, are possible through any Crédit

Agricole cash machine. As more and more Crédit Agricole branches have English-speaking staff, you may find opening an account locally more advantageous.

Barclays Bank   15 rue Jeanne d'Arc, Rouen   ☎ 02 35 71 70 63
                       💻 *www.barclaysbank.fr*
                       This site has information available in English; go to
                       'Destination France'.

General Information

French banking is quite different from banking in the UK. The most noticeable differences are the following:

- French cheques are laid out differently (the amount precedes the payee), and you must state the town where the cheque was written. Note also that, when writing figures, a comma is used in place of a decimal point and a point or space instead of a comma in thousands, e.g. €1.234,56 or €1 234,56.

- You may have to press a button or even enter a code to gain access to a bank.

- Most banks have open-plan desks with receptionists who handle minimal amounts of cash; most cash transactions are carried out by machine. Some banks don't have any cash at the counter. If you want to withdraw money, you're given a card, which you take to a cash machine. This system doesn't always enable you to withdraw the exact amount you want, e.g. €20 or €40, but not €36.

- Receipts aren't always issued when paying in money without a paying-in slip, so ask for a paying-in book (or simply ask for a receipt – *un reçu*).

- When you open an account, you will be given copies of your *relevé d'identité bancaire* (normally called *un RIB* – pronounced 'reeb'), which contains all your account details. As you will need to provide a *RIB* when setting up a direct debit or an account (e.g. with a shop) and when asking anyone (e.g. an employer) to pay money into your account, it's wise to take extra copies.

- There are no cheque guarantee cards, although many shops now insist on identification with cheques.

- Cheques are guaranteed for payment in France, but if you write a cheque without sufficient funds in your account (unless you have an authorised overdraft facility) it may result in a registered letter being sent by the bank demanding that funds are paid into the account within 30 days. If this happens again within 12 months, the account will be closed and you will be unable to hold any account in France for a year and will be blacklisted for three years. You've been warned!

- It's wise to keep at least €30 in your account at all times to cover any unexpected charges. For example, some banks charge to transfer money between accounts of the same bank while others charge each time you access your account online and up to €15 just to 'accept' a letter from you confirming that you've cancelled a direct debit with a third party.

- If your cheque book is lost or stolen, irrespective of which bank you use, call ☎ 08 92 68 32 08 between 8am and 11pm.

Opening a French bank account will provide many benefits – not least the provision of a debit card (*une carte bleue*), which has a microchip and requires you to enter a four-digit PIN rather than sign a receipt. Such a card enables you to use automated petrol pumps (see page 74) and will save you embarrassment and hassle in shops where the staff are unfamiliar with UK credit cards and either won't accept them or don't know how to 'swipe' them. Most *cartes bleues* can be used all over Europe.

Moneo

Moneo is a system designed to eliminate the need to carry small change. A Moneo card has an annual cost of €8 and is then 'charged' with up to €100. It can be used to buy a newspaper, a loaf of bread or even a bar of chocolate in shops, cafés, newsagents and bakeries displaying the Mon€o sign, of which there's an increasing number. The card can be used for purchases up to €30 and, once the credit is used, it can be re-charged at your bank. Cards are ordered from your bank; you must have a French bank account to obtain one.

Business Services

Employment Agencies

Agence Nationale pour l'Emploi (ANPE)
🖥 *www.anpe.fr*

The main offices of ANPE are listed in the relevant chapter. Independent companies, which are only allowed to offer temporary employment, include the following:

Vedior Bis   🖥 *www.vediorbis.com*

Adecco   🖥 *www.adecco.fr*
Manpower   🖥 *www.manpower.fr*

New Businesses

Agence Pour la Création d'Entreprise
🖥 *www.apce.com*
This is an excellent website for anyone thinking of starting up
a business in France, and part of the site is available in
English. Alternatively, ask at your *mairie* for details of the
local Chambre de Commerce, where staff are usually very
approachable and keen to help new businesses in their area.

Communications

Telephone

Fixed Line Telephone Services

Telephone installations must be carried out by France Télécom, but
telephone services are also available from a number of other operators,
some of which are listed below.

France Télécom   🖥 *www.francetelecom.fr*   ☎ 1014
                  The website has an English option.
                  France Télécom has a dedicated
                  English-language helpline   ☎ 08 00 36 47 75

One.Tel   🖥 *www.onetel.fr*   ☎ 3238

Tele2   🖥 *www.tele2.fr*   ☎ 08 11 24 00 10

These companies can prove to be cheaper than France Télécom, especially
for international calls, which are often the same tariff day and night, but
you should always compare before deciding. France Télécom's standing
charge is payable for the line, even if you use another service provider. It's
worth noting that some UK non-geographical numbers (e.g. beginning
0870 or 0345) are accessible only via a France Télécom phone call.

Useful Numbers

French Directory Enquiries   ☎ 4357

International Directory Enquiries
and dialling information   ☎ 3212

BT Direct   ☎ 08 00 99 00 44
For making reverse-charge calls to the UK, etc.

Mobile Telephones

All France Télécom shops sell mobile phones (*portable* or, increasingly, *mobile*), there are mobile phone shops in most town centres, and hypermarkets sell a good selection of handsets and connection packages. Reception in rural areas can be poor, with some quite large areas having no reception at all. There are three service providers in France: Bouygues (pronounced 'bweeg'), Orange and SFR. If your mobile phone is lost or stolen, contact the appropriate number below:

Bouygues	💻 *www.bouyguestelecom.fr*	☎ 08 25 82 56 14
Orange	💻 *www.orange.fr*	☎ 08 25 00 57 00
SFR	💻 *www.sfr.fr*	☎ 06 10 00 19 00

Public Telephones

These are located all over towns and villages, in railway stations, bars and cafés. The new kiosks are Perspex and usually only accept cards; however, if there's a group of three or more kiosks, one may accept coins. All public phones allow international calls and there's a button with a double flag symbol, which you can press for the telephone display to appear in different languages.

Telephone cards are available from post offices, railway stations, cafés, banks and anywhere you see the sign *Télécarte en vente ici*. Cards don't have a standard design, as they're used for advertising. You usually need a telephone card for internet access at a public facility such as a post office.

Telephone Directories

Directories usually incorporate both yellow pages (*les pages jaunes*) and white pages (*l'annuaire* or *les pages blanches*) in a single book, back to back, although they may come separately. All listings in the residential section are in alphabetical order within each commune, so you need to know the commune where someone lives in order to find his number.

If you don't have a directory or would like a copy for a neighbouring department, they can be obtained by phoning ☎ 08 10 81 07 67. If it's for a different department it will cost €12.50 for just a yellow pages or €24.46 for both yellow pages and residential listings. The line is often busy, so keep trying: choose option 1; you will be asked to tap in your phone number and will then be put through to an operator.

Special Rate Phone Numbers

Special rate numbers normally start with 08 or 09 (mobile numbers start 06). Numbers beginning 09 are charged at high rates and are to be avoided if possible. The cost of calls to numbers beginning 08 varies greatly (see below), and you're advised to be wary of numbers for which the charge isn't specified. You should also avoid numbers starting with 00, as calls may be routed via another country. Common 08 prefixes include the following:

● 0800, 0805, 0809 – free call (known as *numéros verts*);

● 0810, 0811 – local call rates (known as *numéros azur*);

● 0836 – calls vary from free to €1.35 for connection plus 34 centimes per minute;

● 0899 79 – €1.35 for connection plus 34 centimes per minute.

Internet Access

There are a number of internet service providers (ISPs) in France, and the following websites can help you to choose the best provider for you.

        🖳 *www.club-internet.fr*
        🖳 *www.illiclic.com* (operated by La Poste)
        🖳 *www.freesurf.fr*
        🖳 *www.wanadoo.fr* (operated by France Télécom)
        🖳 *www.tiscali.fr*

The best way to get connected is to go to a public internet access provider (see below) and register an address and obtain the dial-up numbers, etc. so that you can then go online at home. Note that software may need to be installed in your computer. Alternatively, you can register with Wanadoo by phone (☎ 3608), when you will be given all the access codes and phone numbers immediately.

Wanadoo offers a number of dial-up packages, which can work out cheaper than paying for access calls on a per minute basis if you spent more than a certain time online.

Public Internet Access

All France Télécom shops have internet access, as do many post offices. Public places that offer access usually require a telephone card.

Broadband

High-speed lines or broadband (*le haut débit* or *l'ADSL*) are gradually becoming more widely available, although not as common in rural areas. However, the French government plans to have high speed lines available throughout the country, including rural areas, by 2007. To find out if broadband is currently available where you are, go to 🖳 *www.france*

telecom.fr and on left of the front page click on '*ADSL & TV*', then in the left hand column click on '*Internet haut débit*', then '*Tout sur l'ADSL*', then on the right hand side below '*l'ADSL disponsible chez vous*' enter your phone number and it will tell you straight away if high-speed lines are available to you.

There are various tariffs available for high-speed connections. Wanadoo and France Télécom offer ADSL packages, usually entailing a set fee plus a monthly payment. Offers are changing all the time and are frequently advertised on TV and on the relevant websites. More information can be obtained from 🖳 *www.francetelecom.fr* and 🖳 *www.adsl-france.org*.

Useful Web Addresses

The following is a selection from the myriad websites accessible:

🖳 *www.voila.fr* – A French search engine.

🖳 *www.pagesjeunes.fr* – Yellow pages. This site has the option at the bottom to convert the site to English.

🖳 *www.meteoconsult.com* – Weather site. (Alternatively call ☎ 08 99 70 11 11 and press '1' for the weather forecast in English.)

🖳 *www.service-public.fr* – This is the official gateway to the French civil service.

🖳 *www.google.com* – Although this is an English-language search engine, when foreign websites are located it gives you the option of translating the web page into English – the results are never less than entertaining!

Television & Radio

Whether your television (TV) set will work in France is dependent on which model you have. Most televisions bought in the UK in the last few years should work in France, as most now have the capability to pick up both Secam and PAL signals. If you buy a television in France, you may find that it's sold without a stand.

If you're learning French, watching French TV with subtitles is a good idea. If subtitles are available, they can be found on Teletext 888. If you have a TV guide, the programme may have a symbol of an ear to show that it has subtitles, which are generally for the hard of hearing but will do just as well for foreigners!

It's possible to receive British television broadcasts in France but a satellite dish is needed and you must ensure that you're aware of the legalities before proceeding. There are various British suppliers and installers of satellite who will give you all the information you need, including the following company, which has a comprehensive website:

> Big Dish Satellite
> Mouriol, Milhaguet, 87440 Marval   ☎ 05 55 78 72 98
> 🖥 *www.bigdishsat.com*

Licence

To watch TV in France you need a licence, costing €116.50 for colour and €74.31 for black and white. This fee covers all the television sets that you own in France, even if in different locations such as a caravan or holiday home. As in the UK, when a television set is purchased, the shop must inform the authorities and a television licence bill will duly arrive (unlike the UK, it takes several months!).

If you bring a British TV into France that's capable of receiving French programmes, you should notify the Centre Régional de la Redevance Audiovisuelle (CRRA) within 30 days.

> CRRA   ☎ 01 49 70 40 00
> 🖥 *www.service-public.fr*

Radio

There's a wide variety of local and national stations that can be received in the area, some of which are detailed below.

Station	FM Frequency	Description
BBC Radio 4	94.8	British Radio 4
Classique	99.0	Primarily classical music
Cocktail	89.2	A mix of modern chart music
Culture	91.8, 94.5	Primarily talk and intellectual discussion
Europe 1	100.8, 106.7	A wide variety of music
Europe 2	88.3, 96.8, 101.8	Current chart music
Fun Radio	96.	Current chart music
France Bleu Basse Normandie	102.2	A wide variety of current music

France Bleu Haute Normandie	95.1, 101.6	A wide variety of current music
Info	105.6	Talk
Inter	92.7, 89.8, 94.1	Talk and a variety of music
Musiques	90.2, 95.6, 97.4, 103.7	A mix of classical and 'cultural' music
Normandie FM	103.6	Current, easy-listening music
Nostalgie	99.3, 106.4	'Golden oldies'
NRJ	101.4, 102.9	Current chart music
Radio Albatros	88.2	Local radio with a variety of current music
Radio Manche	93.4	Local radio with a variety of current music
RCF	103., 94.9	The Catholic radio station
RTL	107.5	A wide variety of music
RTL 2	106.1	A wide variety of music
Skyrock	89.6, 107.0	Current chart music

Entertainment

Cinemas

Some French cinemas show English-language films in their original version, i.e. in English with French subtitles. These are identified by the letters *VO* (*version originale*) next to the title. (*VF* indicates that a film has been dubbed into French.)

English-language Books

Libraries and book shops stocking books in English are listed in each chapter. Library membership will require one piece of identification and proof of address such as a utility bill. There's often a nominal charge per annum for membership to the library.

Festivals

There are many annual festivals in this region, just a small selection of which are listed in this book. Dates vary each year, so only the month has been given.

Public Holidays

The official French public holidays (*jours fériés*) are listed below. Note, however, that when a holiday falls on a Saturday or Sunday, another day off isn't usually granted 'in lieu', but when a holiday falls on a Tuesday or Thursday, the day before or the day after may also be taken a holiday, either officially or unofficially, to make a four-day weekend; this practice is known as 'making a bridge' (*faire un pont*).

Date	Holiday	French
1st January	New Year's Day	*Jour de l'An*
March/April	Easter Monday (1)	*Lundi de Pâques*
1st May	Labour Day	*Fête du Travail*
8th May	VE Day	*Fête de la Libération/Victoire 1945*
May (2)	Ascension Day	*Jour de l'Ascension*
14th July	Bastille Day	*Fête Nationale*
15th August	Assumption Day	*Fête de l'Assomption*
1st November	All Saints' Day	*Toussaint*
11th November	Armistice Day	*Fête de l'Armistice*
25th December	Christmas Day	*Noël*

Notes:
1. Good Friday isn't a public holiday in France.

2. Ascension Day is the sixth Thursday after Easter.

Shrove Tuesday (*Mardi Gras*) in February is given by some businesses as a staff holiday.

Video & DVD Hire

DVDs are widely available and are usually viewable in English, but check the back of the case before buying or renting: there will be a Union Jack and/or the words *Sous-titres* (sub-titles) and *Langues* (languages) with *'Anglais'* in the list that follows. Some video shops also hire out DVD players (*lecteurs DVD*).

Medical Facilities & Emergency Services

Ambulances

Ambulances are operated privately in France. If an ambulance has been agreed or requested by a doctor or medical establishment, the cost can be reclaimed if you're registered with the French social security system. In the event of a medical emergency dial ☎ 15.

Doctors

French doctors and dentists have flexible working hours and doctors may have an 'open surgery' during the week, or even at certain times every day, when no appointment is necessary; you just go and wait your turn.

You don't need to register with a doctor or dentist when you arrive in France; simply call when you need an appointment, although you're now required to appoint a 'regular doctor' (*médecin traitant*). There's a charge each time you visit or they visit you (more expensive in the evenings) which is partially reclaimable if you're registered with French social security or if you're on holiday from the UK and have an E111 form (**in an emergency only; you cannot reclaim the cost of routine treatment**). Remember to keep all receipts, including those of any prescriptions and the labels from any medicines prescribed, to send with your claim. An E111 is valid from a year up to three years depending on the issuing office. They're free from post offices in the UK, so if you aren't living permanently in France it's advisable to renew yours regularly.

When you go to a doctor or dentist in France, he will give you a form with details of the treatment given, his details and reference number. Ensure that you give your British address if you intend to reclaim these costs with your E111. This form should be attached to your E111 and sent to the Caisse Régionale Assurance Maladie (CRAM – see **Health Authority** on page 72).

If you intend to be in France for a long period or permanently, it's recommended to ask your UK doctor for a print-out of your medical record. He may not be able to give you copies of the actual written records, but should be willing to provide a print-out (although you may be charged), which you should take with you to your French doctor on your first visit.

Emergencies

In the event of an emergency, dial one of the following numbers:

Any medical emergency
SAMU (Service d'Aide Médical d'Urgence)   ☎ 15

Police (see page 72)
Gendarmes   ☎ 17

Fire or accident not requiring medical help (see below)
Sapeurs-Pompiers   ☎ 18

The *SAMU* are often the first on the scene in the event of an accident. You should call the police first and they will contact the *SAMU*, or you can call them as well.

If you need to call any of the above numbers, you will be asked a series of questions. Below are examples of what you may be asked (with English translations) and a selection of possible responses.

1. Your name and phone number:
    Quel est votre nom et numéro de téléphone?
    [Give your surname first, then your first name, then a contact telephone number]

2. The nature of accident or problem:
    Quelle est la nature de l'accident?
    Il/elle s'est écroulé(e) (S/he has collapsed/fainted)
    Il/elle est tombé(e) d'une échelle/un arbre (S/he has fallen off a ladder/tree)
    Il/elle a eu une crise cardiaque (S/he has had a heart attack)

3. Your exact address/position and how to get there:
    Quelle est votre adresse exacte et pouvez-vous me donner des directions?
    [Give the address/location using the following vocabulary]
    au carrefour (at the crossroads)
    au coin (on the corner)
    tournez à droite/gauche (turn right/left)
    tout droit (straight on)
    après/avant (after/before)
    sur votre gauche/droite (on the left/right

4. How many people are involved:
    Combien de personnes sont impliquées?
    une/deux/trois personnes (one/two/three people)

5. The condition of any injured parties:
    Quels sont les blessures?
    Il/elle est inconscient(e) (S/he is unconscious)
    Il/elle a une hémorragie (S/he is bleeding)
    Il/elle souffre beaucoup (S/he is in a lot of pain)
    Il/elle a une fracture de la jambe/du bras (S/he has broken a leg/arm)

6. What treatment has been given:
    Quel médicament a été préscrit?
    [Give name of medication] ·
    Aucun (None)

A number of other useful emergency numbers are listed below.

Advice

To find a counsellor in your area	☎ 05 55 60 01 23
🖳 *www.find-a-counsellor-in-france.com*	

Electricity Emergency

Calvados		☎ 08 10 33 30 14
Eure	Les Andelys	☎ 08 10 333 127
	Bernay	☎ 08 10 333 227
	Evreux	☎ 08 10 333 027
Manche	Cherbourg	☎ 08 10 35 35 50
	Saint Lô	☎ 08 10 33 30 50
Orne	L'Aigle	☎ 0810 333 261
	Alencon	☎ 0810 333 061
	Flers	☎ 0810 333 161
Seine-Maritime	Le Havre	☎ 0 810 333 376
	Rouen	☎ 0 810 333 076

Gas Leak

Calvados		☎ 08 10 03 10 00
Eure	Brionne	☎ 02 32 44 93 85
	Evreux	☎ 02 32 38 44 66
	Vernon	☎ 02 32 51 27 62
Manche	Avranches	☎ 02 33 60 48 48
	Cherbourg	☎ 02 33 95 05 87
	Saint Lô	☎ 02 33 05 16 73

Orne	L'Aigle	☎ 02 33 25 00 66
	Alençon	☎ 02 33 26 00 50
	Flers	☎ 02 33 64 38 62

Seine-Maritime ☎ 08 10 433 076

Lost or Stolen Bank Cards

	All banks	☎ 08 92 70 57 05
	Banque Populaire	☎ 0892 68 32 08
	BNP Paribas	☎ 08 20 820 002
	Banque Tarneaud	☎ 08 25 00 59 59
	Caisse d'Epargne	☎ 08 25 39 39 39
	Crédit Agricole*	☎ 01 45 67 84 84
	Crédit Lyonnaise	☎ 08 21 80 90 90
	Crédit Mutuel	☎ 05 56 24 48 48
	Société Générale	☎ 08 25 07 00 70
	(*includes Britline* – see page 58)	

If your cheque book is lost or stolen
All banks ☎ 08 92 68 32 08

Pest Control (e.g. Termites)

☎ 08 00 13 31 34

Poisoning

	Centre Anti-Poisons	
	Rennes	☎ 02 99 59 22 22
	Rouen	☎ 02 35 88 44 00

	Centre Anti-Poison Animals	
	Nantes	☎ 02 40 68 77 40

Other emergency numbers are listed in the front of the yellow pages.

Fire Brigade

Members of the fire brigade (*sapeurs-pompiers* or *pompiers*) have a high level of medical training and are usually the first on the scene of any accident, often carrying out medical procedures until the arrival of the *SAMU*. In rural areas, *pompiers* are often 'reserves' and are called to duty by a siren giving three short, very loud blasts.

You can also call the fire brigade if you have a bee or wasp nest in the house or a swarm is presenting an immediate threat. You pay them directly, around €30, for the service.

Health Authority

The Caisse Régional Assurance Maladie (CRAM) deals with medical claims and expenses. You must contact the CRAM in order to join the French social security system. CRAM representatives pay regular visits to some towns (enquire at the *mairie*), in which case you can meet them in person and ask any questions you may have. Otherwise, you need to contact one of the CRAM or Caisse Primaire Assurance Maladie (CPAM) offices listed in the relevant chapter.

Police

There are two main types of police in France: *police nationale* and *gendarmes*. The *police nationale* is under the control of the Interior Ministry and deals with 'general' crime, mostly in urban or semi-urban areas. They're most commonly seen in towns and are distinguished by the silver buttons on their uniforms. At night and in rain and fog they often wear white caps and capes.

The *gendarmerie nationale* is part of the army and under the control of the Ministry of Defence, although it's also at the service of the Interior Ministry. *Gendarmes* deal with serious crime on a national scale and all crime in rural areas where there's no *police* station. They're also responsible for motorway patrols, air safety, mountain rescue, etc. *Gendarmes* wear blue uniforms and traditional caps (*képis*) and have gold buttons on their uniforms. Gendarmes include police motorcyclists (*motards*), who patrol in pairs or threes. Some of the smaller *gendarmeries* are being merged with others and a rural station may be open limited hours, but the local number will always be put through to the station that's on duty.

In addition to the above, most cities and medium-size towns have their own police force, *police municipale* or *corps urbain*, which deals mainly with petty crime, traffic offences and road accidents. They're based at the *mairie* or close by.

All French police are armed with guns.

Motoring

Accidents

In the event of an accident involving two or more cars, it's normal for the drivers to complete an accident report form (*constat à l'amiable*), which is provided by French insurance companies. This is completed by all drivers involved, who must agree (more or less) on what happened. You can write in English or any other language and it's important that you check the particulars (e.g. address) of the other driver(s) listed on the form against something official, such as their driving licence. Take care when ticking the relevant boxes that the form cannot be added to or changed later and be sure that you're happy that you understand what has been written by the other driver(s). A *constat à l'amiable* isn't mandatory, and you can refuse to complete one if the other driver(s) disagree with your interpretation of what happened.

Car Insurance

It isn't necessary to have an insurance 'green card' (although some insurance companies issue one as a matter of course) to drive in France, but you must notify your insurance company of your dates of travel. Insurance for British-registered cars abroad is becoming more difficult, many British insurance companies cutting the length of time they're allowing a car to be abroad, so check carefully with your insurance company. If you're bringing your car to France permanently but cannot re-register it (e.g. because it's a lease car or has been modified), there are some French companies that will insure your car, but for a maximum of 12 months. However, you should read the small print, as cover may apply only for three or six months or even just one month.

AGF Assurfinance
🖳 *www.agf.fr*

AXA Assurance
🖳 *www.axa.fr*

Azur Assurances
🖳 *www.azur-assurances.fr*

GAN Assurances
🖳 *www.gan.fr*

MAAF Assurances
🖳 *www.maaf.fr*

Mutuel du Mans Assurances
🖳 *www.mma.fr*

Europ Assistance, 1 promenade de
la Bonnette, 92230 Gennevilliers   ☎ 01 41 85 85 85
🖳 *www.europ-assistance.com*
Provides international breakdown cover, health and
house insurance and relocation services. The website
is in English.

Car Repairs & Service

Most privately owned petrol stations service and repair cars and some of the large chains, such as Shell and Esso, have a workshop attached. Even small towns will have a repair garage of some description. However, if your car is damaged, you must contact your insurer before having any repairs carried out, as the insurer may specify certain garages to carry out the repairs or insist that a loss-adjuster approve the cost of the repair.

Petrol Stations

Petrol stations in France are generally open much shorter hours than in the UK, occasionally 6am to 10pm, but generally 8am to 7pm and only occasionally 24 hours a day. If a station has a '24/24' sign, this means that petrol can be bought using automated pumps that will only take a credit or debit card with a microchip and a four-digit code, such as French bank cards. Some of the petrol stations with longer opening hours are given below.

Calvados

Caen	Total, 73 avenue Georges Clémenceau Open every day 6am to 10pm.	☎ 02 31 93 02 92

Manche

Cherbourg	Total, 10 avenue Lemonnier Every day 6am to 9.30pm.	☎ 02 33 43 05 99

Orne

Argentan	Elf, 158 route de Falaise Open every day 6am to 10pm.	☎ 02 33 35 25 02
Mortagne	Esso, 16 rue du Faubourg St Éloi Open every day 6am to 10pm.	☎ 02 33 25 18 67

Seine-Maritime

Dieppe	Total France, avenue Canadiens Open every day 5am to 8.45pm.	☎ 02 35 84 86 79
Le Havre	Total, relais de la Halte de Granville, boulevard Léningrad Open every day 6am to 10pm.	☎ 02 35 26 55 00
Rouen	Shell, avenue Aristide Briand Open every day 6am to 10pm.	☎ 02 35 89 44 74

Rules & Regulations

When driving in France, you must have the following in your car at all times:

- Vehicle registration document or, if you're driving a leased or hired car, a letter of authority and a VE103 Hired Vehicle Certificate from the leasing or hire company;

- Your driving licence;

- Vehicle insurance documents;

- A warning triangle;

- Spare bulbs.

It's also advisable to carry a fire extinguisher and a first-aid kit.

Note also the following general rules and regulations relating to driving in France:

- The wearing of seatbelts is compulsory and includes passengers in rear seats when seatbelts are fitted. You (or any of your passengers) can be fined up to €90 for not wearing a seatbelt. Children must be accommodated in approved child seats, and children under ten cannot ride in the front of a vehicle unless it has no back seat.

- Failure to dip your lights when following or approaching another vehicle can cost you up to €750 and a penalty point on your licence, if you have a French licence. (French licenses – *permis de conduire* – work in reverse, with points given with the licence that you can then lose.)

- French traffic lights usually have a small set of lights at eye level, which are handy if you cannot see the main lights (there are rarely lights on the far side of a junction). If the amber light (either a normal round light or an arrow shape) is flashing, you may continue (in the direction indicated, if an arrow shape) but must observe any relevant priority signs. If you shoot a red light, you can be fined €300 and earn four penalty points!

- Watch out for a triangular sign with a red border displaying a large black X. This means that you **don't** have priority at the next junction (which may not be a crossroads) but must give way to the right, however minor the joining road is.

- Always come to a complete stop at junctions when required to (i.e. by a STOP sign) and ensure that your front wheels are behind the white line. Failing to stop behind the line can cost you €750 and four licence points.

- Beware of moped riders. French people are allowed on mopeds from the age of 14, and many youngsters pull out and weave around traffic without looking or indicating; even French motorists give them an extremely wide berth when overtaking!

- The name sign as you enter a village or town marks the start of the urban speed limit (see below) and the name crossed through as you leave marks the end.

- Parking in towns with parking meters is often free between noon and 2pm (times vary).

- All motorists are recommended to use dipped headlights outside towns during the day, although this isn't a legal requirement – yet.

- Finally, don't assume that a British licence plate will prevent you from being stopped. Tickets for motoring offences such as illegal parking and speeding are now sent for payment to the country in which the car is registered.

Further details of French driving regulations can be found in *Living and Working in France* (see page 379).

Speed Limits

Speed limits in France vary according to road conditions, as shown below. When visibility is below 50m (165ft) for any reason (e.g. rain or fog), you must not exceed 50kph (32mph) on any road, including a motorway. Speeds shown are in kilometres per hour with mile-per-hour equivalents in brackets.

Type of Road	Speed Limit	
	Dry Road	**Wet Road**
Motorway	130 (81)	110 (68)
Dual-carriageway	110 (68)	100 (62)
Single-carriageway	90 (56)	80 (50)
Towns	50 (32)	50 (32)

Note: The above limits apply unless otherwise indicated.

If you're caught exceeding a speed limit by 40kph (25mph), your driving licence can be confiscated on the spot.

Pets

France is a nation of dog-lovers, although French people's attitude towards other pets and animals in general (and sometimes also to dogs) can be alarmingly indifferent. The following information may be of use to those importing a pet or buying a pet in France.

● Many restaurants will provide food and water for dogs, some even allowing dogs to be seated at the table! Hotels may provide a rate for pets to stay.

● It's common practice to have third-party insurance in case your pet bites someone or causes an accident; the majority of household insurance policies include this, but you should check.

● Dogs must be kept on leads in most public parks and gardens in France and there are large fines for dog owners who don't comply.

● In 2004 there were some cases of rabies in France and everyone is strongly advised to have all pets vaccinated. If you intend to put a cat or a dog into kennels or a cattery, it must have had a rabies vaccination.

● Rural French dogs are generally kept more as guard dogs than as pets and often live outdoors. Vicious dogs are (usually) confined or chained, but in a small community other 'pet' dogs may be left to wander around the village or hamlet.

● Dogs aren't welcome on the majority of beaches and, if you're staying on a campsite, they must be vaccinated against rabies and wear a collar at all times.

● On trains, pets under 6kg (13lb) which can be carried in a bag are charged around €5, but larger ones must be on a lead and wear a muzzle and will be charged half the normal second-class fare.

● Some Mercure and Formule 1 hotels accept dogs (see page 55 for contact details).

Dog Hygiene

In towns and cities, a variety of schemes are being implemented to keep the streets free of canine waste. The following are some of the schemes already in place.

● Mortagne has special red bins and bag dispensers;

● Cherbourg has bag distributors and *La Pelle Civique*, which is a cardboard shovel and paper bag to be put in the litter bin after use;

● Le Havre has designated sand beds with scoops and bins alongside;

- Rouen has 19 designated areas across the city for dog walking, which are regularly cleaned; a list is available from the tourist office and Hôtel de Ville.

Horse Dentists

Vets in France don't usually deal with horses' teeth and there are specific equine dentists, which are listed in the following chapters. You're advised to book a few weeks in advance and you will be included in their next circuit.

Horse Feed

The feed you need is obviously dependent on how your horses are used and what their current feeding regime is. In any case, until you've established your new suppliers, it's wise to bring over with you any specific feeds.

Your local agricultural Co-op (look out for huge hoppers, sometimes in the middle of nowhere) will sell sacks of feed and often pony nuts. Some have started selling only 'high-performance' nuts, so check carefully. Maize and barley are often available.

A local farmer may be your best source of feed; grain is normally sold whole or as flour (*farine*), although some farmers will grind it for you. An alternative for horses that have come from the UK is whole-grain barley soaked for 24 hours. Your local farmer will also be the best source of hay and straw. See also **Riding Equipment** on page 80.

Spillers export horse feeds to France; to find your nearest supplier visit Spillers' website at 🖳 *www.spillers-feeds.com* or contact:

> SA Sodiva, 7 rue de la Roberdière,
> 35000 Rennes   ☎ 02 99 59 87 05
> 🖳 *www.coopagr-bretagne.fr*

Horse Vet

> Stockwell & Poutas, L'Attache,
> Falaise   ☎ 02 31 90 17 79
> (on the northern outskirts of the town, tucked away behind the Renault garage, opposite Super U supermarket)
> This is a specialist vet in the department of Calvados that deals only with horses, in a large purpose-built building.

Identification

All dogs in France must be tattooed or microchipped with an identity number, enabling owners to recover lost or stolen pets and also preventing a rabies or other vaccination certificate from being used for more than one dog. Tattoos used to be done inside the ear but it may now be done inside the animal's back leg. The costs of the two procedures are similar, although charges aren't fixed and vary considerably according to the veterinary practice – between around €25 and €75 for tattooing and from €35 to €70 for microchipping. The numbers are kept in a central computer by the SPA (see page 80). If you lose your pet, contact the nearest SPA office.

Pet Parlours

Although many dogs are used as guard dogs, millions are kept as pampered domestic pets, and a large number of 'pet parlours' (*salon de toilettage*) are to be found in France.

Pet Travel

Pet Passport Scheme

The Department for Food, Agriculture and Rural Affairs (DEFRA) operates a 'pet passport' scheme (known as PETS) for the benefit of owners wishing to take their pets abroad and bring them back to the UK. Full details of the requirements for re-entry into the UK are available from the DEFRA helpline or website (see below). Alternatively, a company called Dogs Away offers a free eight-page booklet to guide you through the process.

If applying for a pet passport in France, always ensure that you have in your possession the *carte de tatouage* before you start the pet passport process, as unless you have this card, which has your name and address as the registered owner, the registration of the microchip (*puce*) will be refused, along with the rabies vaccination, blood test, etc.

DEFRA   ☎ +44 (0)870-241 1710
💻 *www.defra.gov.uk*
The helpline is accessible from both England and France and the lines are open from 8.30am to 5pm (UK time) Mondays to Fridays.

Dogs Away   ☎ +44 (0)20-8441 9311
💻 *www.dogsaway.co.uk*

Paws 4 Travel
💻 *www.paws4travel.co.uk*

Sea Crossings

Crossing the Channel through the Tunnel reduces the possibility of stress for your pets, as you can remain with them. Some ferry companies may allow you to check your pet on the car deck during the crossing, but this isn't always easy and the car decks can be very noisy and cause more stress to the pet. For contact details of the companies listed below, see page 36.

Eurotunnel

The check-in desk for pets at Coquelles is to the right of the check-in lanes. Animals are checked in before entering the Eurotunnel site. A single journey costs £30 per animal; guide dogs for the disabled are free. You can book via the website but are advised to book by phone, as a limited number of pets are allowed per train.

Hoverspeed

Each pet is charged £18 each way. Bookings aren't possible online and must be made by phone.

P&O Ferries

You must check in at least an hour before departure if travelling with pets.

Seafrance

All travellers with pets must check in at least 45 minutes before departure.

Riding Equipment

Gamm Vert

🖥 *www.gammvert.fr*

These garden centres sell horse feed and some basic equipment, depending on the size of the shop. The website gives the location and opening hours of your nearest shop.

Decathlon

🖥 *www.decathlon.fr*

These large sports shops carry a wide selection of riding accessories and equipment, including the hire of clippers (*tondeuses*), which are available for half or full days.

SPA

The Société pour la Protection des Animaux (SPA) is an organisation similar to the RSPCA in the UK but it isn't a national scheme, so you must contact your departmental branch with any complaints or questions. Details are included in the following chapters.

Veterinary Clinics

Most veterinary surgeries are open Mondays to Saturdays, usually closing for lunch. There are often open surgeries as well as appointments. Where a vet's name isn't given, there's more than one vet at the surgery.

Many vets will deal with horses and other equines but generally those that are used for hacking rather than expensive eventing or competition horses. See also **Horse Vet** on page 78.

Places to Visit

Beaches & Leisure Parks

There are many natural beaches along the Normandy coast and numerous leisure lakes also have sandy beaches and supervised bathing. The lakes may be just for fishing and relaxing beside or there may be a playground, crazy golf and more. Details of all such facilities are given in the following chapters.

Churches & Abbeys

Churches of interest are signposted from main roads and motorways and can be easily identified, e.g. *Eglise XIVème Siècle* = 14th century church.

Professional Services

Architects & Project Managers

As many architects also offer a project management and general building services, they've been listed under **Architects & Project Managers** in the **Tradesmen** sections.

Property

Building Plots

These can be found simply by driving around, as many are advertised by a board saying '*à vendre*' on the edge of the land for sale. Many estate agents have land for sale and, increasingly commonly, *mairies* are selling land, either as individual plots or in 'estates' (*lotissement*) of around 5 to 15 plots at the edge of villages in an attempt to revitalise them. Such land can vary considerably in price (per square metre) according to how keen the *mairie* is to boost the local population; it has been known to sell for as little as €1 per square metre.

There are many companies that specialise in building new houses, and the larger ones may have a stock of building plots (see **Builders** under **Tradesmen** in the relevant chapter).

House Hunting

There are many ways of finding homes for sale in France, including the following:

Estate Agents & Notaires

There are many estate agents across Normandy who have English-speaking staff. You will be taken to a property and shown around by the agent or his representative and won't (usually) be given an address and sent off into the wilderness. Many agents will set aside a whole day to spend with you and many offer a comprehensive after sales services, getting telephone lines and electricity and water supplies transferred for you.

Properties for sale are often listed with several agents and sometimes the sale prices differ. This may simply be because some show the price with fees included, whilst others don't, but check.

Many people are starting property search or selling agencies who aren't actually estate agents themselves but only representatives of estate agents – or should be. If they're legally registered they will have a *carte professionnelle* and will be able to tell you the estate agent that they work with. If in doubt, ask to see their *carte professionnelle* (also referred to as a *carte grise* and not to be confused with a car registration document, which has the same name!) or deal directly with the agent they're working for.

Notaires are the government representatives you must deal with for any property transaction and they often have a supply of property for sale, which can be displayed in their window or on a notice board outside. If you're buying direct from a *notaire*, there's no agency fee but they're allowed to charge a negotiating fee, which is generally lower than an estate agent's fees. Their legal fees are a percentage of the sale price and are fixed by law.

In France it's the purchaser who generally pays the estate agent's fee and you need to allow up to 10 per cent of the purchase price for this and other fees and legal costs.

Internet

There are many sites dedicated to property in Normandy. If you use an English-language search engine such as Google (🖥 *www.google.com*) and type in 'property for sale' and the area or department you're looking for, it will produce a selection of French and English sites.

Private Sales

Many property owners sell privately to avoid paying an agent's commission and put up 'for sale' (*à vendre* or *AV*) signs outside the property.

Property Exhibitions

These exhibitions are held throughout the UK and are packed with almost every English-speaking estate agent from France. Go early, wear comfortable shoes and collect as much information on both estate agents and house buying as you can, to read properly once at home. Many homes that are on display will have been sold by the time you next visit France, but it will give you an immediate picture of what's available, for how much and which agents cover the area you're interested in. For forthcoming shows see 🖥 *www.vivelafrance.co.uk* and the magazine websites listed below.

Magazines

There are many magazines dedicated to French property and living, which contain advertisements by agents and individuals, including the following. They're available in newsagents' unless otherwise stated.

> Everything France
> 🖥 *www.everythingfrancemag.co.uk*
>
> Focus on France
> 🖥 *www.outboundpublishing.com*
>
> France
> 🖥 *www.francemag.com*
>
> French Magazine
> 🖥 *www.frenchmagazine.co.uk*
>
> French Property News
> 🖥 *www.french-property-news.com* (subscriptions only)
>
> Living France
> 🖥 *www.livingfrance.com*

Property Prices

The following information gives an approximate idea of what you can buy within a particular price range. As property prices are constantly changing, these figures should be used only as a guide. Four property categories have been given for each of the towns within the department and the prices were based on property on the market at the end of 2004. These are the **starting** price for properties in each category, in or close to the towns specified. Where an area didn't have any property in a particular category, no prices are given. Over €250,000 the variety of property available becomes very broad; for example, a new three-bedroom house can be the same price as an old five-bedroom property with a large plot in the same area. All prices are in euros.

	Ruin or Land	Requiring Renovation	3-bed Modern(ised)	4+-bed with Character or Land
Calvados				
Bayeux	60,000*	87,000	147,000	195,000
Caen	33,000*	86,000	155,000	190,000
Falaise	26,000	70,000	113,000	145,000
Lisieux	26,000*	74,000	127,000	156,000
Vire	46,000	69,000	110,000	200,000
Eure				
Les Andelys	55,000*	113,000	145,000	230,000
Bernay	25,000	60,000	90,000	147,000
Evreux	20,000*	96,000	155,00	210,000
Pont Audemer	61,000	81,000	145,000	242,000
Manche				
Avranches	41,000	70,000	115,000	210,000
Barneville	40,000	72,000	137,000	200,000
Cherbourg	50,000*	110,000	180,000	230,000
Coutances	45,000	80,000	135,000	200,000
Saint Lô	36,000	68,000	130,000	171,000
Orne				
L'Aigle	15,000*	97,000	130,000	220,000
Alençon	30,000*	50,000	134,000	215,000

Argentan	45,000	82,000	142,000	175,000
Domfront	19,500	62,000	80,000	166,000
Mortagne	35,000	42,000	130,000	196,000
Seine-Maritime				
Dieppe	N/A	80,000	135,000	245,000
Le Havre	42,000	91,000	150,000	190,000
Neufchâtel	40,000	67,000	100,000	180,000
Rouen	30,000*	N/A	155,000	240,000
Yvetot	66,000	86,000	145,000	190,000

* Land only; prices without an asterisk indicate a ruin or property requiring extensive renovation (*caveat emptor*!).

Property Taxes

As an owner/occupier of French property, you will receive two or three tax bills a year. Taxe foncière is a land tax payable by the owner of the property. Even if there are no buildings on the land, this tax will still be due unless the land is being used for agricultural purposes. *Taxe d'habitation* is payable by the occupier of the property on 1st January each year and may include a portion for refuse collection (*ordures*). If not, a separate bill will be issued for this.

For the year during which you buy your property, the vendor will be responsible for paying the *taxe d'habitation*, as he would have been in occupation on 1st January. Even if you become the owner on 2nd January, this tax will still be his responsibility. For *taxe foncière* there's normally an apportionment between the vendor and the seller according to how long they each own the property in that year. This is usually provided for by the *notaire* in the final conveyance deed (*acte de vente*). Although the vendor will be sent the *taxe foncière* bill and must pay it, he will be entitled to immediate reimbursement by the purchaser as soon as he provides proof that he has been billed.

Both *taxe d'habitation* and *taxe foncière* are calculated using the rental value of the property as a base figure. Hence taxes on property in towns and cities are higher than those on properties in small villages. If your property is situated in a tourist area, there may be additional tax included in the *taxe d'habitation* charge for maintaining the area to a higher than normal standard. Also, if there's an exceptional expense, such as improving the sewage system, there may be a separate one-off bill.

You should always pay tax bills promptly, as otherwise you may incur penalties. It isn't uncommon for owners of French property not to receive their tax bills. In this case you should write to the appropriate authority by recorded delivery informing them you haven't received a bill and asking them to send it; otherwise you may have great difficulty convincing them that you aren't liable for the late payment charge.

Purchase Procedure

Once you've found a property, the process to follow in order the complete the purchase is quite straightforward.

There are two forms of standard preliminary contract, a *compromis de vente* and a promesse de vente, *the former being preferable, as it offers you greater protection.* The preliminary contract is usually prepared and signed by the parties, within a week or so of orally agreeing the sale, sometimes on the same day. Before this can occur however, some specialist reports may have to be obtained, particularly if the property is old. These reports (certifying the presence or absence of asbestos, lead and termites) are usually paid for by the vendor.

You should at this time ensure that any conditions that you want are included in the contract and that you understand (and it's clear) what is and what isn't included in the sale. Upon signature of the preliminary contract, the vendor is fully committed to the sale, but the position is different for the buyer. Under French law the buyer has a 'cooling off' period of seven days after receipt of copies of the signed agreement. During this seven day period, he's free to change his mind and withdraw from the agreement without penalty. At the end of this period, the buyer pays a deposit (normally of 10 per cent of the purchase price) to the *notaire* handling the sale.

Under French law, the transfer deed, called the acte authentique, transfers the property to the buyer at completion. This document must be prepared by a *notaire*. The *notaire* can act for both the seller and the buyer, although the buyer will pay his fee. There's nothing to stop you as the seller from instructing your own *notaire*, who will assist the other *notaire* and share the fee with him, although this is rarely necessary. You should remember that the *notaire* doesn't represent the interest of either party in the transaction. He deals with the formalities of checking the title, checking that any loans are paid off and making enquiries of any developments intended in the vicinity of the property. It's common practice for the parties to agree a pre-signature inspection of the property, either on the date of signature, or alternatively the day before.

Buyers need to ensure that their funds are paid into the *notaire*'s account in plenty of time. It's recommended to use a specialist currency dealer in order to change foreign currency to euros. Also, it's essential to have property insurance that's effective on the day of signature – don't rely upon taking over the vendor's policy.

The last part of the sale takes place at the *notaire*'s office, where both parties sign the acte authentique and finalise the financial side of the transaction. The keys to the home are yours as soon as the this procedure is completed.

For comprehensive information on the purchase procedure see this book's sister publication *Buying a Home in France* by David Hampshire (Survival Books – see page 379).

Religion

Anglican Services

Reverend John Porter, Framecourt   ☎ 03 21 04 36 35
Reverend Porter is responsible for the pastoral care of any Anglicans and English Christians who might seek it in northern France.

Catholic Churches

Churches can be found in most communities, and services in the villages are generally held in rotation with other churches in the parish. Notices are displayed on church doors or just inside giving details of forthcoming services. In some small villages, the church doesn't have regular services but is used only on special occasions once or twice a year.

Protestant Churches

For the purposes of this book, all branches of the Protestant Church have been included under this heading.

Restaurants

There are so many restaurants in the region that we've been unable to list them in the following chapters. It's usual for restaurants of all types to offer set menus (*menu* – the menu is *la carte*), which are dishes put together by the chef that complement each other and may change daily. In smaller restaurants, this may be all that's available, although there's usually a choice of two or three dishes for each course.

Routiers

These restaurants can be found on main roads and have a circular logo – half red, half blue. They're usually alongside lorry parking areas and provide meals for drivers which have a reputation for being of good quality and representing good value, the restaurants themselves being clean and tidy. You may be seated canteen style and find yourself next to a 'trucker' but you will get a four-course meal, sometimes with wine included in the price (it's the coffee you have to pay extra for!). Prices vary, but around €10 is usual.

Rubbish & Recycling

Dustmen

The collection of household rubbish (*ramassage*) varies not only between departments but also within areas of each department. It may be collected once or twice a week, even daily in some large towns and there may be separate collections (e.g. weekly or fortnightly) for recyclable waste (see **Rubbish & Recycling** on page 88).

In towns, you may find 'wheelie bins' in the street. If so, you're responsible for putting your rubbish sacks in the bins, which are then emptied once or twice a week. If there's more than one type of wheelie bin, the other(s) are for recycling (see **Rubbish & Recycling** on page 88).

Rural areas may also have wheelie bins, usually brown or grey, with one or two for each group of houses. If there are no bins, rubbish should be put in bin bags and left at the edge of the road, although you're advised to hang them up out of reach of marauding dogs, cats and wildlife; dustmen won't go down drives or onto property. Dustmen often come very early, so bags need to be put out the night before. In towns there's usually a specified time before which you may not put out your rubbish, e.g. around 7pm for collection that evening or in the early hours of the following day.

If collection day falls on a bank holiday, rubbish is generally collected the day before rather than the day after – or the collection may simply be cancelled. The best way to find out what happens in your commune is to speak to your neighbours or enquire at the *mairie*.

In most areas, separate taxes are payable by homeowners for rubbish collection and many French people are fiercely protective of the services for which they pay. You're therefore strongly advised not to put rubbish into a wheelie bin if you're driving a car registered in another department; the same applies if you try to use a rubbish tip in a different department or even a different commune (see **Rubbish Tips** below).

Metal Collection

If the previous occupiers kindly left their old fridge or bedstead in the garden, your *mairie* should be able to put you in touch with your local 'rag and bone man' or arrange for them to be taken away. In some communes, there's a regular (e.g. quarterly) *récupération des objects encombrants*, the dates of which should be advised in advance.

Dieppe   Large unwanted items are collected monthly.

Rouen   Large unwanted items are collected free from your house; to arrange collection call   ☎ 08 00 02 10 21

Recycling

Recycling systems vary both regionally and locally, some areas having no facilities at all whilst others collect recyclable waste from outside your house. Whatever the system, the colour coding is always the same, although yellow and blue are sometimes combined.

● **Blue** – Paper and card, including catalogues, old phone directories and junk mail, but not window envelopes.

● **Yellow** – Packaging, cans (including aerosol cans), tins, drink cartons and plastic milk bottles, but **not** yoghurt pots, oil bottles, plastic bags or the thin plastic that encloses junk mail or six-packs of bottles of water.

● **Green** – All clear and coloured glass, but **not** drinking glasses, medicine bottles, vases or light bulbs and no corks or lids.

Here is a summary of some of the systems currently in place in Normandy:

● Blue and yellow rubbish bags given out free at the *mairie* for collection from outside your property. Glass must be taken to bottle banks.

● Yellow bags given out free for paper, plastic and metal packaging.

● Three different coloured containers provided by the *mairie*, which should already be at the property. These will be emptied from outside your house.

- A single blue container for paper, plastic, metal and glass bottles, emptied from outside your house.

- A series of collection banks, usually for all three categories of recycling. They're often to be found by football pitches, in car parks or near the *mairie*.

- Weekly or monthly collections of garden rubbish from outside the house from around April to November.

- Large blue cages for plastic bottles, blue containers for paper, yellow for other plastic and metal packaging, green for glass.

- Occasionally there are separate containers for coloured and clear glass.

There are many designs of kitchen bin in France that have two or three compartments for the different types of waste. Note that polystyrene cannot be recycled; if you have a large quantity, such as packaging from a household appliance, you can dispose of it at a tip (see below).

Some areas are encouraging the use of compost bins and sell the bins at a reduced price to local residents.

Batteries

Batteries can be recycled in most supermarkets, where you can find containers, usually Perspex, in the foyer or by the customer service desk. Car batteries can be recycled at a rubbish tip (see below).

Clothes & Shoes

Recycling containers for clothes and shoes can often be found in supermarket car parks.

Printer Cartridges

Printer ink cartridges can also be recycled, sometimes in supermarket entrance foyers and sometimes at the *mairie* or library. Toner cartridges can be recycled at the rubbish tip.

Rubbish Tips

Every town and many large villages have a rubbish tip (*déchetterie*); even small communes may have a *décharge*, which is primarily for garden rubbish but may also be used for building rubble.

Déchetteries are clearly marked in towns and outlying areas by a symbol of a hand holding three arrows. Here you can dispose of large metal objects, such as bikes and cookers, as well as motor and cooking oil, glass, paper, clothes and batteries. You aren't allowed to dispose of household rubbish bags, which should be put out for collection from your home.

Some rubbish tips have a maximum quantity of building rubble that they will accept each day from an individual and, if they suspect that you're a tradesman, they will refuse to allow you to deposit at all.

You may have to take proof of a local address when using your rubbish tip, or you may be issued with a pass (available from your *mairie*). If you're driving a car registered in another department (or country), you may be asked where you live or even be prevented from using the tip at all.

Rubbish tips are very rarely open on Sundays or bank holidays. Opening hours may be part days throughout the week or similar to shop hours for larger towns, but always closing for lunch.

Schools

If you're planning to put your children into French school, the first place to go is your *mairie*. They will give you details of the relevant state school for your child's age, but you may have to ask for details of local private (e.g. Catholic) schools. The school week for junior and infant schools is generally Mondays, Tuesdays, Thursdays and Fridays. Some areas also have lessons on Wednesday mornings, as do most secondary schools (*collèges*). There are only a couple of schools in the region that operate on Saturday mornings. School uniform is rarely worn.

Enrolment

To register your children at a school, you must go and see the head teacher, who he will tell you whether there are places and the relevant start date. Take the following with you:

● Details of all vaccinations since birth;

● The name and address of the child's last school (if applicable);

● A copy of his last school report and/or any results you have from any academic tests;

● Evidence of school insurance, which is compulsory in France (see below). At your first meeting, it will be sufficient to say that you've applied for the insurance.

- If your child previously attended a French school, a *certificat de radiation*, which is proof that all contact and dealings have terminated with the previous school. A closing report from a UK school is usually sufficient.

French schools don't provide stationery and will have a long list of stationery and equipment that you must provide, so ask for a copy at an early stage.

Transport

There's a comprehensive network of school buses (*car/bus scolaire*), which collect children in rural areas. An application form for a bus pass can be obtained from the school or the *mairie* and you will need to provide two passport-size photographs. The cost, if any, depends on where you live, how many school-age children there are in the family and what schools they go to.

Holidays

Schools in France are divided into three groups for their holidays so that winter (February/March) and spring (April/May) holidays are staggered, which prevents ski and other resorts from becoming overcrowded. Note that neither the winter nor the spring holiday necessarily coincides with Easter. Due to the summer holidays starting around the end of June, there's no half-term break between the spring and summer holidays. Schools in Eure and Seine-Maritime are group B, while schools in Calvados, Manche and Orne are group A. Calendars are distributed by a wide variety of organisations giving the school holiday dates for the three groups. If a school operates a four-day week, it will give you a list of holiday dates, which may vary by a day or two from the 'official' dates to make up the statutory hours per term.

Insurance

All children must have insurance to attend school in France. Insurance is provided by a number of companies, but Mutuelles d'Assurances Elèves (MAE) is the most popular. The most comprehensive cover is €26.50 and covers your child for all eventualities, both in and out of school. Contact details for MAE are given below. Whichever insurer you use, you must provide the school with a certificate to prove that your child is covered.

General   Mutuelles d'Assurances d'Elèves   ☎ 08 20 00 00 70
               🖥 *www.mae.fr*
               Central helpline open 8.30am to 8pm Mondays to Fridays
               and 8.30am to 5pm Saturdays.

Calvados	4 avenue Parc St André, Hérouville St Clair, Caen	☎ 02 31 43 81 06
Eure	20 rue Borville Dupuis, Evreux	☎ 02 32 39 11 77
Manche	11 route Coutances, Saint Lô	☎ 02 33 57 20 47
Orne	Résidence Front de Sarthe, 7 rue Juiverie, Alençon	☎ 02 33 80 01 51
Seine-Maritime	40 rue Amiens, Rouen	☎ 02 35 71 28 19

Extra Tuition

If your child wants or needs extra help, but not structured lessons, it's worth contacting the local *collège*, as it may be able to recommend a student who is happy to come to your house and spend time with your child going over class notes or lessons. Not only is this cheaper than a qualified teacher but a younger person may be less daunting for your children.

Shopping

Opening Hours

When available, the opening hours of various shops have been included, but they're liable to change and so it's advisable to check before travelling long distances to any specific shop.

Many small businesses are staffed only by members of a family and as a result you may find that the village shop or even the town co-op may close completely for two weeks while the proprietor goes on holiday.

Shop opening hours can change from summer to winter, particularly when school starts in September. Shops that were open all day (*sans interruption*) and on Sunday mornings are suddenly closed for two hours at lunchtime and not open on Sundays at all. Other shops may change their lunchtime closure and close completely on Mondays.

The information in this section relates to shopping in general; details of shops in each department can be found in the following chapters.

Mobile Shops

In rural communities there are various mobile shops, all of which sound their horns loudly as they go through a village. These may include a bakery (*boulangerie*), a butcher's (*boucherie*), a grocery (*épicerie*) and a fishmonger's (*poissonnerie*).

Architectural Antiques

BCA Matériaux, route de Craon, L'Hotellerie
de Flée   ☎ 02 33 94 74 00
💻 *www.bca-materiauxanciens.com*
(25 km north of Angers, alongside the D863 road just north of the village Hotellerie-de-Flée, midway between the market towns of Craon and Segré)
Has a large stock of reclaimed timber; the comprehensive website shows what architectural antiques they have.
Delivers all over France. David Akers speaks English and the website is also available in English.

BCA Matériaux, RN13, route de Paris,
Méry-Corbon   ☎ 02 31 61 62 40
(off the N13 from Lisieux to Caen)
This is a smaller depot of the above company.

Bakeries

Bakeries (*boulangeries*) are usually small family-run businesses that close one day a week and often on Sunday afternoons. They also run delivery vans, going through local villages and hamlets from two to seven days a week, depending on the area.

British Groceries

Many supermarkets are now introducing some 'high demand' British produce to their international sections, e.g. Golden Syrup and HP Sauce. Stock varies with demand and the size of the shop, so keep a look out, especially in hypermarkets and popular tourist areas.

Expatdirect.co.uk   ☎ +44 (0)113 255 0333
💻 *www.expatdirect.co.uk*
This company supplies British produce at supermarket prices and delivers anywhere in France: £14.95 for 30kg of goods.

Chemists'

Even small towns will have a chemist's (*pharmacie*) but they may be open limited hours, such as Tuesdays to Fridays and every other Saturday and Monday. Outside normal opening hours a notice should be displayed giving the address of the nearest duty chemist (*pharmacie de garde*). Alternatively, the *gendarmes* hold a list of duty chemists; dial ☎ 17 or the number of your local *gendarmerie*.

Chemists are trained to give first aid and can also carry out procedures such as taking blood pressure. They can be asked advice on many ailments and without a prescription can give a wider variety of medicines than are available over the counter in the UK. Chemists are also trained to distinguish between around 50 types of mushroom and toadstool and to identify local snakes in order to prescribe the correct antidote for poisoning.

DIY

There are many DIY (*bricolage*) shops in the region, most towns having at least one of the following:

Bricomarché	🖥 *www.bricomarche.com*
Castorama	🖥 *www.castorama.fr*
Mr Bricolage	🖥 *www.mr-bricolage.fr*
Weldom	🖥 *www.weldom.com*

Equipment & Tool Hire

To hire equipment or tools you must take some identification, e.g. a household bill, and must pay a deposit, either by cheque or by debit card.

Frozen Food

Some frozen food (*surgelés*) shops also do home deliveries whilst other companies only sell direct, orders being placed by phone, via the internet or with the driver. The two largest companies that have shops and do home deliveries are:

Picard Surgelés	🖥 *www.picard.fr*
Thiriet Glaces	🖥 *www.thiriet.com*

Garden Centres

M. Andrew Howard, L'Aunay
Samson   ☎ 02 33 35 74 51
(north of Alençon)
English garden plants for sale. Open every day from 10am to 6pm.

The most commonly found garden centres (*jardineries*) are Gamm Vert and Jardiland, the latter being a large shop generally found on retail parks.

Gamm Vert	🖥 *www.gammvert.fr*
Jardiland	🖥 *www.jardiland.fr*

Key Cutting & Heel Bars

Key cutting kiosks and heel bars (*cordonneries*) may be found in hypermarket complexes, outside supermarkets or as independent shops in the high street.

Kitchens & Bathrooms

Specialist shops selling kitchen and bathroom furniture and fittings can often be found in large retail parks. Large DIY shops sometimes sell kitchens and bathrooms.

Markets

Some markets and fairs take place in the centre of towns and villages and can cause streets to be closed; as they're often held on car parks, parking can become difficult. Food markets in France are well worth a visit if you haven't experienced them before (and aren't squeamish), but do check the prices, particularly at indoor markets, which are sometimes higher than you might expect.

Newsagents'

Many general newsagents' (*maison de la presse* or simply *presse*) sell British daily newspapers and even British magazines and paperbacks. They can usually order specific magazines or publications, such as the *TV* and *Radio Times*, on request.

Publications

Le 14, le 50, le 61, le 76, le Caen Poche, Le Havre en Poche, Eure Inter Annonces and *Paru Vendu* are just some of the local 'classified' newspapers, which include advertisements for local events, items for sale, cars, etc. They're free and can be found in *tabacs*, bakeries and other shops.

The following are English-language newspapers for France, published monthly.

The Connexion   ☎ 04 93 32 16 59
🖥 *www.connexionfrance.com*

French News   ☎ 05 53 06 84 40
🖥 *www.french-news.com*

The two weekly newspapers listed below are designed and written for expatriates and can be delivered anywhere in the world. An annual subscription costs between £112 and £118.

The Guardian Weekly   ☎ +44 (0)870-066 0510
🖳 *www.guardian.co.uk/guardianweekly*
Condenses the best of *The Guardian, The Observer, Le Monde* and *The Washington Post* and adds bespoke articles.

The Weekly Telegraph   ☎ +44 (0)1454 642464
🖳 *www.expat.telegraph.co.uk*
Condenses the best of *The Daily* and *Sunday Telegraph* and adds bespoke articles.

Organic Produce

Organic produce (*produits biologiques/bio*) is widely available in supermarkets and hypermarkets. Organic shops are becoming more popular but have a tendency to come and go.

Passport Photos

Kiosks can usually be found in the entrance to supermarkets and in hypermarket centres.

Post Offices

French post offices offer a wide range of facilities, including cash machines and internet access. Some have automated postage machines that can operate in English and allow you to pay by credit card.

Retail Parks

As in the UK, retail parks tend to be on the outskirts of cities and large towns and in France there tends to be a hypermarket at the centre.

Second-hand Goods

Brocantes come in all shapes and sizes and are a cross between an antique shop and a second-hand shop. You can find them in most towns and along main roads and they can be the source of bargains. *Dépôts-vente* – more of a cross between a charity shop and a pawn broker's – are also a good source of second-hand goods, as well as a means of selling unwanted stuff.

Supermarkets & Hypermarkets

French supermarkets advertise heavily on roadside hoardings, often giving directions and distances in minutes, but note that these directions can just stop, leaving you lost and apparently a great deal more than '5 mins' away from the shop. They often advertise at the side of a competitor's shop, when their shop is actually in the next town.

Due to the damage done to the environment by the thin carrier bags currently given away by some supermarkets, they're soon to be banned completely. As a result the shops are encouraging shoppers to buy 'long life' bags, which they will replace free when they wear out.

The most common supermarkets in this region are listed below; the websites will give you the location of the shop nearest to you.

Leclerc	🖥 *www.e-leclerc.com*
Intermarché	🖥 *www.intermarche.com*
Champion	🖥 *www.champion.fr*
Cora	🖥 *www.cora.fr*
Super U	🖥 *www.super-u.com*

Hypermarkets (*hypermarchés*) are one of the best sources of electrical goods and general household items. There aren't as many specialist electrical shops in France as in the UK and it's quite normal to buy your new washing machine from a hypermarket. Hypermarkets tend to be situated in retail parks on the outskirts of towns and cities and the buildings themselves are often small shopping precincts with a variety of shops and services. There are four main hypermarket chains in Normandy. Individual stores are listed in the following chapters. The company websites are given below.

Carrefour	🖥 *www.carrefour.com*
Leclerc	🖥 *www.e-leclerc.com*
Géant	🖥 *www.geant.com*
Auchan	🖥 *www.auchan.com*

Note the following general points regarding store opening times:

- Very few supermarkets open on Sundays – occasionally on Sunday mornings but never in the afternoon – and no hypermarkets open on Sundays.

- Opening hours can change from summer to winter, with longer lunchtime closing and later evening opening in the summer.

- Larger shops may open all day Mondays to Fridays, others only on Fridays and Saturdays, closing for lunch the rest of the week, while the smallest shops generally close for lunch every day and possibly Monday mornings.

Wines & Spirits

There aren't as many off-licences (*caves*) in France as in the UK, as hypermarkets and supermarkets sell the majority of alcoholic drinks. Some of the specialist shops listed under this heading sell table wine by the litre, usually starting at just over €1 per litre, but you must take your own container. Suitable containers with taps can be bought at DIY shops and large supermarkets.

Sports & Outdoor Activities

A selection of the activities available in each department is provided in the following chapters; full details are available from tourist offices and *mairies*. Not surprisingly, large towns have the widest range of facilities.

Note that many 'physical' sports require a licence. The relevant club will have the forms and a medical may be required, which your doctor can carry out as a standard consultation.

Tourist Offices

Tourist offices hold details of local events throughout the year and are a good source of general information and local guide books. Details of relevant regional and departmental offices are given in the following chapters; opening hours are current but may change slightly from year to year.

> Comité Régional du Tourisme
> de Normandie   ☎ 02 32 33 79 00
> Le Doyenné, 14 rue Charles Corbeau, Evreux
> 🖳 *www.normandy-tourisme.org*
> 🖳 *www.normandie-pays.com*

The Paris tourist office, given below, can provide information for the whole of France.

> Office de Tourisme de Paris, 25 rue
> des Pyramides, 75001 Paris   ☎ 08 92 68 30 00
> 🖳 *www.paris-touristoffice.com*

Tradesmen

Almost every commune has a tradesman (*artisan*) of some description, from carpenter (*menuisier*) or builder (*maçon*) to electrician (*électricien*) or plumber (*plombier*). One way to find out what local tradesmen there are is to look through the phone book in the residential listing for your commune; tradesmen will have their profession next to their name and address. The best way, however, is to ask at the *mairie*; it's likely that the *Maire* will even give you a personal introduction.

Using local French tradesman has the advantage that they know the materials they will be working with, are familiar with the systems in place in your property and, as they live locally, have a reputation to maintain. The increasing influx of Britons and other foreigners to rural France means that more and more French artisans are willing to communicate in a mixture of French and English, drawings and sign language (see also **Translation** below).

Registered builders in France have their work guaranteed for ten years and must be fully insured to cover any accident or damage to themselves, you or your property. To check whether a tradesman is registered to work in France, go to 🖳 *www.cofacerating.fr*, click on the Union Jack at the top and under 'For more information on' click on 'A company'; this takes you to a form where you enter the tradesman's telephone number. If he's registered, the company information will appear; a big red cross indicates that he isn't registered.

Should you decide to use an un-registered tradesman – either French or foreign – you should be aware that, if there's an accident, you will be personally and financially liable; you will have no warranty on the work carried out and you won't be able to claim the low tax rate (5.5 per cent instead of 19.6 per cent) available until the end of 2005 for renovation work. You could have additional problems if you need to make an insurance claim involving the work (e.g. in the case of a flood or subsidence).

Note also that a tradesman's insurance doesn't cover them for all work, but only for the skills for which they're registered; for example, your builder may offer to sort out your electrics, but he may not be registered as an electrician and hence not insured for that work.

Just as you would in the UK, ensure that you obtain several quotes, if possible see some work already done and think you will get along with a tradesman before engaging him.

Further details of finding and supervising builders in France can be found in *Renovating and Maintaining Your French Home* (Survival Books – see page 379).

The following website has details on English-speaking tradesmen that are French registered.

🖳 *www.artisan-anglais.com*

Planning Permission

If you want to make any alterations to your home – even painting the window frames a different colour – you must first visit the *mairie*. There are strict regulations (which vary from commune to commune) governing what can and cannot be done and a strict procedure that must be followed for certain types of work. This is too a complex subject to describe here. For full details, refer to **Renovating and Maintaining Your French Home** (Survival Books – see page 379).

Translation

If you have a small amount of text that you need translated, the Altavista website (🖥 *www.altavista.com*) can translate up to 150 words from a variety of different languages. This isn't an accurate translation and should never be relied on for legal or professional purposes, but it will give you the gist of the information.

Another website that offers translations is 🖥 www.wanadoo.fr; go to '*traduction*' on the left hand side under the heading '*Utile & pratique*'. It can translate both typed in text and websites.

Utilities

Electricity

Électricité de France/Gaz de France (EDF/GDF) is one company for the whole of France but operates its gas and electricity divisions separately. The numbers below are for general information; emergency numbers can be found on page 69.

In France electricity bills are in two parts: consumption (*consommation*) and a monthly standing charge (*abonnement*). Electricity consumption is charged according to one of a range of tariffs. The standing charge is related to how much power (calculated in kilowatts or kW) you have available to you at any time: the more power you have available, the higher the standing charge. Your consumption charge is also related to the amount of power you have available, the charge per unit being higher the more power is available.

Your electricity bill, under '*votre facture en détail*', will tell you what your standing charge is per month (…€/*mois*). Under *montant à prélever* it will give you your existing allowance of kW at any one time, e.g. '*puissance 6kW, code 024*'. If you qualify for cheap rate hours (*heures creuses*), it will also show the relevant times, which are usually from 1 to 7am and from noon to 2pm.

If you use more than the power available, the trip switch is triggered and you will be thrown into darkness and left to fumble for a torch. To prevent repeated 'tripping' of the system, you may need to uprate your supply to cover your expected maximum power consumption at any one time (e.g. running the dishwasher, washing machine and cooker all at once), although this will cost you more.

An alternative is to install a piece of equipment called a *délesteur*, which is a tiny computer wired into your system: when the system is overloaded, it automatically switches off apparatus in order of priority (pre-determined by you, e.g. hot water tank and tumble drier before lights, alarm or plug sockets).

Like most other utility bills, electricity bills are normally issued bi-monthly in France. As your meter will be outside the property and accessible from the street (you mustn't block access to it), it may be read without your knowing. If a reading hasn't been taken, your electricity bill will be estimated (indicated by an *E* alongside the figures). If the estimate is higher than the actual reading, you can take your bill to your local office (listed in subsequent chapters) and you will be sent an amended bill in the form of a credit to your account.

Gas

Gas (*gaz*) can be 'natural' (from a main supply), butane or propane. If you aren't on mains gas (*gaz de ville*), which is generally available only in larger towns and residential areas, you will need a tank (*citerne*), which provides propane gas, or bottles to provide butane. If you use gas only for cooking, bottles are sufficient; if you have gas central heating, a tank is essential. The main difference between natural and butane or propane gas is that the latter burn much hotter (take care when trying to simmer milk!) and appliances designed for natural gas will need to have the injectors changed to a smaller size. If the appliance is new, it should come with two sizes of injector (the larger size is for natural gas and usually the one that comes fitted).

If there's already a tank at the property, you will be required to pay a deposit for it and, when it has been filled up, the price of a full tank of gas, irrespective of how much was left in it. The gas company will credit the previous owners with what was left in the tank. The deposit can be as much as €1,000 and a tank full of gas as much as €900, so take this into account when considering purchasing the property. Instead of a deposit, you can choose to pay a monthly charge for the tank.

You can monitor your gas consumption using the gauge on a tank and re-order when it drops to the red line. You may find that the gas company will come automatically when they believe you should be due for a refill or phone you if they're going to be in the area to see if you want more gas delivered. The driver will give you a delivery note stating the quantity delivered, the price per kg and the total due. If the bill is large, you may be able to send two cheques, one dated a month after the other, but ask your supplier first.

The first time you buy bottled gas, you must pay a deposit for the bottle plus the price of the gas; when you have a bottle refilled, you pay only for the gas. You don't need to take the paperwork with you for refills, just the empty bottle. The deposit is around €25 but varies slightly according to the gas you choose. Bottles, which don't have gauges but can simply be shaken to ascertain how much gas is left gas, are available from petrol stations and many garden centres.

Water

Water in France is supplied by a variety of organisations, from national companies to individual communes – in the latter case with bills sent out by the *mairie*.

Wood

To find a local supplier of firewood, ask a neighbour or at the *mairie*, as many farmers in the region supply suitable wood. When ordering wood, you must specify how much you want in an arcane measure called a *stère*, which is roughly 0.6 cubic metres (many people erroneously believe it's one cubic metre) or 500kg of wood. You may also need to specify whether it's for burning now or in a few years and whether it's for a large open fire or a log burner. Wood for log burners is slightly more expensive, as it has to be cut smaller. You can of course order the longer length and cut your own for the log burner. Electric and petrol chainsaws (*tronçonneuses*) are available from all DIY shops from the autumn onwards and can also be hired from certain outlets. Depending on the age and type of wood, expect to pay around €20 to €25 per cubic metre.

Six cubic metres (around ten *stères*) should be enough for a winter if you're only using fires and log burners for cold days or in the evenings. If fires are your only source of heating, you will need more, depending of course on how many fires you have and whether you have a wood-burning cooker.

Wood varies in suitability for use on an open fire. Good and unsuitable woods are listed below.

Good Woods

- Apple (*pommier*) – produces a good scent;

- Ash (*frêne*) – burns well and produces plenty of warmth whether green or brown, wet or dry;

- Beech (*hêtre*) – almost smokeless;

- Chestnut (*châtaignier*) – needs to be aged;

- Oak (*chêne*) – must be old and dry;

- Pear (*poirier*) – produces a good scent.

Unsuitable Woods

- Birch (*bouleau*) – bright and fast burning;

- Elm (*orme*) – doesn't burn well;

- Fir (*sapin*) – bright and fast burning;

- Poplar (*peuplier*) – fast burning and produces a bitter smoke.

Chimney Sweeps

It costs around €45 to have a chimney swept (*ramoné*). The chimney sweep (*ramoneur*) may ask you to sign a form that enables him to charge you a lower rate of VAT. Although you're no longer legally required to have your chimney swept regularly, if you have a chimney fire and are unable to produce a receipt showing that your chimney has been swept recently, you may have difficulty claiming on insurance (check your policy). If using a fire or log burner throughout the winter, you're recommended to have a chimney swept at least once a year anyway. A '*bouchon de ramonage*' is a slow burning brick that performs a similar job to a chimney sweep. Throughout the winter they can found in both supermarkets and DIY shops. This method of cleaning isn't as thorough and therefore should be used in addition to a chimney sweep, not instead. Many plumbers and roofing companies also sweep chimneys.

Château de Crèvecoeur, Lisieux

3

Calvados

This chapter provides details of facilities and services in the department of Calvados (14). General information about each subject can be found in **Chapter 2**. All entries are arranged alphabetically by town, except where a service applies over a wide area, in which case it's listed at the beginning of the relevant section under 'General'. A map of Calvados is shown below.

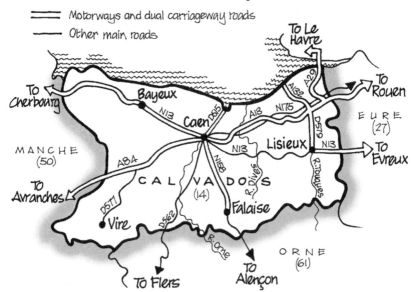

Accommodation

Chateaux

Houlgate   Château de Dramard, Gonneville-
              sur-Mer   ☎ 02 31 24 63 41
              💻 *www.chateaudramard.com*
              (north-east of Caen, a few kilometres east of Cabourg)
              This small 17th century chateau is situated in parkland
              close to the sea. There are two small and two large suites,
              the latter have the option of an extra, adjoining double
              bedroom. English is spoken by the owners. Prices from
              €150 to €260 per night, per suite, including breakfast.

Colombières   Château de Colombières   ☎ 02 31 22 51 65
              ✉ *colombieresaccueil@tiscali.fr*
              (mid-way between Carentan and Bayeux)
              This is an impressive chateau surrounded by a moat and
              the drawbridge is still the only means of entry to the inner
              courtyard. Three bedrooms are available from 1st June to

30th September, from €130 to €180 per night. English is
spoken fluently by the Count and Countess.

Gîtes and Bed & Breakfast

General   Gîtes de France Calvados, 6 promenade
de Madame de Sévigné, Caen   ☎ 02 31 82 71 65
🖳 *www.gites-de-france-calvados.fr*

Clévacances, 8 rue Renoir, Caen   ☎ 02 31 27 90 30
🖳 *www.clevacances.com*
✉ *14@clevacances.com*

Hotels

Various tourist office websites have details of hotel accommodation in
Calvados, including the following:

🖳 *www.bayeux-tourism.com*
🖳 *www.caen.fr/tourisme/*
🖳 *www.calvados-tourisme.com*
🖳 *www.normandy-tourism.org*

Business Services

Computer Services

Caen   Espace Micro, 3 rue Basse   ☎ 02 31 93 37 14
(by the bus station)
Computer sales, repairs and software. Open Mondays to
Thursdays 10am to 11pm, Fridays and Saturdays 10am to
1am, Sundays and bank holidays 10am to 1pm and 3 to
9pm. The long hours are due to the shop also offering
internet access and video/DVD hire.

Falaise   Aservitec Informatique, 19 rue
Georges Clémenceau   ☎ 02 31 90 33 20
This shop deals with all computer services and staff speak
English. Open Mondays to Saturday 9am to noon and 2 to
7pm.

Lisieux   Micro Tech, 52 rue Alençon   ☎ 02 31 62 07 91
Computer sales, repairs (including a home service) and
courses.

Vire   Espace Internet, 30 rue André
Halbout   ☎ 02 31 67 00 01
🖳 *www.espaceinternet.com*

Open Mondays to Fridays 10.30am to 12.30pm and 2.30 to 7pm. Computer sales, repairs and internet access.

Employment Agencies

The main offices of the national employment agency, ANPE, are as follows:

Bayeux	62 bis rue St Patrice	☎ 02 31 51 28 40
Caen	16 clos Herbert	☎ 02 31 46 19 19
Falaise	12 rue Trinité	☎ 02 31 90 06 48
Lisieux	3 chemin Lourdes	☎ 02 31 31 11 07
Vire	3 rue Viverot	☎ 02 31 09 20 90

Communications

France Télécom

General	Dial ☎ 1014 or go to 💻 *www.francetelecom.fr* Local France Télécom shops are listed below.
Bayeux	rue Saint Lô Open Tuesdays to Fridays 9.30am to noon (Thursdays from 10am) and 2 to 6pm, Saturdays 9.30am to 12.30pm and 2 to 5.30pm.
Caen	rue Bellivet Open Mondays to Saturdays 10am to 7pm.
Falaise	1 rue Vauquelin Open Tuesdays to Saturdays 9.30am to 12.15pm and 2 to 6pm.
Lisieux	rue Henri Chéron Open Tuesdays to Saturdays 9.30am to noon (Wednesdays from 10am) and 2 to 7pm.
Vire	16 rue Saulnerie Open Tuesdays to Fridays 9.30am to noon and 2 to 6pm, Saturdays 9.30am to 12.30pm and 2 to 5.30pm.

Internet Access

Bayeux	Micro Sim Plus, 67 rue des Bouchers ☎ 02 31 22 06 02 💻 *www.microsimplus*

Open Tuesdays to Saturdays 10am to 12.30pm and
2.30 to 9pm.
You can also access the internet in the post office by the
Hôtel de Ville.

Caen   Espace Micro, 1–3 rue Basse, place
                     Courtonne   ☎ 02 31 53 68 68
                     (from the tourist office go past the cathedral and straight on
                     towards the old tower; place Courtonne is just behind)
                     This is reputedly the largest cyber café in Normandy with
                     60 computers, open every day 10am to midnight.

Falaise   Aservitec Informatique, 19 rue
                     Georges Clémenceau   ☎ 02 31 90 33 20
                     Open Mondays to Saturday 9am to noon and 2 to 7pm.
                     English spoken.

Lisieux   le Cybercafé, 3 bis avenue Sainte
                     Thérèse   ☎ 02 31 62 83 51
                     💻 www.lecybercafe.net
                     Open Fridays to Wednesdays 2pm to 1am.

Vire   Espace Internet, 30 rue André
                     Halbout   ☎ 02 31 67 00 01
                     💻 www.espaceinternet.com
                     Open Mondays to Fridays 10.30am to 12.30pm and
                     2.30 to 7pm.

Mobile Telephones

See page 62.

Domestic Services

Clothes Alterations

Falaise   Retouches Couture, 30 rue Trinité   ☎ 02 31 90 15 96
                     Open Tuesdays to Saturdays.

Lisieux   Central Retouches, 29 rue 11
                     Novembre   ☎ 02 31 62 94 10

Vire   Top Couture, 2 rue Chênedollé   ☎ 02 31 68 15 92
                     Open Tuesdays to Saturdays.

Crèches & Nurseries

Bayeux   Graine d'Eveil, 24 rue Bouchers   ☎ 02 31 92 75 25

Children from two months to five years old. Open Mondays
1.30 to 5.30pm, Tuesdays and Thursdays 9am to 6pm,
Wednesdays and Fridays 9am to noon and 1.30
to 5.30pm.

Caen	Crèche Halte-Garderie, 18 avenue des Chevaliers	☎ 02 31 73 79 00
Falaise	Halte-Garderie, rue Charlotte Herpin	☎ 02 31 90 05 80
Lisieux	Crèche, place François Mitterrand	☎ 02 31 31 53 10
Vire	Crèche, rue Anne Morgan	☎ 02 31 68 04 12
	Babysitting, Maison Jeunes & Culture, 1 rue des Halles	☎ 02 31 66 35 10

Equipment & Tool Hire

Bayeux	Régis Location, 1 rue Arromanches, St Vigor le Grand 🖳 *www.regis-location.fr* (off the northern ring road)	☎ 02 31 92 17 89
Caen	Loxam, ZI Sud, rue Newton, Mondeville 🖳 *www.loxam.fr* (south-east of Caen, on the N13)	☎ 02 31 35 88 10
Marolles	Espace Emeraude, RN13 (directly east of Lisieux)	☎ 02 31 48 32 32

Garden Services

General	Iain & Anna Geraghy, Chênedouit ✉ *thefrenchgeraghtys@tiscali.fr* Garden design and maintenance covering southern Calvados.	☎ 02 33 36 94 74
Bayeux	Au Comptoir du Bessin, 1 rue Arromanches General garden maintenance.	☎ 02 31 92 17 89
Lisieux	A la Coupe sur Measure Grass cutting and general garden maintenance, either regular contracts or specific tasks.	☎ 02 31 31 37 30

Marquee Hire

Livarot   Levannier-Huet, Le Mesnil Simon   ☎ 02 31 63 15 75
Marquees for hire complete with heating, tables and chairs,
for 30 to 100 people.

Septic Tank Services

Blainville sur Orne   Madeline Yves, ZI Caen Canal,
rue Mer   ☎ 02 31 72 44 44

Hermival les Vaux   Bouillet Sarl, rue Edouard Branly   ☎ 02 31 31 44 00

Entertainment

This section isn't intended to be a definitive guide but gives a wide range
of ideas for the department. Prices and opening hours were correct at the
time of writing, but it's best to check before travelling long distances.

Cinemas

Bayeux   le Méliès, 6 rue Genas Duhomme ☎ 02 31 21 55 47

Caen   Ciné Cité, Centre Commercial
Mondeville 2   ☎ 08 92 70 00 00
(on the south-east outskirts of the city)
A 12-screen complex.

Falaise   l'Entracte, 8 rue de la Fresnaye   ☎ 02 31 90 31 17
💻 *www.falaise.fr*

Lisieux   le Majestic, 7 rue au Char   ☎ 08 92 68 81 06

Vire   le Basselin, place Castel   ☎ 02 31 66 16 40

Festivals

There are many festivals in this department, and just a small selection of
the annual events are detailed here. Further details are available from
tourist offices.

March   Bayeux
Festival d'Art Vocal   ☎ 02 31 51 28 28

Pont L'Evêque
Festival de Musique

May	**Pont d'Ouilly** Fête de la Pentecôte Carnival and parade, music and fireworks at the end of the month.
June	**Caen** Le Marathon de la Liberté ☎ 02 31 27 14 14
	Bayeux Victoire de la Liberté Shows and re-enactments.
July	**Bayeux** Two-day medieval festival. ☎ 02 31 51 28 28
	Vire les Virevoltés ☎ 02 31 66 60 27 🖥 *www.lesvirevoltes.com* A variety of street entertainment, shows and celebrations for all ages in the first two weeks of the month.
July/August	**Across the department** les Promenades Musicales du Pays d'Auge ☎ 02 31 31 06 00 ✉ *culture.et.patrimoine@wanadoo.fr* Concerts throughout the department held in churches, chateaux, parks and gardens.
August	**Bayeux** Calvadose de Rock ☎ 02 31 51 28 28 Music festival.
	Falaise Festival des Jeux Anciens, Château de Guillaume. Festival of toys and games from times gone by.
September	**Caen** Foire Internationale de Caen ☎ 02 31 27 14 14
October	**Caen** Jumping International de Caen ☎ 02 31 27 14 14 This show jumping event has been running for 20 years.
	Fontaine-Henry (north-west of Caen) Annual flower festival at the chateau.
	Trévières (below the N13, north-west of Bayeux) Apple festival.

Libraries

Bayeux	Centre Guillaume le Conquérant, rue aux Coqs ☎ 02 31 51 20 20

Open Tuesdays, Thursdays and Fridays 2 to 6pm, Wednesdays 10am to 12.30pm and 2 to 6pm, Saturdays 10am to 12.30pm and 2 to 5pm. There's a selection of English books in the adult section.

Caen   Place Louis-Guillouard ☎ 02 31 30 47 00
💻 *www.bm@ville-caen.fr*
Tuesdays, Wednesdays, Fridays and Saturdays 9am to 7pm, Thursdays 1 to 7pm. This library has a selection of English books that can be found in sections 813 and 823.

Falaise   rue Gonfroy Fitz Rou ☎ 02 31 41 61 41
Tuesdays, Thursdays and Fridays 2 to 6pm, Wednesdays 10am to 12.30 and 2 to 6pm, Saturdays 10am to 5pm. There's a small selection of English books. If the library is closed or the telephone engaged, your call is automatically diverted to the *mairie*.

Lisieux   Place de la République ☎ 02 31 48 41 00
Tuesdays 2 to 7pm, Wednesdays 10am to noon and 2 to 6pm, Thursdays and Fridays 12.30pm to 6pm, Saturdays 9.30am to 5.30pm. This library does not currently stock any English books.

Vire   14 rue Chênedolle ☎ 02 31 66 27 10
Tuesdays and Thursdays 2 to 6.30pm, Wednesdays 9am to 6.30pm, Fridays 9am to noon and 2 to 6.30pm, Saturdays 9am to noon and 2 to 5pm. This library has a selection of English books.

Theatres

Caen   Théâtre de Caen, 135 boulevard Maréchal Leclerc ☎ 02 31 30 48 20
💻 *www.theatre.caen.fr*
(in the pedestrian area south of the chateau)

         Théâtre d'Hérouville, quartier du Bois, Hérouville St Clair ☎ 02 31 53 67 00
(north-east side of Caen)

Deauville   Théâtre du Casino Barrière, 2 rue Edmond Blanc ☎ 02 31 98 66 00
(on the coast north of Lisieux)

Falaise   Théâtre de Forum, boulevard de la Libération ☎ 02 31 41 66 80

Lisieux	Théâtre de Lisieux Pays d'Auge, 2 rue au Char ✉ *theatre.liseux@free.fr*	☎ 02 31 61 12 13
Vire	le Préau, place Castel	☎ 02 31 66 16 00

Video & DVD Hire

See page 67.

French Teachers & Courses

Bayeux	Greta, route Caen Government-run organisation.	☎ 02 31 21 61 00
Caen	Words & Ways, 15 rue Sadi Carnot 🖥 *www.words-and-ways.com*	☎ 02 31 50 23 79
Falaise	Greta, rue des Champs St Georges (on the bend of the road by the bridge as you go out of the town towards Caen) Government-run organisation.	☎ 02 31 90 28 06
Lisieux	Greta, Lycée Marcel Gambier, rue du Général Leclerc ✉ *greta.paysdauge@ac-caen.fr* Government-run organisation.	☎ 02 31 48 60 00
	Centre d'Etudes Lisieux, 10 boulevard Carnot 🖥 *www.perso.wanadoo.fr/centre.normandie* Residential language courses.	☎ 02 31 31 22 01
Vire	MJC, 1 rue des Halles 🖥 *www.mjc-vire.org* Beginners' and improvers' groups on Wednesday evenings.	☎ 02 31 66 35 10

Leisure Activities

This section isn't intended to be a definitive guide but gives a wide range of ideas for the department. Prices and opening hours were correct at the time of writing, but it's best to check before travelling long distances.

Arts & Crafts

Bayeux	Ecole Municipale des Beaux-Arts,

Impasse du Stade ☎ 02 31 21 57 36
Courses for all ages from seven to adult.

Caen   MJC du Chemin Vert, 1 rue d'Isigny ☎ 02 31 74 13 87
              💻 www.caen.fr/mjc-cheminvert
              (north-east of the city, just inside the ring road at junction 7)
              A wide range of classes are held throughout the week,
              including drawing and sketching, sculpture and modelling,
              pastels, oil painting and painting on porcelain and china.

Vire   MJC, 1 rue des Halles ☎ 02 31 66 35 10
              Sculpture, patchwork and art classes held weekly.

Bouncy Castle Hire

Caen   MJC du Chemin Vert, 1 rue d'Isigny ☎ 02 31 74 13 87
              💻 www.caen.fr/mjc-cheminvert
              (north-east of the city, just inside the ring road at junction 7)
              This organisation has bouncy castles for hire, with or
              without staff. A magician can also come along to the event
              for around an hour.

Bowling

Caen   Bowling, 6 rue Charles Coulomb,
              Mondeville ☎ 02 31 82 53 58
              Open 10am to 4am with 22 bowling alleys, a restaurant,
              pub and live entertainment.

Courseulles sur Mer Bowling de la Mer, place du 6 Juin ☎ 02 31 37 48 58
              💻 www.bowlingdelamer.com
              (on the coast north of Caen)
              Bowling, bar and karaoke just 50m from the beach. Open
              Mondays to Fridays 8pm to 4am, weekends 3pm to 4am,
              school holidays open every day 3pm to 4am. Closed
              Sunday evenings and Mondays from September to Easter.

Bridge

Bayeux   Bayeux Bridge Club, contact
              M. Marie ☎ 02 31 80 11 77

Caen   Ceux de l'OMJ, La Prairie, 11 avenue
              Albert Soret ☎ 02 31 85 25 16
              💻 www.la-prairie.com
              (on the north-west side of the hippodrome, south of the city
              centre)
              The bridge club meets every Tuesday at 2pm.

Lisieux   Club de Bridge, 17 rue Edouard
              Branly ☎ 02 31 62 30 60

Vire   Club de Bridge, Ancienne Mairie de
                Neuville, rue de la Mairie de Neuville ☎ 02 31 68 19 86
                Competitions Monday afternoons and Thursday evenings,
                beginners' courses Monday evenings at 8pm, free play
                Saturdays from 2pm.

Children's Activity Clubs

Bayeux   Centre de Loisirs Educatif Municipal,
                5 place Charles de Gaulle   ☎ 02 31 22 72 31
                Leisure activities for children from 4 to 14 every
                Wednesday and during the school holidays.

Caen   MJC du Chemin Vert, 1 rue d'Isigny ☎ 02 31 74 13 87
                💻 www.caen.fr/mjc-cheminvert
                (north-east of the city, just inside the ring road at junction 7)
                Activities for 3 to 14-year-olds between 7.30am and 6pm
                every Wednesday during term time and school holidays,
                either full or half days, with or without lunch. €6.50 half day,
                €12.30 full day.

                Tandem, 8 rue Nicolas Oresme   ☎ 02 31 29 54 54
                (south-west of the city centre)
                This organisation runs two groups, as follows:

                Atelier d'Eveil Câlin
                A group for babies from two months through to walking age.
                A maximum of eight babies and their parents. Sessions last
                one hour and include movement and massage.

                Atelier Rencontre en Jeux
                This group is for children just walking to 30 months old and
                involves the parents helping their children to discover a
                variety of toys and activities that will assist their
                development.

Lisieux   Lisieux Stella Gym, rue du Général
                Leclerc   ☎ 02 31 62 05 37
                Baby gym.

Choral Singing

Caen   MJC du Chemin Vert, 1 rue d'Isigny ☎ 02 31 74 13 87
                💻 www.caen.fr/mjc-cheminvert
                (north-east of the city, just inside the ring road at junction 7)
                Catherine Maillot runs singing workshops with a show
                arranged at the end of the year. Mondays at 6.30pm.

                Jazz Vocal, La Prairie, 11 avenue
                Albert Soret   ☎ 02 31 85 25 16
                💻 www.la-prairie.com

(on the north-west side of the hippodrome, south of the city centre)
This class meets in groups of four, Mondays at 8.30pm.

Circus Skills

Caen   Compagnie Les Toqués du Tic,
                Tandem, 8 rue Nicolas Oresme   ☎ 02 31 29 54 54
                (south-west of the city centre)
                Groups for various ages from five to adult.

Computer Training

Caen   Atelier Informatique, Tandem, 8 rue
                Nicolas Oresme   ☎ 02 31 29 54 54
                (south-west of the city centre)
                Courses for children, youngsters and adults, covering the
                basics of computer use and packages such as Word, Excel
                and Internet Explorer. Maximum group size of eight people.

Lisieux   le Cybercafé, 3 bis avenue Sainte
                Thérèse   ☎ 02 31 62 83 51
                This internet cafe offers training for all levels. Open Fridays
                to Wednesdays 2pm to 1am.

Vire   MJC, 1 rue des Halles   ☎ 02 31 66 35 10
                Six-week courses for beginners and improvers, Thursday
                and Friday evenings.

Dancing

Bayeux   Centre de Danse, 26 rue de la
                Poterie   ☎ 02 31 92 36 68
                This centre offers ballet, modern dance, jazz, yoga and
                gym classes.

                Association Bayeux Danse Club, Salle
                St Laurent, 46 rue St Laurent   ☎ 06 81 80 49 31
                🖳 www.danse-avenel.com
                Lessons for the waltz, tango, cha cha, etc.

Caen   MJC du Chemin Vert, 1 rue d'Isigny ☎ 02 31 74 13 87
                🖳 www.caen.fr/mjc-cheminvert
                (north-east of the city, just inside the ring road at junction 7)
                A variety of classes. including African, Indian, Latin
                American and Salsa dancing.

                la Prairie, 11 avenue Albert Soret ☎ 02 31 85 25 16
                🖳 www.la-prairie.com

(on the north-west side of the hippodrome, south of the city centre)
Latin American and ballroom dancing.

Falaise

Ecole de Danse, Centre Dumont
d'Urville   ☎ 02 31 40 10 52
Ballet, jazz and keep fit.

Danses du Monde, Salle de Guibray,
19 rue Robert le Magnifique   ☎ 02 31 90 08 86
Folk dancing for beginners and intermediates, first session free.

Lisieux

MJC, 13 boulevard Pasteur   ☎ 02 31 62 09 60
Ballet, jazz, rock, break dancing and classical dances such as waltz, samba, etc. All age groups with various sessions throughout the week.

Vire

MJC, 1 rue des Halles   ☎ 02 31 66 35 10
Latin and modern dance classes for beginners and intermediates.

Ecole de Danse Nadine Leprovost, rue
André Séverin   ☎ 02 31 67 90 70
Ballet, jazz and tap for all ages.

Drama

Bayeux

Atelier Théâtre, Salle St Léon, rue des
Teinturiers   ☎ 02 31 51 83 06
Groups for children and adults.

Caen

MJC du Chemin Vert, 1 rue d'Isigny ☎ 02 31 74 13 87
🖥 www.caen.fr/mjc-cheminvert
(north-east of the city, just inside the ring road at junction 7)
Theatre classes that work on your voice, learning of lines and the preparation of scenes. Groups for children and adults.

la Prairie, 11 avenue Albert Soret   ☎ 02 31 85 25 16
🖥 www.la-prairie.com
(on the north-west side of the hippodrome, south of the city centre)
Drama classes for adult beginners and experienced actors. The first three sessions can be on a trial basis. Free childcare is available between 5 and 8.30pm for children between three and ten.

Dress Making

Bayeux
Club Couture Familiale, La Halle St
Patrice, place St Patrice   ☎ 02 31 80 27 18
Friday afternoons from 2pm.

Caen
la Prairie, 11 avenue Albert Soret   ☎ 02 31 85 25 16
💻 *www.la-prairie.com*
(on the north-west side of the hippodrome, south of the city
centre)
Various dress making and patchwork classes throughout
the week.

Vire
MJC, 1 rue des Halles   ☎ 02 31 66 35 10
Classes on Fridays from September to April.

Flower Arranging

Caen
Art Floral Occidental, La Prairie, 11
avenue Albert Soret   ☎ 02 31 85 25 16
💻 *www.la-prairie.com*
(on the north-west side of the hippodrome, south of the city
centre)
Classes are held one Thursday a month at 9.15am, 2pm
and 6pm. €20 per session including tuition and flowers.
Free childcare is available from 5pm for children between
three and ten.

Gym

Caen
MJC du Chemin Vert, 1 rue d'Isigny ☎ 02 31 74 13 87
💻 *www.caen.fr/mjc-cheminvert*
(north-east of the city, just inside the ring road at junction 7)
A wide variety of exercises classes throughout the week,
including step, stretching and high energy workouts.

Lisieux
Lisieux Stella Gym, rue du Général
Leclerc   ☎ 02 31 62 05 37
Baby gym, gymnastics and adult gym classes.

Vire
MJC, 1 rue des Halles   ☎ 02 31 66 35 10
Aerobic, step and stretching classes; different classes to
cover all ages and levels.

Gyms & Health Clubs

Bayeux
System Form, ZI du Loup Perdu   ☎ 02 31 51 92 71
(opposite the entrance to Weldom DIY shop)
This health club offers gym classes, cardio training, free
weights and a sauna.

Caen   Fleming Sport Center, 1 rue Alexander
                        Fleming, Hérouville St Clair   ☎ 02 31 47 56 71
                        💻 *www.flemingsportcenter.com*
                        (just north of the ring road at junction 4)
                        Swimming pool, gym classes, cardio equipment and
                        personal trainers. Open Mondays to Fridays 9am to
                        9.30pm, Saturdays 9am to 4.30pm and Sundays
                        10am to 1pm.

Ice Skating

Caen   Patinoire, rue Jean de la Varende   ☎ 02 31 30 47 40
                        💻 *www.caen.fr/netsport*
                        (in the south of the city by the hippodrome)
                        Open every day except Mondays in school term time (hours
                        vary according to the school holidays). Gloves are
                        obligatory. Individual and group lessons available. Adults
                        €3.45, under 18-year-olds €2.55. Ice hockey is played here,
                        and there are occasionally themed sessions such as
                        Halloween.

Magic

Caen   MJC du Chemin Vert, 1 rue d'Isigny ☎ 02 31 74 13 87
                        💻 *www.caen.fr/mjc-cheminvert*
                        (north-east of the city, just inside the ring road at junction 7)
                        An introduction to magic that also develops your
                        concentration and mental agility. Courses for all on Monday
                        evenings at 5.30pm.

Music

Bayeux   Ecole Municipale de Musique, place
                        Pommes   ☎ 02 31 92 24 38
                        Individual instruments, orchestra and choir.

Caen   MJC du Chemin Vert, 1 rue d'Isigny ☎ 02 31 74 13 87
                        💻 *www.caen.fr/mjc-cheminvert*
                        (north-east of the city, just inside the ring road at junction 7)
                        Lessons for violin and all types of guitar.

                        la Prairie, 11 avenue Albert Soret   ☎ 02 31 85 25 16
                        💻 *www.la-prairie.com*
                        (on the north-west side of the hippodrome, south of the city
                        centre)
                        Piano and clarinet lessons.

Falaise   Ecole de Musique, résidence Dumont
                        d'Urville, rue de la Résistance   ☎ 02 31 90 43 45

| Lisieux | Ecole Nationale de Musique & Danse, 3 place Georges Clémenceau | ☎ 02 31 48 31 85 |

Photography

Bayeux   Société Photographique,
              La Bajocasse   ☎ 02 31 22 88 51
              Specialising in old photography, collections and restoration.
              Contact Mlle Herouard.

Caen   MJC du Chemin Vert, 1 rue d'Isigny ☎ 02 31 74 13 87
              💻 www.caen.fr/mjc-cheminvert
              (north-east of the city, just inside the ring road at junction 7)
              Association Photos Arts Verts. This group covers the
              practical side of taking photographs, development in black
              and white and colour and displays of the finished results.
              Groups meet Mondays at 6.30pm and Fridays at 5.30pm.

Scouts & Guides

Bayeux   Scouts de France, 5 rue Franche   ☎ 02 31 51 95 15
              Three age groups from 8 to 21.

Caen   Scouts de Caen, 34 route de Caen,
              Rots   ☎ 02 31 26 04 98
              (north-west of Caen, off the N13)

Lisieux   Association des Scouts de France   ☎ 02 31 31 35 34
              Contact M. Vandewiele.

Vire   Scouts de France, Groupe St François☎ 02 31 67 39 47
              Contact M. Elyn.

Social Groups

Rotary Club

Bayeux   Rotary Club de Bayeux   ☎ 06 83 82 01 74
              Organised by M. Vigneau.

Lisieux   Rotary Club, Hôtel Mercure, RN13   ☎ 02 31 61 17 17
              Contact M. Fontaine.

Town Twinning

Bayeux   Bayeux-Dorchester   ☎ 02 31 92 10 20
              Meetings and events between the two towns, contact M.
              Bonnet.

Caen   Association pour le Jumelage Caen-

| | Portsmouth, 120 rue de la Délivrande | ☎ 02 31 93 06 44 |

| Lisieux | les Amis de Taunton
Contact Karin Carel. | ☎ 02 31 31 26 88 |

| Vire | Association de Jumelage Vire-Totnes | ☎ 02 31 66 60 29 |

Welcome Groups

| General | Accueil des Villes Françaises (AVF)
🖳 *www.avf.asso.fr*
Some towns have a branch of this organisation, which is specifically to help newcomers settle into the town. The site is available in English. |

| Bayeux | Bayeux AVF Accueil, 1 rue
Cuisiniers | ☎ 02 31 51 87 29 |

(in a beautiful old building on the corner of rue St Martin, which is a partially pedestrian street)
Various groups, including French conversation and a meeting group for young women.

| Caen | AVF, 2 avenue du 6 Juin | ☎ 02 31 86 02 60 |

| Vire | AVF, 1 rue des Augustines | ☎ 02 31 67 25 15 |

Stamp Collecting

| Bayeux | Amicale Philatélique Bayeusaine
Contact Mme Lepailleur. | ☎ 02 31 92 15 40 |

| Caen | Club Philathélique de la Folie
Couvrechef, 3 rue des Luthiers | ☎ 02 31 47 65 74 |

| Vire | Groupement Philatélique Virois
Contact M. Koch. | ☎ 02 31 67 00 90 |

Yoga

| Bayeux | Centre de Danse et Yoga de Bayeux,
26 rue de la Poterie | ☎ 02 31 92 36 68 |

| Caen | MJC du Chemin Vert, 1 rue d'Isigny | ☎ 06 62 57 23 27 |

🖳 *www.caen.fr/mjc-cheminvert*
(north-east of the city, just inside the ring road at junction 7)
Yoga classes and shiatsu workshops.

| Lisieux | MJC, 13 boulevard Pasteur | ☎ 02 31 62 09 60 |

Monday and Wednesday evenings, Thursday and Friday
mornings.

Vire   MJC, 1 rue des Halles   ☎ 02 31 66 35 10
                      Classes for adolescents, adults and seniors.

Medical Facilities & Emergency Services

Ambulances

See page 68.

Doctors

English-speakers may like to contact the following doctors:

Bayeux   Dr Marie-Noëlle Lavier, 6 rue
                     St Martin   ☎ 02 31 10 14 10

Caen   Dr Patrick Delahaye, 7 place St Gilles ☎ 02 31 93 08 84
                              for the duty doctor   ☎ 02 31 34 31 31

Falaise   Dr Macé, 3 boulevard de la
                     Libération   ☎ 02 31 40 06 90

Lisieux   Dr Hitier, 18 boulevard Pasteur ☎ 02 31 62 13 98

Vire   Dr Leribaux, 5 rue Notre Dame   ☎ 02 31 68 03 55

Gendarmeries

Bayeux   avenue Conseil   ☎ 02 31 92 94 00

Caen   12 rue Daniel Huet   ☎ 02 31 35 55 55
+
Falaise   route de Caen   ☎ 02 31 41 65 50

Lisieux   12 boulevard Duchesne Fournet   ☎ 02 31 62 02 45

Vire   1 rue des Tribunaux   ☎ 02 31 68 07 90

Health Authority

General   Assurance Maladie du Calvados, boulevard
                     du Général Weygard, Caen   ☎ 08 20 90 41 77
                     🖳 *www.cpam14.fr*

This is the main office for the department. Other offices are listed below.

Bayeux	59 bis rue Port en Bessin	☎ 02 31 51 15 50
Falaise	25 rue Amiral Courbet (behind the covered market)	☎ 02 31 90 00 01
Lisieux	cour Matignon	☎ 02 31 48 62 90
Vire	12 rue Emile Desvaux	☎ 02 31 66 20 20

Hospitals

All the following hospitals have an emergency department.

Bayeux	Centre Hospitalier, 13 rue de Nesmond	☎ 02 31 51 51 51
Caen	CHU, avenue Côte de Nacre	☎ 02 31 06 31 06
Falaise	Centre Hospitalier, boulevard des Bercagnes	☎ 02 31 40 40 40
Lisieux	Centre Hospitalier, 4 rue Roger Aini	☎ 02 31 61 31 31
Vire	Centre Hospitalier, 4 rue Emile Desvaux	☎ 02 31 67 47 47

Nightlife

This section isn't intended to be a definitive guide but gives a wide range of ideas for the department. Prices and opening hours were correct at the time of writing, but it's best to check before travelling long distances.

Bayeux   Loch Ness Café, 67 rue Montfiquet   ☎ 02 31 51 71 71
🖳 *www.lenoctambule.com*
Pool, video games, darts and football evenings with concerts throughout the summer. Open 7.30pm to 2am, Fridays and Saturdays until 3am.

Pub Fiction, 14 rue du Petit Rouen   ☎ 02 31 10 17 41
This bar is open Mondays to Thursdays 8pm to 2am, Fridays and Saturdays until 3am. There's a giant screen, music, concerts and theme evenings.

Caen

**Big Band Café, 1 avenue du Haut
Crépon, Herouville St Clair**   ☎ 02 31 47 96 13
(north-east side of Caen)
Part of a large complex including a concert venue, with
rehearsal rooms and music studios available
for hire.

**Bowling du Calvados, 6 rue
Charles Coulomb, Mondeville**   ☎ 02 31 82 53 58
(on the A13 east off the ring road)
Open noon to 4am with a restaurant, pub, karaoke, live
entertainment, bowling and pool tables.

**Café le Régent, 3 avenue de la
Libération**   ☎ 02 31 93 75 75
Open from 7am to 1am the following morning, every day.
There's a pool room upstairs open every day from 2.30pm
to 1am.

Canal Café, quai Vendeuvre   ☎ 02 31 86 73 00
🖳 *www.lerapporteur.fr/canalcafe*
This bar has a DJ every Wednesday and various concerts.
Open from 6pm to 4am.

le Carre, 32 quai Vendeuvre   ☎ 02 31 38 90 90
(overlooking the marina in the centre of town)
This club requires smart attire: no jeans or trainers allowed.
Open Tuesdays to Sundays 10.30pm to 5am.

le Dakota, 54 rue de Bernières   ☎ 02 31 50 05 25
This bar and nightclub is open Fridays and Saturdays from
6pm to 4am.

**el Cubanito Café, 12 avenue de la
Libération**   ☎ 02 31 94 34 16
(east of the chateau)
A Cuban bar with oriental cuisine and a large selection of
rum. Open from 11am to 1am.

the Glue Pot Pub, 18 quai Vendeuvre   ☎ 02 31 86 29 15
(south-east of the chateau in the city centre, alongside the
Bassin St Pierre section of the river)
An evening bar that has concerts at the weekends, open
Mondays to Saturdays 4pm to 4am, Sundays 8pm to 2am.

le Loft, route de Paris, Mondeville   ☎ 02 31 84 14 10
(on the south-east side of Caen, next to the BMW garage)
This music bar is open Thursdays to Saturdays from
7.30pm to midnight.

O'Donnell's Irish Pub, 20 quai
Vendeuvre ☎ 02 31 85 51 50
🖳 *www.odonnells-pub.com*
(south-east of the chateau in the city centre, alongside the
Bassin St Pierre section of the river)
A typical Irish pub with live concerts and a giant screen
for watching major sporting events. Open every day,
Sundays to Wednesdays 4pm to 2.30am, Thursdays
and Fridays 4pm to 4am, Saturdays
2pm to 4am.

l'Orient Express, rue du 11
Novembre ☎ 02 31 72 81 64
(near the river and the hippodrome)
Open from 2.30pm to 4am, with video games and 38
tables: pool and French billiards.

le Régent Cubain, 11 avenue de la
Côte de Nacre ☎ 02 31 44 83 47
Cuban music, *tapas* and summer concerts. Open
until 1am.

Courseulles sur Mer Bowling, 6 place du 6 Juin ☎ 02 31 37 48 58
🖳 *www.bowlingdelamer.com*
(on the coast to the north-west of Caen)
Bowling, pool tables, video bar and karaoke. Normally open
Tuesdays to Fridays 8pm to 4am, Saturdays and Sundays
3pm to 4am. (September to Easter closes at 8pm on
Sundays. During school holidays opens daily from 3pm to
4am.)

Deauville Casino Barrière de Deauville, 2 rue
Edmond Blanc ☎ 02 31 98 66 00
(on the coast north of Lisieux)
This casino also has a restaurant and theatre.

Lisieux le Bowling, rue de Paris ☎ 02 31 62 19 30
Bowling and pool tables.

le Club 98, 98 quai des Remparts ☎ 02 31 61 07 07
This nightclub is open from 11pm Thursdays to Saturdays
and bank holidays.

Luc sur Mer Casino Luc sur Mer, 20 rue Guynemer ☎ 02 31 97 32 19
(directly north of Caen, overlooking the sea)
This casino has a restaurant, live shows and gaming
machines as well as Black Jack, poker and roulette. The
casino is open from 9pm, the gaming machines
from 10am.

Perrières	le Lagon Bleu, Sur les Roches	☎ 02 31 40 10 97

(north-east of Falaise)
Discotheque.

Pont L'Evêque	Festival, route de Rouen	☎ 02 31 64 35 94

This disco is open Fridays, Saturdays and bank holidays.

Subles	l'Aurore Dancing, 3 route de St Paul du Vernay	☎ 02 31 92 64 33

(south-west of Bayeux on the D572)
Tea dances (ballroom and Latin American). Appropriate attire to be worn. Thursdays and Sunday 3 to 7pm and Saturdays 10pm to 3am.

Vire	Far West Café, 79 avenue de la Gare	☎ 02 31 68 91 51

This disco is open Wednesdays to Saturdays 11pm to 5am.

le Tiffany/le Tropique, route de Champ du Boult   ☎ 02 31 68 62 27
Two different discos within the same complex. Open 11pm to 5am. Smart clothes: no trainers, sports clothes or scruffy jeans.

Pets

Farriers

General	Anthony Gouya, Anguerny	☎ 06 07 53 76 58

(based north of Caen)

Pet Parlours

See page 79.

Riding Equipment

Lisieux	Horse Wood, route de Paris	☎ 02 31 32 57 20

💻 *www.horsewood.com*
(on the RN13 opposite the Leclerc supermarket in the south-east of the town)

SPA

Bayeux	SPA de Balleroy, 6 rue Verdun	☎ 02 31 21 61 37

Veterinary Clinics

See page 80.

Places to Visit

This section isn't intended to be a definitive guide but gives a wide range of ideas for the department. Prices and opening hours were correct at the time of writing, but it's best to check before travelling long distances.

Animal Parks & Aquariums

Courseulles sur Mer   Maison de la Mer, place Charles de Gaulle   ☎ 02 31 37 92 58
✉ *maison.de.la.mer@wanadoo.fr*
(on the coast north of Caen)
This aquarium specialises in wildlife in the Channel with giant sea turtles and a collection of shell fish from all over the world. There's an underwater viewing tunnel, and guided tours are available if booked. Open February to June and September 10am to 12.30pm and 2 to 6pm, July and August 9.30am to 7pm, October to January 2 to 6pm on Wednesdays, weekends and every day in the school holidays.

Honfleur   Naturospace, boulevard Charles V   ☎ 02 31 81 77 00
✉ *damico@naturospace.com*
The largest tropical butterfly house in France, with a large variety of tropical plants from across the world. Fully accessible for the disabled. Open February and March, October and November every day 10am to 1pm and 2 to 5.30pm, April to September every day 10am to 1pm and 2 to 7pm, July and August 10am to 7pm. Adults €7.10, 3 to 14-year-olds €5.70.

Jurques   Zoo Jurques   ☎ 02 31 77 94 12
💻 *www.zoodejurques.com*
Lions, tigers, cheetahs, giraffes, wolves and other animlas. A vivid aerial display of parrots and other shows organised throughout the day. There's an adventure playground and the café is open Easter to October. The zoo is open mid-February to end of March and 1st October to 1st November from 1.30 to 5.30pm, April 10am to 6pm, May to August 10am to 7pm, September 11am to 6pm. Adults €10.30, under 12s €6.

Lisieux   Espace de Liberté, Hermival les Vaux   ☎ 02 31 62 17 22
💻 *www.cerza.com*
This animal park has tigers, lions, rhinoceros, hippopotamus and more. A 3km (2mi) 'train' journey takes you past the animals, or there are two circuits you can walk. Two restaurants overlook the park and animals. Open February, March, October and November every day 10am to 5pm, April to June and September 9.30am to 6.30pm, July and August 9.30am to 7pm.

Trouville sur Mer   Natur'Aquarium, 17 rue de Paris   ☎ 02 31 88 46 04
💻 *www.natur-aquarium.com*
This aquarium has 70 tanks, including sea water,
freshwater and tropical, and features insects and reptiles
as well as fish. Open Easter to June, September and
October 10am to noon and 2 to 7pm, July and August
10am to 7.30pm, November to Easter
2 to 6.30pm.

Vire   Lac de la Dathée   ☎ 02 31 43 52 56
(south-west of the town, off the D76)
This lake was formed as a result of the construction of a
dam nearby in 1977. The surrounding area has become a
bird reserve and has an observatory.

Beaches & Leisure Parks

Pont L'Evêque   Parc de Loisirs, Lac de Pont L'Evêque   ☎ 02 31 65 29 21
💻 *www.normandie-challenge.com*
(north of Lisieux)
A large lake and park area open from Easter to 1st
November with a sandy beach, pedalos, jet skis, canoes,
sailing, crazy golf, horse riding, bar/restaurant and many
additional activities in summer.

Boat, Train & Wagon Rides

Boat Trips

Caen   Bateau l'Hastings, Quai Vendeuvre   ☎ 02 31 34 00 00
💻 *www.perso.wanadoo.fr/bateau-lhastings.com*
(just to the south-east of the château)
Offering a panoramic view of the city's monuments, this
vessel departs from the heart of Caen on a two-and-a-half
hour trip along its waterways and canals. Dinner trips are
also available, with set menus from €19.50 to €25.50 plus a
€10 children's menu. Diners must do a return trip. Adults
€12 return, €8 one-way; children €6.50 return, €4.50 one-
way.

Port de Plaisance, Bassin Saint Pierre   ☎ 02 31 95 24 47
💻 *www.caen-plaisance.com*
(The Bassin Saint Pierre is the part of the river that goes up
towards the chateau in the centre of the city.)
There are various activities available here: primarily the
yacht club, which organise trips such as collecting shell fish
and canoeing. Moorings are also available, with rates from
€6.28 per day to €418 per year.

Grandcamp Maisy   Colonel Rudder, 11 rue Aristide
Briand   ☎ 02 31 21 42 93

✉ *noellevicquelin@aol.com*
Guided tours of the landing beaches from April to October, with departure times dependent on the tide. There are two trips available: short and long. Adults €10 & €16, under 12-year-olds €6.50 & €10.

Train Rides

Lisieux

le Petit Train de Lisieux   ☎ 02 31 62 98 00
This 'train' drives through the town giving a commentary as you pass places of interest. Departs from rue Carmel, just behind the tourist office. €5.10 for adults, €3.60 for under 12s.

Wagon Rides

Caen

Carriage Rides, place Saint Pierre   ☎ 02 31 27 14 14
A horse-drawn carriage ride through the historic centre of Caen. From the second week in July to the end of August, Tuesdays to Saturdays from 10.30am to 12.30pm and 2 to 5.30pm. Departures every half hour. Adults €8, children €4. No booking.

Chateaux

Balleroy

Château de Balleroy   ☎ 02 31 21 60 61
🖳 *www.château-balleroy.com*
(south-west of Bayeux)
The chateau has many beautifully furnished rooms, including the Regency-panelled dining room with an oak parquet floor and the cantilevered staircase, which was an engineering marvel of the period. Open from mid-March to 30th June and 1st September to mid-October Wednesdays to Mondays 10am to 6pm, 1st July to 31st August every day from 10am to 6pm. There's also a balloon museum in the stables (see **Museums, Memorials & Galleries** on page 136); the two can be visited separately but a combined ticket is better value:
€6.86 for adults and €5.35 for children. Free for children under seven.

Caen

Château Ducal   ☎ 02 31 27 14 14
🖳 *www.caen.fr/tourisme*
(in the very centre of the city)
Constructed around 1060 by William the Conqueror, this is one of the largest fortified and enclosed castles in Europe. Free entry all year with guided tours in July and August from Mondays to Saturdays (11am in French, 3pm in English), departing from the entrance Porte Saint Pierre. €4 for the guided tour.

Falaise	Château Guillaume le Conquérant ☎ 02 31 41 61 44

There's an audio-visual tour that gives an insight into medieval society, some of the important inhabitants of the castle, their wars and their feasts. This fortress was built by the dukes of Normandy with two keeps and a round tower. Open daily from mid-February to the end of December 10am to 6pm, 7pm in July and August. Closed Tuesdays and Wednesdays from October to December and February. Guided tours in English during July and August at 11.30am and 3.30pm, other months 11.30am only. Adults €5.50, 6 to16-year-olds €3.50.

Fontaine Henry	3 place du Chateau ☎ 02 31 80 00 42

🖥 *www.chateau-de-fontaine-henry.com*
(north-west of Caen, a few miles in from the coast) Overlooking the Mue valley, this chateau has tall, steep roofs and a richly sculpted facade, the result of 15th and 16th century architectural styles. Open Easter to 15th June and 16th September to 2nd November weekends and bank holidays from 2.30 to 6.30pm, 16th June to 15th September every afternoon except Tuesdays from 2.30 to 6.30pm. There are evening shows with costumes and music on Fridays in July and August. Adults €6, 8 to 16-year-olds €4; evening shows €8 adults, 6 to 16-year-olds €6.

Vendeuvre	Musée et Jardins du Chateau de Vendeuvre ☎ 02 31 40 93 83

🖥 *www.vendeuvre.com*
(north-east of Falaise) The chateau, which has been in the Vendeuvre family since the 18th century, is beautifully furnished with period pieces. It houses an extraordinary collection of dog beds from the 17th to 19th centuries and, in the kitchens, a display of 18th century utensils. The world's largest collection of miniature furniture is on show in the chateau's Orangery, with over 750 pieces, including silverware and furniture from the 16th century. Outside, Les Jardins d'Eau are three gardens in which fountains have been concealed amidst unusual constructions such as a maze, Chinese bridge and temple. Open May to September every day from 11am to 6pm (July and August until 6.30pm), April, October and the first two weeks of November Sundays and bank holidays from 2 to 6pm (Easter holidays every day 2 to 6pm).

Churches & Abbeys

Bayeux	Cathédrale Notre Dame, rue Lambert Leforestier ☎ 02 31 92 14 21

(in the town centre)

This cathedral was started in the 11th century and was last modified in the 19th with the addition of the copper dome on the gothic tower. Open January to March 9am to 5pm, April to June 9am to 6pm, July to September 8.30am to 7pm, October to December 8.30am to 6pm. Guided tours available daily in the summer months. Adults €4, under 15s free. No visits during church services.

Caen

Abbaye aux Hommes, Hôtel de Ville, Esplanade J.M. Louvel   ☎ 02 31 30 42 81
(in the city centre, south-west of the chateau)
The buildings that were occupied by the men of the abbey are now the head office of the city hall of Caen. Building was started in 1066 under the rule of William the Conqueror but was not completed until the 13th century. The Abbatiale St Etienne has Roman and Gothic architecture and houses the tomb of William the Conqueror. Free access from 8.15am to noon and 2 to 7.30pm except during church services. Guided tours every day except 1st January, 1st May and 25th December. €2 for the tour, free on Sundays. Underground parking available at the Hôtel de Ville.

Abbaye aux Dames, place Reine Mathilde   ☎ 02 31 06 98 98
(directly east of the chateau in the city centre)
Founded by Queen Mathilde around 1060, the Eglise de la Trinité is one of the most important structures of Roman art in Normandy and houses the queen's tomb. The buildings took until the 13th century to finish and sheltered the monks until the Revolution. They later became a hospital, then a hospice and after careful restoration are now home to the regional government (*Conseil Régional*). Open to the public from 2 to 5.30pm; free entry. Guided tours are available every day at 2.30pm and 4pm, except 1st January, 1st May and 25th December.

Vire

Eglise Notre Dame, place Notre Dame
Built in the 13th century in a primitive gothic style and later enlarged in a variety of different styles. Restored in 1948 after the bombardments of 1944.

Miscellaneous

General

Battlebus   ☎ 02 31 22 28 82
🖳 *www.battlebus.fr*
This company, run by a British/French couple, is based in Bayeux and specialises in tours of the D-Day landing sites and battlefields. The tour guides are either British or speak fluent English. There are a variety of standard full day tours, and private tours can be arranged to your itinerary.

Standard tours cost €75 per day with entry to museums included; credit cards and cheques aren't accepted.

Bayeux

Bayeux Tapestry, Centre Guillaume le Conquérant, rue de Nesmond   ☎ 02 31 51 25 50

A unique 11th century masterpiece, 70m (225ft) long, depicts the conquest of England by William the Conqueror. Recorded information is available in English. Open all year except the second week of January from Mondays to Fridays and from the afternoon of the 24th December to the morning of the 26th December inclusive and the afternoon of the 31st December to the morning of the 2nd January inclusive. Mid-March to 30th April and 1st September to 1st November 9am to 6.30pm, 1st May to 31 August 9am to 7pm, 2nd November to mid-March 9.30am to 12.30pm and 2 to 6pm. Adults €7.40, over ten-year-olds €3, including the audio guide.

Atelier du Bessin, 5 place aux Pommes   ☎ 02 31 21 98 00

Workshop showing the art of decorating porcelain (*faïence*) with modern and traditional designs. Open Mondays to Saturdays 10am to 7pm. Free entry.

Caen

Parc Festyland, Bretteville sur Odon   ☎ 02 31 75 04 04
🖳 *www.festyland.com*
(on the east side of Caen city centre; from the ring road take the airport turn-off)
This activity park includes full-size dinosaurs (not real ones!) and a lake that can be crossed via a rope bridge. There's a small chateau-style playground for younger children, an 180° cinema called Le Dôme, a roller coaster and water slides where you sit in small boats (be prepared to get wet!). There's also a *crêperie*, snack bars and a large picnic area. Various shows are put on throughout the season. Open from the first Sunday in April to 30th June and September, weekends, Wednesdays and school holidays 11am to 6pm, July and August every day 10.30am to 7pm. Dogs aren't allowed. Adults €11, under 12s €9.

Caumont

l'Evente Le Souterroscope, route de Saint Lô   ☎ 02 31 71 15 15
🖳 *www.souterroscope.com*
(north of Vire, west of Caen)
Souterroscope takes you underground through 400m of tunnels to four immense underground caverns. Open mid-February to mid-December 10am to 5pm Tuesdays to Saturdays, May, June and September 10am to 6pm Sundays, July and August every day. Open all bank holidays. Adults €9.45, 4 to 12 year-olds €4,50.

Lisieux

Hippodrome de Lisieux, route de Paris ☎ 02 31 31 03 28
(east of the town near the retail park)
Various events are held at this horse racing track
throughout the year and there's a restaurant on site.

Mosles

le Labyrinthe de Bayeux, Ferme de
la Fresnée   ☎ 02 31 10 06 21
(north-west of Bayeux)
A huge maze consisting of 2m-high corn plants, with
entertainment and games to enjoy whilst trying to find your
way out. Picnic area and snack bar. Open mid-July to the
end of August every day from 10.30am to 7pm, Thursdays
open additionally 8.30 to 11pm, September weekends only
10.30am to 7pm. Adults €6.50, 4 to 12-year-olds €5.50,
under fours free.

Noron

la Poterie, Atelier Ceramique Turgis ☎ 02 31 92 57 03
🖳 www.poterie-turgis.com
(south-west of Bayeux on the D572)
One of the three major pottery villages in France,
where the art has been practised for four generations. Free
visits to the workshops all year, 9am to noon and 2 to
6.30pm.

Museums, Memorials & Galleries

Arromanches

Musée du Débarquement, place du
6 Juin   ☎ 02 31 22 34 31
🖳 www.normandy1944.com
(on the coast north-east of Bayeux)
This museum tells the story of the construction and
work of the artificial port at Arromanches, which was the
key to the success of the Battle of Normandy. Open daily.
Winter hours 9.30am to 12.30pm and 1.30 to 5.30pm,
summer hours 9am to 7pm, closed January. Adults €6,
children €4.

Balleroy

Musée des Balloons, Château de
Balleroy   ☎ 02 31 21 60 61
🖳 www.château-balleroy.com
(south-west of Bayeux)
This international balloon museum is located in the
stables of the chateau and was the world's first museum
dedicated to ballooning. Open from mid-March to 30th June
and 1st September to mid-October Wednesdays to
Mondays 10am to 6pm, 1st July to 31st August every day
10am to 6pm. The museum and chateau can be visited
separately, but a combined ticket is better value: €6.86 for
adults and €5.35 for children. Free for children
under seven.

Bayeux

Mémorial de la Bataille de Normandie, boulevard Fabian Ware   ☎ 02 31 51 46 90

(south-west side of the town, near the military cemetery)
Just a few minutes from the beaches of the Normandy
landings, this museum retraces the 77 days of conflict.
Open 1st May to mid-September 9.30am to 6.30pm, mid-
September to 30th April 10am to 12.30pm and 2 to 6pm,
closed the last two weeks of January. Adults €5.50, children
over ten €2.60.

Musée Baron Gérard, Hotel du Doyen, rue Lambert Leforestier   ☎ 02 31 92 14 21

(opposite the cathedral in the centre of the town)
A collection of art, porcelain, lace and paintings plus various
temporary exhibitions. Open every day except 1st January
and 25th December 10am to 12.30pm and 2 to 6pm (July
and August until 7pm). Adults €2.60, children €1.50.

Galerie du Duc Guillaume, 18 rue des Cuisiniers   ☎ 02 31 51 98 15

(in the centre of the town, just north of the cathedral)
This art gallery displays work from a selection of artists
plus old engravings and books from the region. Open
Monday afternoons to Saturdays 10am to noon and 3 to
6.30pm.

Caen

Mémorial de Caen, esplanade Dwight Eisenhower   ☎ 02 31 06 06 44

🖳 *www.memorial-caen.fr*
(from the north ring road around the city take exit 7)
This memorial includes a media library, bookshop,
restaurant and children's play area and is constantly
expanding. Free child-minding is available for under tens
for the duration of their parents' visit. There's an
International Park with various gardens extending over 35
ha (85 acres) and various halls depicting events of the
Second World War and the cold war. Open daily from 9am
to 7pm (6pm in winter, 8pm in July and August). Closed
25th December, 1st January, and the first two weeks of the
school term in January. Adults €16.50 to €18, 10 to 18-
year-olds €14 to €16 (rate varies according to the time of
year). Free for under tens. Allow up to a full day for the visit.

Musée des Beaux Arts, Château Ducal   ☎ 02 31 30 47 70

(in the centre of the city)
One of the most prestigious art museums in France with
paintings, prints and contemporary art on permanent
display and various temporary exhibitions throughout the
year. Bookshop and café. Open 9.30am to 6pm, closed

Tuesdays and some bank holidays. €4 entry during an exhibition, €3.20 at other times, free to under 18s and for everyone on Sundays.

Musée de Normandie, Château
Ducal   ☎ 02 31 30 47 60
🖳 *www.ville-caen.fr/mdn*
(in the centre of the city)
This museum shows the evolution of life in Normandy and houses various exhibitions each year. Open 9.30am to 6pm, closed Tuesdays and some bank holidays. €1.60 entry, free for under 18s and for everyone on Sundays.

Musée de La Poste et des Techniques
de Communication, 52 rue Saint
Pierre   ☎ 02 31 50 12 20
✉ *musee.poste.caen@wanadoo.fr*
(a pedestrian street directly south of the chateau)
Located in a historic building in the centre of Caen, the exhibits show the history of the French postal system from the earliest deliveries, on horseback, to the introduction of stamps, telephones and Minitel (a French system that preceded the internet). Open 16th June to 15th September and school holidays, Tuesdays to Saturdays 10am to noon and 2 to 6pm, the remainder of the year Tuesdays to Saturdays 1.30 to 5.30pm. Adults €2.50, children €1.

Clécy

Musée du Chemin de Fer Miniature,
Les Fours   ☎ 02 31 69 07 13
(between Vire and Falaise, near the D562)
A model railway covering 310m2 with 15 trains travelling through highly detailed miniature landscapes and with a thousand road vehicles as well as locomotives, rolling stock and many other scale models. Open March to Easter, October and November Sundays 2 to 5pm, Easter Saturday to September every day 10am to noon and 2 to 6pm. Closed Mondays in September and from December to February.

Colleville sur Mer

Big Red One Assault Museum,
Hameau Le Bray   ☎ 06 72 89 36 18
(on the D514 coast road north-west of Bayeux)
A museum of the 1st Infantry Division at Omaha Beach. A collection of equipment and uniforms, with archives and a film show. Guided tours in English on request. Open every day, March to May and September to November 9am to noon and 2 to 6pm, June to August 9am to 7pm. Adults €5, under 16s €3.50.

Falaise
Automates Avenue, boulevard de la
Libération   ☎ 02 31 90 02 43
A museum of window displays from Paris shops
from 1920 to 1950 with automated displays and incredible
attention to detail. Open April to October every day 10am to
12.30pm and 1.30 to 6pm, October to March weekends,
bank holidays and school holidays 10am to 12.30pm and
1.30 to 6pm (Sundays 2 to 6pm). Closed from the
second week of January to the first week
of February.

Le Molay Littry
Musée de la Mine, rue de la Fosse
Frandemiche   ☎ 02 31 22 89 10
🖳 www.ville-molay-littry.fr
(west of Bayeux on the D5)
An ancient mining site and unique coal basin in Normandy.
This is one of the oldest mining museums in France and
includes a reconstruction of a mining gallery. Open every
day February to November 9.30am to noon and 1.30 to
6pm. Adults €5.40, children €3.

Port en Bessin
Musée des Epaves Sous-Marines, route
de Bayeux   ☎ 02 31 21 17 06
(on the coast north of Bayeux)
The result of 25 years of underwater exploration, this
museum displays the personal effects and wreckage that
sank to the seabed around 6th June 1944. Open 10am to
noon and 2 to 6pm. Adults €6, children €3.

Parks, Gardens & Forests

Bayeux
Jardin Public de Bayeux, 55 route de
Port en Bessin   ☎ 02 31 51 26 61
(north-west of the town centre)
Designed in 1859, this garden has a large pond surrounded
by flowers, two pavilions and three greenhouses. A giant
beech tree is the focal point in the garden and was
classified as a natural monument in 1932. Open April to
September 9am to 8pm, October to March 9am to 7pm.
Free entry.

Caen
Jardin des Plantes, 5 place Blot   ☎ 02 31 30 48 30
(to the west of the château and university in the centre of
the city)
The history of plants covering more than three centuries
and including varieties typical of Normandy plus rock
plants, exotics and those used for medicinal purposes.
Horticultural shows are held here every other year. There's
a picnic area within the gardens. Open all year Mondays to
Fridays from 8am, weekends from 10am, 1st January and
25 December from 2pm. The closing time of the gardens

varies according to the time of year. Allow around two hours for a visit. Free entry.

Parc Floral de la Colline aux Oiseaux, avenue Amiral Mountbatten   ☎ 02 31 30 48 30
(in the north-west of the city, next to the ring road; take exit 7)
These gardens were designed in 1994 for the 50th anniversary of the Normandy landings with the whole park dedicated to peace. There are 17ha (42 acres) of gardens, and the rose garden contains some 15,000 plants, which are in flower from May to September. There's also a picnic area, mini-golf course and snack bar at the site. Open all year from 10am (1st January and 25th December from 2pm), the closing time dependent on the time of year. Allow up to three hours for a visit. Free entry.

Castillon

Jardins de Castillon   ☎ 02 31 92 56 03
✉ *colette.saintebeuve@waika9.com*
(south-west of Bayeux)
A succession of varied gardens, each with its own theme – from water to Japanese, English and scented gardens – and three terraces marked out with distinctive topiary and a maze. Open Mondays to Saturdays from 15th May to 30th October (every day in June and July), 2 to 5.30pm. Adults €7 including a plan of the garden.

Mezidon Canon

Château de Canon   ☎ 02 31 20 71 50
(between Caen and Lisieux)
These gardens were designed in 1775 and have Italian statues, long avenues leading to a main courtyard, a variety of flower gardens, traditional French gardens and English gardens. Open Easter to 30th May, weekends and bank holidays from 2 to 6pm, June to September afternoons 2 to 7pm (except Tuesdays).

Thury Harcourt

Parc et Jardins du Château d'Harcourt   ☎ 02 31 79 72 05
(south of Caen)
Gardens spread over three levels within a 70ha (170-acre) park. Open 2.30 to 6.30pm, every day May to September and on Sundays and bank holidays in April. Adults €4.30 peak season, €3.80 off-peak, €1.60 12- to16-year-olds, free for under 12s.

Regional Produce

Asnelles Meuvaines la Calvadosienne, Chemin des Roquettes   ☎ 02 31 21 33 52
✉ *la.calvadosienne@acsea.asso.fr*
(near the coast north-east of Bayeux)
Oyster farm where you can learn about the breeding, treatment and growth of oysters. Oysters can be tasted and

bought. Open Mondays to Fridays 8am to noon and 1.30 to 6pm, Saturdays 9.30am to 12.30pm and 2.30 to 6pm. Check visiting times in advance, as they can depend on the tide. Adults €3.50, children €2.

Bernesq   la Grange au Mohair, La Hamonière   ☎ 02 31 22 47 52
                       Mohair 'factory', where the goats are bred and there are guided tours of the workshops where clothes are made from their wool. Open all year Mondays to Saturdays 10am to noon and 2 to 5.30pm.

Le Breuil en Auge   Château du Breuil   ☎ 02 31 65 60 00
                       🖳 *www.chateau-breuil.fr*
                       (directly north of Lisieux)
                       This calvados producing chateau has an exceptional barrel store (*chais*) and produces one of the finest quality spirits in the department. Open every day from 9am to noon and 2 to 6pm.

Coudray Rabut   la Distillerie Christian Drouin,
                       RN177   ☎ 02 31 64 30 05
                       🖳 *www.coeur.de.lion.com*
                       (2km north of Pont L'Evêque, on the left hand side of the road)
                       Listed as a 'site of excellence', this calvados distillery is housed in half-timbered buildings. The method uses old casks, double-distillation stills and the juice of apples grown on site. The distillery has won over 380 medals. Open Mondays to Saturdays 9am to noon and 2 to 6pm. Visits must be booked with M. Dufois.

Isigny sur Mer   Isigny Sainte Mère, 2 rue du Docteur
                       Boutrois   ☎ 02 31 51 33 88
                       🖳 *www.isigny-ste-mere.com*
                       Located in the village of a similar name these are the production facilities of the cheese Isigny Sainte Mère. Visitors are shown how milk is turned into butter, *crème fraîche*, camembert and other products, as well as the daily routines of dairy manufacturing. There are video displays and a visitor's route with commentary and product tasting at the end. The factory is open to visitors all year by appointment, preferably in the mornings.

                       Normandie Caramels, Zone Artisanale
                       Isypole   ☎ 02 31 51 66 50
                       🖳 *www.caramels-isigny.com*
                       (on the border with Manche, directly north of Saint Lô and west of Bayeux)

For those with a sweet tooth this is an ideal place to visit, local dairy products being used to make caramels. Visits Mondays to Fridays at 10am between April and September. Free entry.

Guéron | Cidrerie Marcel Viard ☎ 02 31 92 09 15
💻 *www.cidrerieviard.com*
(directly south of Bayeux, just south of the N13 by junction 37)
A selection of apple varieties are used to produce apple juice and cider. Shop open 9am to noon and 2 to 6pm Mondays to Fridays (except bank holidays) all year. Visits at 4pm (July and August 10.30am and 4pm). Free tastings.

Rots | la Ferme de Billy, 31 rue de l'Eglise ☎ 02 31 26 50 51
💻 *www.vauvrecy.com*
(north-west of Caen, in the direction of Bayeux)
Small producer of apple juice, cider, calvados and *pommeau*. Open from 1st April to 30th September Tuesdays to Saturdays.

St Benoît d'Hébertot Fromagerie Maître Pennec, RN175 ☎ 02 31 64 39 49
💻 *www.fromageriemaitrepennec.com*
(north of Lisieux, directly south of Honfleur)
Over 65 Normandy cheeses are made here, from the traditional to innovative. Other regional products on sale include jam, honey and cider. Open Mondays to Friday 9am to 7pm, weekends 2 to 8pm.

Professional Services

The following offices have an English-speaking professional.

Accountants

Caen | KPMG, 1 rue Claude Bloch ☎ 02 31 46 31 46

Solicitors & Notaires

Caen | Mauduit Peltier Peltier, 80 boulevard Dunois ☎ 02 31 29 56 00

Religion

Anglican Services in English

Caen | Chapelle de la Miséricorde, rue Elie de Beaumont ☎ 02 31 73 18 80
💻 *www.caen.stgeorgesparis.com*
(just off Fossés St Julien)

Services on Sundays at 5.30pm October to May, during school terms only. All denominations welcome. Coffee and biscuits are served afterwards and there's an occasional visit to the local *crêperie*. Contact Joan Boyer for more information.

Catholic Churches

Bayeux	Cathédrale Notre Dame	
	Presbytère, 4 rue Général de Dais	☎ 02 31 92 01 85
	Services on Sundays at 10.30am.	
Caen	Eglise St Pierre	
	Presbytère, 2 pass Sohier	☎ 02 31 93 46 13
Falaise	Eglise St Gervais	
	Services on Sundays at 9.30am.	
Lisieux	Cathédrale St Pierre	
	Presbytère, 22 place Mitterrand	☎ 02 31 62 09 82
	Services Mondays to Fridays at 6pm, Sundays at 11am.	
Vire	Eglise Notre Dame	
	Presbytère, 17 rue Chanoine Trêche	☎ 02 31 68 00 70
	Services on Saturdays at 8pm, Sundays at 11am.	

Protestant Churches

Selected churches are listed below.

Bayeux	Eglise Evangélique, 19 rue St Exupère	☎ 02 31 21 88 72
	Eglise Réformée de France, 3 impasse Prud Homme	☎ 02 31 51 85 57
Caen	Eglise Evangélique, rue du Vaugueux	☎ 02 31 93 12 74
	Eglise Réformée de France, 19 rue Mélingue	☎ 02 31 86 28 99
Lisieux	Eglise Evangélique, 28 rue du Camp Franc	☎ 02 31 61 17 63
	Eglise Réformée, 7 rue du Professeur Ramon	☎ 02 31 87 13 95
Vire	Eglise Réformée, place St Thomas	☎ 02 31 68 23 27

Synagogue

Caen	46 avenue de la Libération (north-east of the city centre)	☎ 02 31 43 60 54

Restaurants

See page 87.

Rubbish & Recycling

See page 88.

Shopping

When available, the opening hours of shops have been included, but these are liable to change, so it's advisable to check before travelling long distances to a specific shop.

Architectural Antiques

Castillon en Auge	Lafosse Matériaux Anciens, Le Bourg	☎ 02 31 63 84 91

Department Stores

Caen

Galeries Lafayette, 108 boulevard
Maréchal Leclerc   ☎ 02 31 39 31 00
(in the pedestrian streets south of the chateau)
Open Mondays to Saturdays 9.30am to 7.30pm.

Printemps, 28 rue St Jean   ☎ 02 31 15 65 50
💻 *www.printemps.com*
(on a partially pedestrian road south of the chateau)
Open Mondays to Saturdays 9.30am to 7pm.

Lisieux

Nouvelles Galeries, 5 rue des
Mathurins   ☎ 02 31 31 34 47
Open Mondays to Fridays 9.15am to 7.15pm, Saturdays
9am to 7.15pm.

DIY

See page 95.

Frozen Food

Bayeux	Picard Sugelés, route Vaux sur Aure	☎ 02 31 22 34 58
	💻 *www.picard.fr*	
Caen	Thiriet, ZA Vallée Barrey, Mondeville	☎ 02 31 34 93 16
	💻 *www.thiriet.com*	
Lisieux	Thiriet, 16 rue Edouard Branly	☎ 02 31 48 68 68

Garden Centres

See page 95.

Hypermarkets

See **Retail Parks** on page 147.

Kitchens & Bathrooms

See page 96.

Markets

Arromanches — Wednesdays

Balleroy — Tuesday mornings

Bayeux — rue St Jean on Wednesdays
(east of the river in the town centre, past the tourist office)

place St Patrice on Saturdays
(north-west side of the town centre)

Caen — Daily food market at place Courtonne, 8am to 7pm
(south-east of the chateau)

rue de Bayeux to rue du Clos des Roses, Tuesdays 8am
to 1.30pm
(north-east of the chateau, next to the stadium)

Grâce de Dieu/place du Commerce, Tuesday
mornings

boulevard Leroy/place du Dr Henri Buot, Wednesday
mornings

rue de la Défense Passive, Wednesday mornings

avenue Charlemagne/rue Lucien Nelle Wednesday mornings

place de la Liberté, Thursday mornings

avenue Président Coty, Thursday mornings

place Saint Sauveur, Friday mornings
(just north-east of Abbaye aux Hommes)

boulevard Leroy/place du Dr Henri Buot, Saturday mornings

place Champlain, Saturday mornings

Quai Vendeuvre, Sundays 7.30am to 2.30pm
(alongside the Bassin St Pierre, south-east of the chateau)
Caen's largest market.

Falaise	Saturday and Wednesday mornings.
Grandcamp Maisy	September to June market Tuesday and Saturday mornings; July and August markets Tuesday and Sunday mornings
Honfleur	Saturday mornings around the church tower
Isigny sur Mer	Wednesday and Saturday mornings
Lisieux	Saturday mornings at place de la République; in July and August there's a Wednesday evening market at place François Mitterrand.
Le Molay Littry	Tuesday, Thursday and Sunday mornings
Vire	Friday mornings at place du Château
	Small Tuesday market by the Hôtel de Ville

Organic Produce

Bayeux	Vivre Au Naturel, rue St Malo ☎ 02 31 21 33 95 Open Tuesdays to Saturdays 9.30am to noon and 3 to 7pm.

Caen	la Vie Claire, 3 rue Basse ☎ 02 31 93 66 72

la Vie Claire, 3 rue Basse   ☎ 02 31 93 66 72
(near the bus station)
Open Tuesdays and Fridays 9.30am to 7pm, Wednesdays, Thursdays and Saturdays 10am to 7pm.

Falaise   Marjolaine, 16 rue Trinité   ☎ 02 31 40 98 01
Open Tuesdays to Saturdays 10am to 12.30pm and 3 to 7pm.

Lisieux   le Cabas, 8 rue d'Alençon   ☎ 02 31 31 10 56
Open Tuesdays to Fridays 10am to 12.30pm and 2 to 7pm, Saturdays 10am to 12.15pm.

Vire   Vire Nature, 33 rue du Haut Chemin ☎ 02 31 68 18 35
Open Tuesdays to Saturdays 9.30am to 12.30pm and 2.30 to 7.15pm (Saturdays until 6.45pm).

Retail Parks

Caen   Mondeville 2
       🖳 *www.carrefour.com*
(on the south-east outskirts of the city, accessible from junction 16 of the ring road)
Probably the largest retail park in Normandy (certainly the largest in Calvados) and its largest hypermarket with an extensive shopping centre within the same complex, including cafés, mobile phone shops, a games arcade, a shoe and key bar and jewellers'. The hypermarket is open Mondays to Saturdays 9am to 9.30pm (Fridays till 10pm). Main shops include:
* 4 Murs – painting and decorating;
* Buffalo Grill – steak house-style restaurant;
* Carrefour – hypermarket;
* Conforama – furniture, household appliances and electrical goods;
* Darty – electrical goods;
* Gémo – clothes;
* Leroy Merlin – DIY equipment;
* Mondial Moquette – carpets;
* Office depot – office supplies;
* Pier Import – gifts and household furnishings;
* Le Scalaire – pet supplies;
* Toys R Us – toys.

Lisieux   ZA de l'Espérance, 64 avenue Victor
       Hugo   ☎ 02 31 62 11 14
       🖳 *www.e-leclerc.com*
(south–east of the town)
Within this complex are a travel agent's, chemist's, café, dry cleaner's, shoe and key bar, photo booth, business card

machine and photocopier. Open Mondays to Saturdays
9am to 7.15pm (Fridays until 8pm). Main shops include:

- Aubert – baby clothes and goods;
- BUT – general furniture and household
  accessories;
- Cuisines Plus – kitchens and bathrooms;
- Feu Vert – tyre and exhaust centre;
- La Halle aux Chassures – shoes;
- Horse Wood – equestrian goods;
- Intersport – sports goods;
- King Jouet – toys;
- Leclerc – hypermarket;
- McDonald's;
- Thiriet – frozen food.

Vire

There's a retail park on the northern outskirts of the
town.

Shops include:

- Brico Jardi Bati – garden centre and DIY equipment;
- Bricomarché – DIY equipment;
- BUT – general furniture and household accessories;
- Casa – gifts and household furnishings;
- Expert – electrical goods;
- Intersport – sports goods;
- Jouet Club – toys;
- Style Eco – clothes.

Second-hand Goods

See page 97.

Wines & Spirits

See page 98.

Sports & Outdoor Activities

The following is just a selection of the activities available, the large towns
having a wide range of sports facilities. Full details are available from the
local tourist office or the *mairie*.

Aerial Sports

Flying

Asnelles   Gold Beach Evasion, 2 rue Maurice
                        Schumann   ☎ 02 31 22 75 80
                        💻 *www.goldbeachevasion.com*
                        (north-east of Bayeux)

Introductory microlight flights. Open all year 9am to 7pm.

Bayeux

Aéro Club Ailes du Calvados, la Coquerie,
Nonant ☎ 02 31 51 87 51
(the aerodrome is just south-east of the town)

Association Aéronautique de Bayeux et
du Bessin ☎ 02 31 92 46 69
This club deals with everything involving microlights. Run
by M. Simonet.

Caen

Aviation Service Normandie, Aéroport
de Caen-Carpiquet ☎ 02 31 75 20 89
Introductory flights and sightseeing flights over the D-Day
beaches. English spoken. Prices from €65 per person,
based on three people.

Aéroclub Régional de Caen, Aéroport
de Caen-Carpiquet ☎ 02 31 26 52 00
Flying club offering courses.

Courseulles sur Mer Vols en ULM ☎ 06 14 14 36 96
(on the coast north of Caen)
Introductory flights from €40, flights over the landing
beaches with commentaries in English on request. Training
courses also available, open all year.

Hang-gliding

Pont d'Ouilly

Plaine Altitude, rue de la 5ème
République ☎ 02 31 69 39 31
💻 *www.plaine-altitude.com*
(directly west of Falaise)
Tandem or solo, courses or introductory flights.

Parachuting

Caen

Para Club de Caen et du Calvados,
Aéroport de Caen-Carpiquet ☎ 06 08 28 54 01

Archery

Bayeux

Compagnie des Archers de Bayeux,
Aire Couverte, Stade Henry Jeanne,
allée du Jardin Botanique ☎ 02 31 92 71 22
Training Mondays, Wednesdays and Fridays at 5.30pm.
Contact M. Bougeneaux.

Caen

les Archers de Caen, rue Albert 1er ☎ 02 31 83 75 15

Falaise	les Archers de Guillaume, Salle David Bon, Ecole Carnot, rue Prémontres ☎ 02 31 90 85 00 Held in a hall dedicated to archery, suitable for wheelchair-bound archers. During the summer, training is held behind the municipal stadium to the east of the town.
Lisieux	MJC, 13 boulevard Pasteur ☎ 02 31 62 09 60
Vire	USMV, 14 bis route de Caen ☎ 02 31 67 67 97 Contact M. Buot.

Badminton

Caen	Conquérant Badminton Club, 15 rue du Carel ☎ 02 31 50 03 15
Falaise	ESF Badminton ☎ 02 31 90 85 00
Lisieux	CAL Badminton, Gymnase Terray & Gymnase Cerdan, both rue Roger Aini ☎ 02 31 32 38 80 Various courses and competitions held throughout the week for all age groups.
Vire	USMV, 14 bis route de Caen ☎ 02 31 67 67 97

Boules/Pétanque

Bayeux	Amicale Bouliste Bayeusaine, Stade Henry Jeanne ☎ 02 31 22 38 63 Contact M. Charpin.
Caen	Amicale Boules Loisirs Paul, rue de Secqueville ☎ 02 31 74 50 03 There are many *boulodromes* throughout the city, including route de La Guerinière, rue de Franqueville, rue Maréchal Gallièni and rue des Boutiques.
Falaise	Boules courts on avenue du Général Leclerc (on the left going out of the town, just past the public garden) The local *boules* group meets on Friday afternoons from 3 to 6pm (every afternoon from May to September). Competitions held at weekends.
Lisieux	Pétanque Lexovienne, Boulodrome Hauteville, boulevard Winston Churchill ☎ 02 31 31 50 43
Vire	Boules Lyonnaises – USMV, 14 bis route de Caen ☎ 02 31 67 67 97

Bungee Jumping

La Ferrière Harang   Hackett Bungy, Viaduc de la
Souleuvre   ☎ 02 31 66 31 66
(south of junction 41 of the A84 and north of Vire)
Bungee jumping, giant aerial runways and adventure
courses. Open April to mid-November weekends and bank
holidays (every day July to mid-September).

Canoeing & Kayaking

Caen   Canoë Club Caennais, 4 quai
Caffareli   ☎ 02 31 82 46 34

Vire   Base de Voile – Lac de la Dathée   ☎ 02 31 66 01 58
Kayaks available to hire by the hour or half day.

Clay Pigeon Shooting

Falaise   Ball Trap Club d'Eraines, Le Stand André
Rabet, route de Damblainville   ☎ 02 31 90 85 00
(on the north-east outskirts of the town past the stadium)
There's also training at Ferme de St Léger, la Hoguette
from the first Saturday in February to the last
Saturday in September from 2 to 6pm and from the
first Sunday in March to the third Sunday in September
9am to noon.

Pont L'Evêque   Parc de Loisirs, Lac de Pont L'Evêque ☎ 02 31 65 29 21
🖥 *www.normandie-challenge.com*
(north of Lisieux)
Laser clay pigeon shooting, €25 per hour; booking
required. Open from Easter to 1st November.

Climbing

Bayeux   CSB Escrime, COSEC St Julien, chemin
du Moulin Morin   ☎ 02 31 21 44 39
Training on Wednesdays and Fridays. All welcome from
six-year-olds upwards.

Caen   la Prairie, 11 avenue Albert Soret   ☎ 02 31 85 25 16
🖥 *www.la-prairie.com*
(beside the hippodrome, south of the city centre)
The Club Alpin Français meets one Friday each month at
8.30pm.

Escalade Aventure, Quartier Savary,
Hérouville St Clair   ☎ 02 31 94 19 86

(next to Collège Varignon, 1 quart Savary)
This specialist site has 150 climbing routes for various
levels plus an adventure course.

Falaise   la Grimp'ante, avenue de Verdun   ☎ 02 31 90 85 00

Vire   MJC Salle Omnisports, 1 rue
                    des Halles   ☎ 02 31 66 35 10
                    Indoor climbing walls. 13-year-olds to adults welcome
                    Thursday evenings. Outdoor climbs also arranged.

Cycling

Bayeux   AC Bayeux   ☎ 02 31 51 98 36
                    Cycling club open to all from six years old.

                    Tandem, 2 Hameau de la Rivière, St
                    Vigor le Grand   ☎ 02 31 92 03 50
                    Bicycle hire, sales and repairs. Open Tuesdays to
                    Saturdays March to October, December and January,
                    9.30am to noon and 2 to 6.30pm.

Caen   Amicale Cyclo Touriste Caennaise, la Prairie,
                    11 avenue Albert Soret   ☎ 02 31 85 25 16
                    🖳 *www.la-prairie.com*
                    (on the north-west side of the hippodrome, south of the city
                    centre)
                    Cycle rides on the first Thursday of each month, departing
                    at 8.30pm.

                    Vélodrome, boulevard André Detolle   ☎ 02 31 74 33 03
                    400m cycle track.

                    Club Alpin Français, 92 rue de Geôle   ☎ 02 31 86 29 55
                    Mountain biking club.

Falaise   VTT Club Falaisien,
                    This is a club for mountain bikers, from the age of four.
                    Regular training for all levels and a group ride on the last
                    Sunday of each month, meeting outside the shop 'Flash
                    Bike' (15 rue Trinité); under 16s must be accompanied by
                    an adult.

Lisieux   Cycles F. Billette, 20 rue au Char   ☎ 02 31 31 45 00
                    Bicycle hire.

                    Vélo Club Lexovien, Stade Bielman,
                    rue Paul Cornu   ☎ 02 31 31 38 50
                    This club organises rides, competitions and mountain biking
                    and has children's groups of different ages.

Vire	Base de Voile – Lac de la Dathée ☎ 02 31 66 01 58
	(south-west of the town)
	Bicycle hire. Open every day from June to September.

MJC, 1 rue des Halles   ☎ 02 31 66 35 10
Bicycle hire.

Vélo Club du Bocage   ☎ 02 31 09 08 79
Cycling club. Contact M. Josset for current information, meetings and training.

Fencing

Caen   Escrime Club de Caen, 135 rue
de Bayeux   ☎ 02 31 85 50 50

Falaise   Escrime Club Robert le Magnifique, La Salle
d'Armes, rue de la Résistance   ☎ 02 31 90 85 00
This club meets and trains weekly, organising regular competitions.

Lisieux   Cercle d'Escrime de Lisieux, Gymnase
Alain Mimoun, rue St Hippolyte   ☎ 06 11 74 88 59

Fishing

Maps are available from fishing shops and tourist offices showing local fishing waters. If there's a lake locally, permits will be on sale in nearby *tabacs* and fishing shops and at the *mairie*.

Agy   la Truite du Moulin, Moulin d'Agy   ☎ 02 31 21 97 96
(5km south-west of Bayeux, towards Saint Lô)
Fishing by weight or by whole or half days. Drinks available, picnic tables and children's playground. Open 7am to 7pm March to October.

Caen   Club Mouche Cormel-Lois, Salle
Polyvalent du Parc, rue du Calvaire,
Cormelles le Royal   ☎ 02 31 82 37 27
(south-east of the city, on the N13 past Mondeville)
Fishing club open to all ages from six.

Falaise   l'Etang du Colvert, route de Robehomme
Bavent   ☎ 02 31 78 10 73
Three-hectare (seven-acre) fishing lake including trout and salmon, closed Tuesdays.

Planquery   les Etangs de Planquery   ☎ 02 31 21 60 88
💻 *www.etangsdeplanquery.com*

(south-west of Bayeux near Balleroy)
Specialising in large trout. Open every day all year Sundays
to Thursdays 6.30am to 7.30pm, Fridays and Saturdays
6.30am to 10pm.

St Vigor le Grand

Squale: la Pêche de A à Z, 2 chemin
de la Rivière   ☎ 02 31 92 74 64
🖳 *www.squalefishing.com*
(on the eastern outskirts of Bayeux)
Everything for the fisherman, including sea, river and lake
fishing; courses and introductory lessons plus sea permits
and motor boats. Open all year round Mondays to
Saturdays 9am to 12.30pm and 2 to 7pm.

Vire

l'Ecluse & Lac de la Dathée   ☎ 02 31 68 29 67
(south of town centre and south-east of Vire)
Both these lakes allow fishing. Contact Pierre Pinel for
further information.

Football

Bayeux

Football Club, Stade Henry Jeanne,
allée du Jardin Botanique   ☎ 02 31 21 10 50
Training, matches and a football school for six-year-olds
upwards.

Caen

ASL Chemin Vert, 3 rue Pierre
Corneille   ☎ 02 31 73 79 49

Falaise

Football Club de Falaise   ☎ 02 31 90 85 00

Lisieux

CAL Football, Stade Bielman, rue
Paul Cornu   ☎ 02 31 62 24 82
Various training sessions throughout the week for all age
groups, including a ladies' team.

Vire

Association du Football Virois, 12 bis
route de Caen   ☎ 02 31 67 67 98

Golf

Bieville Beuville

Golf de Caen, route de Caen   ☎ 02 31 94 72 09
                                        restaurant ☎ 02 31 47 58 78
🖳 *www.formulegolf.com*
(just north of Caen)
18-hole course, par 72, 6053m, plus a practice green and
driving range. Lessons are available for adults and juniors.
Green fees from €31 to €41 during the week and €38 to
€45 at weekends. Three-day Holiday Passes are available,

allowing you to play on this and 16 other golf courses in Normandy, Brittany and the Loire; details of the courses included in this scheme are available on the website. Passes cost €90 January to March and October to December, €123 April to September.

Carcelles Secqueville	Golf de Garcelles	☎ 02 31 39 09 09

🖥 *www.golfdegarcelles.com*
(directly south of Caen, off exit 13 from the ring road towards Falaise)
An 18-hole, 5716m course and a six-hole beginners' course. The main course has woodland and water obstacles. Green fees: November to March weekdays €27.50, weekends €33; April to June and September to October weekdays €37.50 weekends €45; July and August €40 every day. Clubs, trolleys and golf carts available for hire. Individual and group lessons.

Port en Bessin	Omaha Beach Golf Club, Ferme St Sauveur	☎ 02 31 22 12 12

🖥 *www.omahabeachgolfclub.com*
(just in from the coast, north-west of Bayeux)
27-hole international golf club with three nine-hole courses and a full competition calendar. Green fees for 18 holes: March and October to mid-November €42; April to June and September €27; July and August €50; mid-November to February €27. Individual lessons, golf cars, clubs and trolleys available. Open mid-March to mid-November from 8am to 7pm, the remainder of the year 10am to 5pm.

Hockey

Caen	Hockey Club de Caen, rue Jean de la Varende	☎ 02 31 38 86 42

Ice hockey.

Lisieux	CAL Hockey sur Gazon, gymnase Terray, rue Roger Aini	☎ 02 31 31 56 45

Field hockey with various teams from 12-year-olds through to seniors. Training Friday evenings from 6pm.

Vire	USMV, 14 bis route de Caen	☎ 02 31 67 67 97

Field hockey.

Horse Riding

Bayeux	Centre Equestre de Bayeux, route du Molay Littry, St Loup-Hors	☎ 02 31 92 24 59

🖥 *www.pro.wanadoo.fr/centrequestre.bayeux*

(on the southern outskirts of the town)
Riding school, hacks and full- or half-day courses. Open all
year except the Christmas holidays.

Mesnil Clinchamps	Centre Equestre de la Renarderie, route de St Sever	☎ 02 31 67 62 96

🖳 *www.renarderie.com*
(directly west of Vire)
Lessons, courses and hacks in the nearby forest.

Perrières	Rando Loisirs	☎ 02 31 90 60 10

(north-east of Falaise, towards Lisieux)
Hacks. Clubhouse and accommodation available.

Rocques	La Chevauchée, Chemin de la Boutonnerie	☎ 02 31 32 29 92

(north-east of Lisieux)
Lessons, courses and hacks.

Tracy sur Mer	Cherokee Equitation Loisirs, la Ferme de la Petite Noë	☎ 06 12 06 03 96

(on the coast north of Bayeux)
Hacks on horses and ponies, including through woods
and across beaches. Suitable for beginners and open
all year.

Judo

Bayeux	CSB Judo, COSEC St Julien, chemin du Moulin Morin	☎ 02 31 92 89 58

Training sessions Wednesday and Friday evenings.

Caen	MJC du Chemin Vert, 1 rue d'Isigny	☎ 02 31 74 13 87

🖳 *www.caen.fr/mjc-cheminvert*
(north-east of the city, just inside the ring road at junction 7)
A variety of courses throughout the week for children from
five years old and adults.

Falaise	Judo Club de Falaise, avenue du Général de Gaulle	☎ 02 31 90 85 00

Lisieux	MJC, Dojo, rue Roger Aini	☎ 02 31 62 09 60

Various classes on Tuesdays, Wednesdays and Fridays.
Six-year-olds to adults.

Vire	USMV, 14 bis route de Caen	☎ 02 31 67 67 97

Motorsports

Karting

Démouville   César Karting de Caen, Parc d'Activité
du Clos Neuf   ☎ 02 31 72 20 00
🖥 *www.cesar-france.com*
(just to the east of Caen, junction 30 on the A13)
A leisure complex that includes quad bikes and karting for
juniors and adults. Open every day from 3pm. This centre
also offers a variety of driving courses using VW Golf cars.

Caen   Karting Indoor, 133 Cours Caffarelli,
Mondeville   ☎ 02 31 83 09 53
🖥 *www.karting-indoor-caen.com*
(on the eastern outskirts of the city)
Karting for adults and children, quad bikes and a café that
overlooks the track for those not keen on participating.
Open Mondays to Thursdays 2 to 10pm, Fridays and
Saturdays 2pm to midnight, Sundays and bank holidays
2pm to 7pm. Adults €17 for 15 minutes, students €15,
seven to 14-year-olds €14; adults €30 for half an hour.

Motorbikes

Bayeux   Bayeux Moto Club   ☎ 02 31 22 73 23
Social meetings and rides out, including the local police
motorcyclists.

Caen   Caen Moto Club   ☎ 02 31 82 21 59

Falaise   Moto Club de Pierrefitte en Cinglais ☎ 02 31 90 85 00
This club welcomes everyone from beginners upwards,
concentrating on motocross. Contact Patrick Postel.

Quad Bikes

Asnelles   Gold Beach Evasion, 2 rue Maurice
Schumann   ☎ 02 31 22 75 80
🖥 *www.goldbeachevasion.com*
(north-east of Bayeux)
Jeeps and quad bikes. Open daily all year from 9am to 7pm.

Caen   Karting Indoor, 133 Cours Caffarelli,
Mondeville   ☎ 02 31 83 09 53
🖥 *www.karting-indoor-caen.com*
(on the eastern outskirts of the city)
Quad bikes and karting. Open Mondays to Thursdays 2 to
10pm, Fridays and Saturdays 2pm to midnight, Sundays
and bank holidays 2pm to 7pm.

Paintball

Caen   Paint Ball Fury, 37 rue de Québec   ☎ 02 31 74 19 09
Open to all over 16s.

Pont L'Evêque   Parc de Loisirs, Lac de Pont L'Evêque   ☎ 02 31 65 29 21
💻 *www.normandie-challenge.com*
(north of Lisieux)
Open from Easter to 1st November. €30 per hour; booking essential.

Potholing

Caen   Club Alpin Français, 92 rue de Geôle   ☎ 02 31 86 29 55

Rollerskating

Bayeux   There's a skate park on boulevard d'Eindhoven.

Caen   Roller Skating Hockey Caen, Halle aux
Granges, 15 rue du Carel   ☎ 02 31 85 25 12
In-line hockey, courses and group skating for all levels.

               Get High Skate Park, 1 rue Pierre
Anne   ☎ 02 31 83 54 42
💻 *www.gethigh-skatepark.com*
Open to everyone from six-year-olds upwards.

Lisieux   MJC, Gymnase Louison Bobet, rue
Jean Bouin   ☎ 02 31 62 09 60
Various sessions held here and at the roller rink at Hauteville, boulevard Winston Churchill. Competitions Mondays and Fridays at 6pm.

Sand Surfing

Asnelles   Club Loisirs Nautiques, Cale
de l'Essex   ☎ 02 31 22 71 33
💻 *www.nautique-asnelles.ass.fr*
(north-east of Bayeux)
This is an established sand surfing centre that is open every day, weekdays 8.30am to noon and 1.30 to 5.45pm and at low tide at weekends. A ten-hour course costs €110 for 8 to 18-year-olds, €145 for adults. Sea canoeing trips also available.

Colleville sur Mer   Eolia Normandie, Le Cavey   ☎ 02 31 22 26 21
💻 *www.eolia.fr.st*

(on the coast north-west of Bayeux)
Beginners' lessons and trips along the coast, on monohulls
and catamarans, all year round. Office open 10am to noon
and 2.30 to 6pm.

Shooting

Bayeux   BTC Tir, la Carrière de St Martin   ☎ 02 31 92 53 60
                Open to all from seven years old. Contact M. Lechevallier.

Lisieux   Loxovii Tir, Stand de Tir, rue Joseph
                Guillonneau   ☎ 06 60 93 19 40
                Saturdays and Wednesdays 2.30pm to 6pm, Sundays
                9.30am to noon.

Vire   Stand de Tir, rue André Malraux   ☎ 02 31 68 17 11
                Contact M. Pruneau.

Swimming

Bayeux   Piscine Municipale de Bayeux, avenue
                de la Vallée des Prés   ☎ 02 31 92 07 64
                Two pools, sauna and solarium. Closed Sunday afternoons,
                Monday mornings and bank holidays. Indoor pool open all
                year.

Caen   Stade Nautique, avenue Albert
                Sorel   ☎ 02 31 30 47 47
                🖳 *www.caen.fr/netsport*
                (in the south of the city by the hippodrome)
                Two main pools and a paddling pool indoors, plus a 50m
                pool and separate diving pool outdoors. Outdoor pools
                open all year from 10am to 8pm Mondays to Thursdays,
                Fridays until 10pm and weekends to 6pm. Indoor pools
                open every day but hours vary according to the
                school holidays. Swimming lessons for all ages and
                all abilities.

                Piscine du Chemin Vert, rue
                de Champagne   ☎ 02 31 73 08 79
                Two indoor pools open to the public daily all year, but hours
                vary according to the school holidays.

                Piscine de la Grâce de Dieu, avenue
                Père Charles de Foucauld   ☎ 02 31 52 19 78
                Two indoor pools open to the public every day, hours
                varying according to the school holidays. Swimming
                lessons, aqua gym and aqua step classes available.

At all the above pools swimming hats must be worn and shorts aren't allowed, only swimming trunks.

Condé sur Noireau | Espace Aquatique, route de Vire ☎ 02 31 69 02 93
(directly east of Vire)
Open every day, all year round, this water park has a conventional pool and separate pools with water jets, games and a slide.

Falaise | Centre Aquatique, chemin
de la Vallée ☎ 02 31 41 69 00
This swimming centre also has an area for cardio training.

Piscine Municipale, rue des Ursulines ☎ 02 31 90 18 70

Lisieux | le Nautile, rue Joseph Guillonneau ☎ 02 31 48 66 66
✉ *lenautile@cclisieuxpaysdauge.fr*
Water complex with fifty metre water chute and a selection of different pools, including some outdoor. Open every day except the 24th, 25th December and 1st January.

Vire | Centre Aquatique Aquavire, Parc
de l'Europe ☎ 02 31 66 30 60
(on the north side of the town centre, by the railway line)
A water complex with several pools, chute, 'beach' volleyball, steam room, sauna and spa. The complex is open every day, longer hours in the school holidays.

Piscine d'Eté, route de Maisoncelles
la Jourdan ☎ 02 31 68 00 94
Outdoor pool next to the campsite. Open in summer only.

Tennis

Bayeux | Complexe Eindhoven, rue Louvière ☎ 02 31 21 13 71
Municipal indoor courts.

Tennis Club de Bayeux, boulevard
d'Eindhoven ☎ 02 31 92 23 05
Outdoor training at Stade Henry Jeanne, allée du Jardin Botanique.

Caen | Tennis Club de Caen, rue de
la Chapelle ☎ 02 31 30 46 53
(north of the ring road)
Ten outdoor courts, eight indoor. Open every day but hours vary according to the time of year. Contact Fabienne Kintzinger.

Falaise	All-weather tennis courts by the campsite in the town, indoor courts by the stadium to the east of the town.
Lisieux	Stade Bielman, 7 bis rue Paul Cornu ☎ 02 31 62 26 80 The tennis club is open Mondays to Fridays 10am to 9pm, Saturdays and Sundays 9am to 5pm.
Vire	14 bis route de Caen ☎ 02 31 67 75 56 Eight municipal courts including four indoor.
	Club de Tennis ☎ 02 31 67 67 97

Tree Climbing

St Gatien des Bois	le Val des Cimes ☎ 02 31 65 49 96 🖥 *www.levaldescimes.com* Adventure course up in the trees, with five courses to suit all ages and abilities. Full safety equipment provided. From €13 for those over 1.50m tall and €10 for those under.

Vintage Cars

Bayeux	Retro Auto Club ☎ 02 31 92 65 33 Rallies, drives and competitions. Contact Mme Delaunay.
Lisieux	Auto-Rétro Lisieux ☎ 02 31 62 62 09 Contact Christian Maintrieu.

Walking

General	Comité Départemental de la Randonnée Pédestre du Calvados, 8 Promenade du Fort, Caen ☎ 02 31 38 22 04 🖥 *www.randoleconquerant.net*
Caen	ATSCAF du Calvados, 2 boulevard du Général Vanier ☎ 02 31 85 32 82
Falaise	Local walking route maps are available from the tourist office for €1.50 each, or €12.00 for a set of ten. ☎ 02 31 90 17 26
Vire	Guides are available from the tourist office (€6 to €8) detailing 46 routes in the area, ten around Vire.
	MJC, 1 rue des Halles ☎ 02 31 66 35 10 This organisation arranges regular walks; details are displayed in the foyer.

Watersports

Jet Skiing

Pont L'Evêque   Parc de Loisirs, Lac de pont L'Evêque ☎ 02 31 65 29 21
                 🖳 *www.normandie-challenge.com*
                 Open from Easter to 1st November. Booking required.

Rowing

Caen   Société Nautique de Caen et du Calvados,
        avenue de Tourville   ☎ 02 31 93 36 14

Sailing

Grandcamp Maisy   Ecole de Voile, 82 quai Crampon   ☎ 02 31 22 14 35
                   Sailing and windsurfing with qualified instructors. Minimum
                   age five.

Caen   Société des Régates de Caen-Ouistreham,
        quai Georges Thierry   ☎ 02 31 97 00 25

Lisieux   Croisière Côte Fleurie   ☎ 02 31 31 51 43
           Despite not being on the coast, this sailing club owns two
           yachts, 11m and 12.50m long, which sail in the Channel
           and the Atlantic. All levels of sailors welcome.
           Contact M. Leboucher for details of forthcoming trips
           and training.

Vire   MJC, 1 rue des Halles   ☎ 02 31 66 35 10
        Sailing boats, catamarans, surf boards, rowing boats and
        canoes for hire.

Scuba Diving

Tracy sur Mer   Centre de Plongée YCPWATP, Câle
                 Tracy   ☎ 02 31 22 31 01
                 🖳 *www.arromanches-plongee.com*
                 (north of Bayeux)
                 Diving on the wrecks offshore, introductory sessions and
                 training for levels 1 to 3. Open every day from April
                 to the end of October and weekends the rest of
                 the year.

Lisieux   Lexoprofonde, le Nautile, rue Joseph
           Guillonneau   ☎ 06 87 22 90 68
           ✉ *president@lexoprofonde.com*
           Wednesdays and Thursdays at 8pm and Sundays
           at 8am.

Vire	Bélouga Subaquatique	☎ 02 31 67 01 94
	Contact Daniel Rizi.	

Windsurfing

Grandcamp Maisy	Ecole de Voile, 82 quai Crampon	☎ 02 31 22 14 35
	Sailing and windsurfing with qualified instructors. Minimum age five.	

Vire	Base de Voile – Lac de la Dathée	☎ 02 31 66 01 58
	Windsurfing, rowing and kayaking.	

Tourist Offices

General	Comité Départemental du Tourisme,	
	8 rue Renoir, Caen	☎ 02 31 27 90 30
	🖳 *www.calvados-tourisme.com*	

Bayeux	3 rue St Jean	☎ 02 31 51 28 28
	🖳 *www.bayeux-tourisme.com*	
	Open January to March, November and December Mondays to Saturdays 9.30am to 12.30pm and 2 to 5.30pm; April, May, September and October Mondays to Sundays 9.30am to 12.30pm and 2 to 6pm; June to August Mondays to Saturdays 9am to 7pm, Sundays 9am to 1pm and 2 to 6pm.	

Caen	Hôtel d'Escoville, place Saint Pierre	☎ 02 31 27 14 14
	🖳 *www.caen.fr/tourisme*	
	Open July and August Mondays to Saturdays 9am to 7pm, Sundays 10am to 1pm and 2 to 5pm; October to March Mondays to Saturdays 9.30am to 1pm and 2 to 6pm, Sundays 10am to 1pm; April to June and September Mondays to Saturdays 9.30am to 6.30pm, Sundays 10am to 1pm. Closed in the afternoon on 11th November and all day 25th December and 1st January. All other national holidays open 10am to 1pm and 2 to 5pm.	

Falaise	boulevard de la Libération	☎ 02 31 90 17 26
	🖳 *www.otsifalaise.com*	
	🖳 *www.falaise.fr*	
	Open May to September Mondays to Saturdays 9.30am to 12.30pm and 1.30 to 6.30pm (15th June to 15th September also open Sundays 10am to noon and 3 to 5pm and bank holidays 10am to noon and 3 to 5pm); October to April Mondays to Saturdays 9.30am to 12.30pm and 1.30 to 5.30pm.	

| Lisieux | 11 rue d'Alençon | ☎ 02 31 48 18 10 |

💻 *www.ville-lisieux.fr*
Open June to September Mondays to Saturdays 8.30am to
6.30pm, Sundays and bank holidays 10am to 12.30pm and
2 to 5pm; October to May Mondays to Saturdays 8.30am to
noon and 1.30 to 6pm.

Vire   square de la Résistance   ☎ 02 31 66 28 50
💻 *www.vire-tourisme.com*
💻 *www.vire.com*
Open July and August Mondays to Saturdays 9.30am to
6.30pm; September to June Mondays to Saturdays 9.30am
to 12.15pm and 1.45 to 6pm.

Tradesmen

Architects & Project Managers

Bayeux   Daligaux Van Nieuvenhuyse, 5
rue Royale   ☎ 02 31 21 16 25
Architect.

Builders

General   PD Gough Building Services, la Villaise,
Plouasne   ☎ 02 96 86 46 18
✉ *pdgough@tiscali.fr*
General building including renovation, electrical, plumbing
and heating. English-speaking tradesman.

Bayeux   SBB, 2 rue St Loup   ☎ 02 31 10 00 46
New building and renovation work.

Caen   Denis Bertin, 9 impasse Pascal   ☎ 02 31 82 62 22

Falaise   Christian Levesque, Cantepie
Beaumais   ☎ 02 31 40 03 55

Lisieux   SEEL, 30 avenue Georges
Pompidou   ☎ 02 31 31 35 64
General builder and carpenter.

Vire   Grisanti Maladry, 40 rue Armand
Gasté   ☎ 02 31 67 25 44
General building work including stonework, carpentry,
plastering and tiling.

The following companies specialise in new construction.

Bayeux	Hervé Entreprises, 8 rue de la Résistance	☎ 02 31 92 17 97
Caen	Bessin Pavillons, 2 boulevard Detolle	☎ 02 31 71 20 50
Lisieux	SECTI, 97 rue Henri Chéron	☎ 02 31 48 27 60

Carpenters

Many carpentry firms that make wooden windows and doors also work in aluminium.

Bayeux	Lamy, Père & Fils, route d'Andrieu	☎ 02 31 92 37 93
	Roofing, insulation, skylight installation and general carpentry.	
Caen	Prod'homme, 167 rue d'Auge	☎ 02 31 34 73 24
Falaise	Philippe Lemoine, avenue d'Hastings	☎ 02 31 40 00 43
	General carpentry including staircases, furniture and kitchens.	
	Pourrit, 49 avenue d'Hastings	☎ 02 31 90 03 28
	Roofing and external carpentry.	
Lisieux	JP Riquier, Marolles	☎ 02 31 62 59 32
	General carpentry and restoration work.	
Vire	Besnier Menuiseries, ZI, 20 rue de l'Artisanat	☎ 02 31 67 21 59

Chimney Sweeps

Bayeux	Esnault, boulevard Montgomery	☎ 02 31 51 66 66
Caen	Joël Bion, 16 bis rue Neuve, Bourg l'Abbé	☎ 02 31 85 74 63
Falaise	Pourrit, 49 avenue d'Hastings	☎ 02 31 90 03 28
Lisieux	Au Petit Savoyard, Le Beau Soleil, St Philbert des Champs (just north-east of Lisieux)	☎ 02 31 64 77 18

Electricians

General   Craig Hutchinson, 158 rue Henri-Veniard,
                        St Georges des Groseillers   ☎ 06 73 11 40 89
                        ✉ *craighutchinson@aol.com*
                        All electrical work from small jobs to complete re-wiring.
                        English-speaking.

Bayeux   Leclerc Sarl, 90 rue St Loup   ☎ 02 31 92 07 99
                        General electrical work including alarms.

Caen   AS Entreprise, 3 rue du Parc des
                        Sports   ☎ 02 31 74 50 98

Falaise   Duval & Antoine, 21 rue du Champ
                        St Michel   ☎ 02 31 40 70 05
                        Plumbing, heating and electrical work.

Lisieux   ABIE, les Mesnil Eudes   ☎ 02 31 62 52 40
                        General electrics, installation and repair.

Vire   Clarélec, rue de l'Artisanat   ☎ 02 31 67 20 10

Painters & Decorators

Bayeux   Franck Lefranc, 27 avenue Georges
                        Clémenceau   ☎ 02 31 21 39 88

Caen   Didier Gagneux, boulevard des
                        Alliés   ☎ 02 31 85 40 14

Falaise   Thierry Canonne, 81 avenue
                        d'Hastings   ☎ 02 31 40 08 12

Vire   Peinture Levernier, rue Armand
                        Gasté   ☎ 02 31 67 53 22

Plumbers

Bayeux   JY Bellamy, St Vigor le Grand   ☎ 02 31 92 68 18
                        Plumbing, heating and electrics, installation, repair and
                        maintenance.

Caen   Gérard Mauger, 153 bis rue
                        de Bayeux   ☎ 02 31 73 14 14
                        Plumbing and heating, installation, maintenance and
                        repairs.

Falaise	Lesenechal Lenoir, 9 rue St Gervais Plumbing, electrics and heating.	☎ 02 31 40 06 49
Lisieux	Noël Allaire, Hameau de Villers Glos Heating, plumbing and bathrooms.	☎ 02 31 63 64 60
Vire	JP Tréol, 5 impasse Roger Eng Plumbing, heating and bathrooms.	☎ 02 31 68 98 93

Utilities

Electricity & Gas

| General | EDF/GDF Services Calvados, 5 rue
du Marais, Caen
🖥 *www.edf.fr*
🖥 *www.gazdefrance.com* | ☎ 08 10 333 433 |

EDF/GDF local offices are listed below (these don't have direct telephone numbers).

Bayeux	rue de la Résistance
Falaise	9 avenue du Général de Gaulle
Lisieux	51 boulevard Sainte Anne
Vire	rue Raymond Berthout

Heating Oil

| Ouistreham | DMS, rue Gloriette Trevières
🖥 *www.dca-fioul.com*
Oil, wood and coal. | ☎ 02 31 36 35 35 |
| Falaise | Combustibles de Normandie, route
de Putanges
Oil, wood and coal. | ☎ 02 31 90 11 23 |

Water

The main water supply companies are listed below. If you aren't covered by one of these, your *mairie* will have details of your water supplier.

| General | Compagnie Générale des
Eaux | *emergencies* ☎ 08 11 90 08 00 |

31 boulevard Bertrand, Caen	☎ 02 31 15 58 00
14 rue du Général Leclerc, Lisieux	☎ 08 10 33 31 11

Lyonnaise des Eaux
4 rue Grand Clos, Langrune sur Mer	☎ 08 10 38 43 84
14 rue du Général Leclerc, Lisieux	☎ 08 10 88 48 84

SAUR, 7 bis rue Ursulines, Falaise	☎ 08 10 14 91 49

château Gaillard, Les Andelys

4

<u>Eure</u>

This chapter provides details of facilities and services in the department of Eure (27). General information about each subject can be found in **Chapter 2**. All entries are arranged alphabetically by town, except where a service applies over a wide area, in which case it's listed at the beginning of the relevant section under 'General'. A map of Eure is shown below.

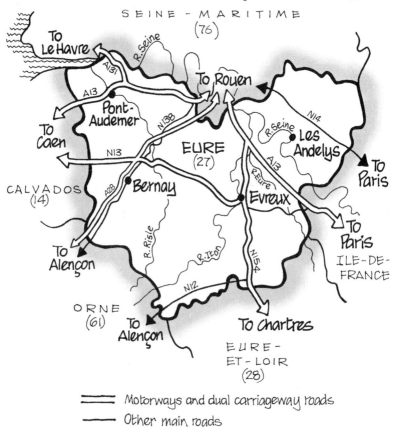

══════ Motorways and dual carriageway roads

─────── Other main roads

Accommodation

Chateaux

Brionne   Manoir d'Hermos, St Eloi de
                      Fourques   ☎ 02 32 35 51 32
                      (in the north of the department and north-east of Evreux)
                      💻 *www.hermos.fr.st*
                      A 16th century manor within a large park where guests
                      can cycle or fish. English is spoken and the manor is

open all year round. Double rooms from €46 to €62
including breakfast.

Gîtes and Bed & Breakfast

General   Gîtes de France, 9 rue de la Petite Cité,
                 Evreux   ☎ 02 32 39 53 38
                 💻 *www.gites-de-France-eure.com*
                 Bookings can be made by phone or the internet.

                 Clévacances Eure-et-Loir, 10 rue
                 du Docteur Maunoury, Chartres   ☎ 02 37 84 01 00
                 ✉ *28@clevacances.com*

Hotels

Various tourist office websites have details of hotel accommodation in
Eure, including the following:
                 💻 *www.normandy-tourism.org*
                 💻 *www.ot-pays-evreux.fr*

Business Services

Computer Services

Evreux   Buzy Informatique, impasse de
                 Cocherel   ☎ 02 32 38 10 10

Pont Audemer   PC Technology, 7 rue du Général
                 Leclerc   ☎ 02 32 41 48 49
                 New and second-hand computers, advice, training and
                 repairs.

Gaillon   ASM Gestion Informatique, 4 rue du
                 Chef de la Ville   ☎ 02 32 53 39 72
                 💻 *www.asmgestion.fr*
                 (south-west of Les Andelys)
                 Computer sales, repairs and software.

Employment Agencies

The main offices of the national employment agency, ANPE, are as follows:

Bernay   rue Val Couture   ☎ 02 32 47 47 47

Evreux   11 rue Buzot   ☎ 02 32 39 85 69

Pont Audemer   place André Delarue   ☎ 02 32 20 25 20

Communications

France Télécom

General	Dial ☎ 1014 or ☎ 08 00 10 14 27 or go to 🖥 *www.francetelecom.fr* Local France Télécom shops are listed below.
Les Andelys	rue Marcel Lefèvre Tuesdays to Saturdays 10am to noon and 2 to 7pm.
Bernay	Place Paul Dérou Tuesdays to Fridays 9.30am to 12.30pm and 2 to 7pm, Saturdays 9.30am to 1pm and 2.30 to 6pm.
Evreux	rue Docteur Oursel Mondays to Fridays 9.30am to 7pm, Saturdays 9.30am to 12.30pm and 2 to 7pm.
Pont Audemer	16 rue Jean Jaurès

Internet Access

Bernay	Bibliothèque, rue de la Charentonne ☎ 02 32 47 42 00 Open Tuesdays, Thursdays and Fridays 2 to 6pm, Wednesdays 10am to 6pm (10am to noon and 2 to 6pm in school holidays) and Saturdays 10am to noon and 2 to 5.30pm.
Evreux	Forum Espace Culture, 18 rue de la Harpe ☎ 02 32 31 20 59 🖥 *www.forum.alsatia.com* Open Mondays 2 to 7pm, Tuesdays to Saturdays 10am to 7pm.
Pont Audemer	Netcité, rue de la Brasserie ☎ 02 32 41 08 15 🖥 *www.net-cite.org* (behind the Hôtel de Ville) Open Mondays and Thursdays 1 to 6pm, Wednesdays 3 to 6pm or by appointment.
Pressagny l'Orgueilleux	l'Estaminet, 46 route des Andelys ☎ 02 32 21 10 88 🖥 *www.lestaminet.com* (10km from Les Andelys) Open April to September Mondays, Wednesdays and Thursdays 11.30am to 10pm, Fridays 11am to midnight, Saturdays 11am to 1am, Sundays 11am to 8.30pm; October to March Mondays, Wednesdays and Thursdays 11am to 3pm and 6 to 10pm, Fridays 11am to 3pm and

6pm to midnight, Saturdays 11am to 1am, Sundays 11am
to 8.30pm. Closed Tuesdays all year.

Mobile Telephones

See page 62.

Domestic Services

Clothes Alterations

L'Andelys	Travaux Couture, 55 rue Marcel Lefèvre	☎ 02 32 54 58 02

Open Tuesdays to Fridays and Saturday lunchtimes.

Bernay	Bernay Retouches, 4 rue Robert Lindet	☎ 02 32 43 23 27

Open Tuesdays to Saturdays.

Evreux	Magiq'Couture, 22 rue des Lombards	☎ 02 32 31 33 29

Crèches & Nurseries

Les Andelys	Crèche Familiale Halte-Garderie, rue Flavigny	☎ 02 32 54 48 04
Bernay	Halte-Garderie, place Magdelaine Hue	☎ 02 32 43 13 64

Children from three months to five years old. Open
Mondays to Fridays 8.30 to noon and 1.30 to
5.30pm.

Evreux	Halte-Garderie, allée des Soupirs	☎ 02 32 38 98 23
Pont Audemer	Halte d'Enfants 'La Marelle', allée Pierre de Coubertin	☎ 02 32 42 22 50

Open Mondays to Fridays 8am to noon and 1.30 to 6pm
(Fridays 5.30pm).

Equipment & Tool Hire

Bernay	Yaqu'à Louer, RN138, route de Broglie	☎ 02 32 46 48 48

Open Mondays to Saturdays.

Evreux	Laho Equipement, rue Jean Monnet	☎ 02 32 62 18 70

🖳 *www.laho.fr*

Pont Audemer   Régis Location, rue 8 Mai   ☎ 02 32 42 12 12

Garden Services

Bernay   les Papillons Blancs, 2 rue des
                    Ménages   ☎ 02 32 43 78 10
                    Garden design and general maintenance.

                    Serge Paviot, Valailles   ☎ 02 32 44 10 00
                    🖳 www.arbresetvie.com
                    Tree surgery and all tree-related services.

Evreux   Jardin Services, 9 rue des Cottages   ☎ 02 32 39 47 94

Pont Audemer   Vert et Bleu, St Siméon   ☎ 02 32 57 28 88
                    Garden design, garden building work, lighting, fencing and
                    gates.

St Symphorien   JP Deglatigny, Maison Baron   ☎ 02 32 42 03 52
                    (just south of Pont Audemer)
                    General garden maintenance, plus painting and decorating.

Marquee Hire

Les Andelys   Erisay, Vezillon   ☎ 02 32 54 06 33
                    🖳 www.erisay.fr
                    Marquees, china and cutlery for hire; outside catering and
                    function rooms available.

Picture Framing & Restoration

Les Andelys   Galerie Tuffier, 22 rue Marcel Lefèvre ☎ 02 32 54 09 57
                    🖳 www.galerie-tuffier.com

Septic Tank Services

Bernay   SAVB, ZI du Parc Expo   ☎ 02 32 43 02 12
                    Emptying and cleaning of septic tanks.

Glisolles   JP Benteyn, 65 allée Mont Planté   ☎ 02 32 37 67 31
                    (west of Évreux)
                    Emptying and cleaning of septic tanks.

Entertainment

This section isn't intended to be a definitive guide but gives a wide range
of ideas for the department. Prices and opening hours were correct at the
time of writing, but it's best to check before travelling long distances.

Cinemas

Les Andelys	Cinéfil Cinéma Palace, 19 rue Sellenick	☎ 08 92 68 69 29
Bernay	le Rex, rue Lobrot	☎ 02 32 43 04 92
Evreux	Ciné Zénith, route St Sauveur 💻 *www.cinezenith.com* Ten-screen cinema complex in the town centre.	☎ 08 92 69 78 92
Pont Audemer	le Royal, boulevard Pasteur	☎ 02 32 41 10 46

Festivals

There are many festivals in this department and just a small selection are given here. More information is available from tourist offices or the department's website 💻 *www.cdt-eure.fr*.

May	Le Vaudreuil Fleurs et Jardins, Patrimoine de Normandie Regional garden festival over two days at the beginning of the month.	☎ 02 32 59 02 74
	Evreux Côté Jardin, Château de Trangis Two-day garden festival towards the end of the month.	☎ 06 60 07 69 54
June	Le Neubourg Festival Régional de l'Agriculture Regional agricultural show over four days towards the end of the month.	☎ 02 32 78 80 00
September	Giverny Festival de Giverny International pop singers and bands perform over a ten-day period. A special bus runs from Vernon to Giverny daily during the festival.	☎ 06 11 65 71 36
October	Evreux Festiv'Art, Halle des Expositions A two-day art and craft show at the end of the month.	☎ 02 32 39 41 81

Libraries

Les Andelys	rue Marville Open Mondays 4 to 6pm, Wednesdays 2.30 to 4.30pm and Saturdays 10am to 12.30pm. There are currently no English-language books in this library.	☎ 02 32 54 05 10

Bernay	rue de la Charentonne	☎ 02 32 47 42 00

✉ *centre.culturel.multimedia@bernay27.fr*
Open Tuesdays, Thursdays and Fridays 2 to 6pm,
Wednesdays 10am to 6pm (10am to noon and 2 to 6pm in
school holidays) and Saturdays 10am to noon and 2 to
5.30pm. This library has a selection of books in English.

Evreux	Square Georges Brassens	☎ 02 32 78 85 00

✉ *mediatheque.mairie@evreux.fr*
(a modern building directly opposite the tourist office, set
back between two old buildings)
Open Tuesdays, Thursdays and Fridays 1.30 to 7pm,
Wednesdays 10am to 7pm and Saturdays 10am to
12.30pm and 1.30 to 6pm. There's a selection of English
books on the second floor.

Pont Audemer	quai François Mitterrand	☎ 02 32 56 46 99

Open Mondays 1.30 to 5.30pm, Wednesdays 10am to
5.30pm, Fridays 10am to noon and 1.30 to 5.30pm and
Saturdays 10am to 4pm. There are no English books
currently available in this library.

Theatres

Bernay	le Piaf, 11 boulevard Dubus	☎ 02 32 43 02 98
Evreux	le Cadran, Palais de Congrès, boulevard de Normandie	☎ 02 32 29 63 00
	🖥 *www.lecadran.com*	
	Scène Nationale, place de Gaulle	☎ 02 32 78 85 20
	Théâtre Mega Pobec Chapelle, rue de la Cavée Boudin	☎ 02 32 31 34 44
	🖥 *www.megapobec.com*	

Video & DVD Hire

Les Andelys	Vidéo Club, avenue du Général de Gaulle	☎ 02 32 54 53 68

Mondays 4 to 8pm, Tuesdays to Fridays 9.30am to noon
and 3.30 to 8pm, Saturdays 10am to 12.30pm and 3 to
8pm, Sundays 10am to 12.30pm and 4 to 8pm. There is
also a 24-hour automatic dispenser.

Bernay	Cinébank, 2 rue Robert Lindet	☎ 02 32 44 57 57

There are three automatic dispensers and the shop is open
Mondays to Fridays 4.30 to 7pm, Saturdays 10am to noon
and 4.30 to 7pm.

Evreux	Vidéo Première, 6 rue des Lombards ☎ 02 32 33 74 66
	Tuesdays, Wednesdays, Fridays and Saturdays 11am to 12.30am, Thursdays 11am to 8.30pm, Sundays 2 to 9pm. There are also two automatic dispensers open 24 hours a day.
Pont Audemer	Vidéo Rex, 3 bis rue du Général Leclerc ☎ 02 32 42 32 59
	There's a 24-hour automatic dispenser outside the shop.

French Teachers & Courses

Bernay	Formation Continue Greta, Lycée Clément Ader, route de Rouen ☎ 02 32 43 77 40
	A government-run organisation.
Evreux	Greta de l'Eure, 32 rue Pierre Brossolette ☎ 02 32 38 81 70
	A government-run organisation.
Pont Audemer	Etablissement Privé STP Formation, 7 impasse Henri Godon, St Germain Village ☎ 02 32 20 11 50
	(south-west outskirts of the town)

Leisure Activities

This section isn't intended to be a definitive guide but gives a wide range of ideas for the department. Prices and opening hours were correct at the time of writing, but it's best to check before travelling long distances.

Arts & Crafts

Les Andelys	Club d'Aquarelle, Maison des Associations, rue Maurice Delarue ☎ 02 32 71 04 75
	Weekly classes for children and adults.
Bernay	Bleu Banane, 8 rue Jacques Philippe Bréant ☎ 02 32 44 83 92
	Classes in drawing, painting and watercolours, plus calligraphy, pottery and oil painting for children, teenagers and adults.
Evreux	Dessin Peinture Adultes, Maison de Quartier, 5 rue Pierre et Marie Curie ☎ 02 32 38 39 37

Art classes on Thursday mornings and evenings, patchwork and embroidery classes on alternate Saturday mornings.

Bridge

Les Andelys   Andelys Bridge Club, 78 rue de la
Sous-Préfecture   ☎ 02 32 71 04 75
Tuesdays 8pm, Thursday 1.30pm.

Bernay   Bridge Club de Bernay, 17 rue Auguste
Leprévost   ☎ 02 32 43 13 40
Practice Mondays 2.30pm, competitions Wednesdays 2pm and Thursdays 8pm.

Evreux   Bridge, MJC d'Evreux, 1 avenue
Aristide Briand   ☎ 02 32 31 86 80
Introductory sessions on Mondays and Fridays from 2 to 6pm.

Pont Audemer   Bridge Club de Pont Audemer   ☎ 02 32 57 00 34
Contact M. Haize.

Children's Activity Clubs

Bernay   MJC, place de la République   ☎ 02 32 43 00 89
🖥 www.mjcbernay.net

Evreux   MJC d'Evreux, 1 avenue Aristide
Briand   ☎ 02 32 31 86 80

Choral Singing

Les Andelys   Institut de Musique et de Danse
J. Ilbert, 8 boulevard Nehou   ☎ 02 32 71 04 75

Bernay   Chorale la Charentonne la Gabelle,   ☎ 02 32 43 14 29
4 rue du Général de Gaulle.

Evreux   Rythmes et Chansons, Salle Polyvalente,
Maison de Quartier de la Madeleine   ☎ 02 32 33 46 48
Classic and contemporary, every Wednesday 6 to 8pm (closed during the school holidays). Contact Paulette Morel.

Pont Audemer   Col Canto, Centre des Cordeliers, 2 rue
Notre Dame du Pré   ☎ 02 32 56 37 06
Choir for boys and girls. Rehearsals on Wednesdays 6 to 7.15pm.

Computer Training

Evreux   Maison de l'Enfant, 4 avenue Aristide
                        Briand   ☎ 02 32 33 47 39
                        Adult instruction Thursday evenings 6 to 8pm.

Dancing

Les Andelys   Institut de Musique et de Danse J. Ilbert,
                        8 boulevard Nehou   ☎ 02 32 71 04 75
                        Ballet and modern dance for all levels.

Bernay   Centre de Danse Guesara, 8 rue des
                        Fontaines   ☎ 02 32 44 59 72

                        Ecole de Danse Classique, Salle
                        Shinsei, 12 bis rue de la Risle   ☎ 02 32 43 40 76
                        Ballet.

Evreux   Ecole de Danse, ALSM, 34 chemin de
                        Sacquenville   ☎ 02 32 33 24 25
                        Ballet, jazz, ballroom and Latin American dancing. Held in
                        the dance studios at the ALSM.

                        Ecole de Danse, 19 rue de Barrey   ☎ 02 32 39 69 85
                        Ballet, jazz and tap classes, children and adults.

Pont Audemer   Cours de Danse, Centre des Cordeliers,
                        2 rue Notre Dame du Pré
                        Ballet, jazz and keep-fit classes, plus Rock 'n' Roll and
                        ballroom dancing on Friday evenings. There's no contact
                        telephone number; simply go along and ask for Mme
                        Mounier.

Drama

Les Andelys   Art'Onde, Maison des Associations,
                        rue Maurice Delarue   ☎ 02 32 71 04 75
                        Production of shows including theatre, music and
                        dance.

                        Théâtre de la Chouette, Maison des
                        Associations, rue Maurice Delarue   ☎ 02 32 71 04 75
                        Groups for children, teenagers and adults.

Evreux   Atelier Théâtre, Association JAE, 45 rue
                        St Germain   ☎ 02 32 33 05 14
                        Workshops for children and adults.

Gardening

Bernay	Société d'Horticulture, rue Jacques-Philippe Bréant	☎ 02 32 43 19 64

Gym

Les Andelys   Rythmes et Loisirs, Gymnase Henri
               Boyer, rue Maurice Delarue   ☎ 02 32 71 04 75
               Various classes including stretching and step.

Evreux   la Maison de Quartier, Gymnase Jean
               Jaurès   ☎ 02 32 38 39 37
               Various classes throughout the week.

Pont Audemer   Guilhène Fitness, Salle d'Armes, place
               du Général de Gaulle   ☎ 02 32 41 17 52
               Thirteen classes held throughout the week from Mondays
               to Saturdays plus a run on Mondays at 7.15pm from in front
               of the complex.

Gyms & Health Clubs

Evreux   Euro Fitness, 9 rue Dulong   ☎ 02 32 38 40 18
               Cardio and weight training, personalised programmes, 35
               gym classes per week plus sauna and sun beds. Mondays
               to Fridays 9am to 9pm Saturdays 9am to 6pm.

Music

Les Andelys   Institut de Musique et de Danse J Ibert,
               8 boulevard Nehou   ☎ 02 32 54 09 82
               A wide range of instruments including flute, piano, violin,
               guitar, trumpet, saxophone and drums.

Bernay   Ecole de Musique, la Gabelle, 4 rue
               du Général de Gaulle   ☎ 02 32 43 00 43
               ✉ ema.ccbe@wanadoo.fr

Evreux   ALSM, 34 chemin de Sacquenville   ☎ 02 32 33 24 25
               Drum, piano and guitar lessons.

               MJC d'Evreux, 1 avenue Aristide
               Briand   ☎ 02 32 31 86 80
               Flute, acousitc and electric guitar, saxophone, violin, piano
               and harp.

Pont Audemer   Ecole de Musique et de Danse, 75 rue
               de la République   ☎ 02 32 41 06 07

(in the old Hôtel de Ville in the centre of the town)
Large selection of orchestral instruments.

Needlework

Les Andelys   De Fil en Aiguille, Maison des
Associations, rue Maurice Delarue   ☎ 02 32 71 04 75

Evreux   Couture, Maison de Quartier, 5 rue
Pierre et Marie Curie   ☎ 02 32 38 39 37
Various classes on Mondays and Thursdays.

Photography

Bernay   Photo Vidéo Club de Bernay, la
Gabelle, 4 rue du Général de Gaulle   ☎ 02 32 45 58 22
Meetings on Wednesdays from 6.30pm.

Evreux   Photo Club, ALSM, 34 chemin de
Sacquenville   ☎ 02 32 33 24 25
Meetings every Friday at 8.30pm.

Scouts & Guides

Bernay   Guides de France, Secteur de Bernay ☎ 02 32 43 51 09
Contact Mme Berrier.

Pont Audemer   Scouts et Guides de France   ☎ 02 32 41 05 56
Contact M. Vittecoq.

Social Groups

Rotary Club

Les Andelys   la Chaîne d'Or, 27 rue Grande, Le Petit
Andely   ☎ 02 32 71 04 75

Bernay   Rotary Club de Bernay, le Soleil d'Or,
la Rivière Thibouville, Nassandres   ☎ 02 32 45 00 08

Pont Audemer   Rotary Club de Pont Audemer   ☎ 02 32 56 96 84
Contact M. Pépy.

Town Twinning

Les Andelys   Amitiés Irlandaise, Maison des
Associations, rue Maurice Delarue   ☎ 02 32 71 04 75
Although not an official town twinning, this group has the
objective of cultural and sporting exchanges with
Ireland.

Bernay   Comité de Jumelage de la Ville de Bernay, Mairie
                    de Bernay, place Gustave Héon   ☎ 02 32 43 14 49
                    Twinned with Haslemere in Surrey.

Evreux   Comité de Jumelage   ☎ 02 32 31 82 60
                    Twinned with Rugby in Warwickshire.

Pont Audemer   Comité de Jumelage   ☎ 02 32 41 44 15
                    Twinned with Ringwood in Hampshire.

Welcome Groups

General   Accueil des Villes Françaises (AVF)
                    💻 *www.avf.asso.fr*
                    Some towns have a branch of this organisation, which is
                    specifically to help newcomers settle into the town. The site
                    is available in English.

Bernay   Bernay Bienvenue, la Gabelle, 4 rue
                    du Général de Gaulle   ☎ 02 32 46 27 50
                    Not an AVF group but one that welcomes everyone and
                    organises various activities including art, cookery, sewing
                    and walks.

Spas

Evreux   Erawan Spa, 12 rue Roosevelt   ☎ 02 32 33 50 70
                    (to the left of the bowling complex)
                    This oriental spa offers a variety of massage and health
                    treatments from one hour to three hours.

Stamp Collecting

Les Andelys   Cercle Philatélique Andelysien, Maison
                    des Assocations, rue Maurice Delarue ☎ 02 32 71 04 75
                    Meets the first and third Sunday of each month from 9 to
                    11am.

Bernay   Cercle Philatélique, 17 rue Auguste
                    Leprévost   ☎ 02 32 43 12 79
                    Meetings the third Sunday of each month from 9.45am to
                    noon.

Evreux   Cartophilie et Philatélie, ALSM, 34
                    chemin de Sacquenville   ☎ 02 32 33 01 02
                    Meets the first Thursday of each month from 2.30 to 5pm.
                    Contact M. Rogron.

Pont Audemer   Amicale Philatélique   ☎ 02 32 41 06 11
                    Contact Michèle Rousse.

© Val Gascoyne

▲ Lyons-la-Forêt, Eure
© Joe Laredo

▲ Etretat, Seine-Maritime
© Survival Books

© Joe Laredo

▲ Honfleur, Calvados
© Survival Books

© Joe Laredo

▲ Barges on the River Seine © Joe Laredo

© Joe Laredo

▼ Barneville, Manche
© Val Gascoyne

◄

Château Gaillard, Les Andelys,
Eure © Joe Laredo

© Joe Laredo

▲ Typical Norman barn © Joe Laredo

© Joe Laredo

© Joe Laredo

► Louviers Church, Eure
© Joe Laredo

▲ *Kite festival, Dieppe, Seine-Maritime*
© *Survival Books*

▲ *Fécamp Cathedral,*
Seine-Maritime © *Joe Laredo*

▲ *Hunting, Eure*
© *Joe Laredo*

▲ *Harvesting* © *Joe Laredo*

◀
Mist on the River Seine
© *Joe Laredo*

Yoga

Les Andelys	Cercle des Amis du Yoga, Maison des Associations, rue Maurice Delarue	☎ 02 32 71 04 75
Bernay	Cours de Yoga, MJC, place de la République	☎ 02 32 43 00 89
Evreux	la Maison de Quartier, 5 rue Pierre et Marie Curie	☎ 02 32 38 39 37

Evreux — Classes held Tuesday and Friday evenings at various locations.

Pont Audemer	Yoga de l'Energie, place du Général de Gaulle	☎ 02 32 41 06 25

Pont Audemer — Monday evenings and Thursday afternoons.

Medical Facilities & Emergency Services

Ambulances

See page 68.

Doctors

English-speakers may like to contact the following doctors:

Les Andelys	Groupe Médical, 6 rue Louis Pasteur	☎ 02 32 54 05 91
Bernay	Dr Sandin, 11 rue Albert Glatigny	☎ 02 32 43 00 11
Evreux	Dr Dissoubret, 2 rue Victor Hugo	☎ 02 32 33 01 28
	duty doctor out of hours	☎ 02 32 33 33 33
Pont Audemer	Dr Casasole, 8 quarter boulevard Pasteur	☎ 02 32 41 37 78

Gendarmeries

Les Andelys	21 rue de la Libération	☎ 02 32 54 03 17
Bernay	rue Gambetta	☎ 02 32 47 83 10
Evreux	rue Buzot	☎ 02 32 29 57 17
Pont Audemer	11 bis rue Prés Coty	☎ 02 32 41 00 17

Health Authority

Les Andelys	rue de Flavigny	☎ 02 32 54 71 80
Bernay	24 rue Guillaume de la Tremblaye	☎ 08 20 90 41 73
Evreux	1 bis place St Taurin	☎ 02 32 29 22 40
Pont Audemer	7 rue Jules Ferry	☎ 02 32 20 30 60

Hospitals

All the hospitals detailed below have emergency departments.

Bernay	Centre Hospitalier, rue Anne de Ticheville	☎ 02 32 45 63 00
Evreux	Centre Hospitalier Intercommunal Eure Seine, 17 rue St Louis	☎ 02 32 33 80 00
Louviers	Hôpital Intercommunal Louviers Val de Reuil, 2 rue St Jean, Louviers (west of Les Andelys) This is the nearest hospital to Les Andelys.	☎ 02 32 25 75 00
Pont Audemer	Centre Hospitalier de la Risle, 64 route Lisieux	☎ 02 32 41 64 64

Nightlife

This section isn't intended to be a definitive guide but gives a wide range of ideas for the department. Prices and opening hours were correct at the time of writing, but it's best to check before travelling long distances.

Beaumont le Roger	De Bouche à Oreille, 3 rue Jules Ferry ☎ 02 32 45 57 27 🖳 *www.lebao-beaumont.com* Dinner concerts and shows with a variety of musical acts including Brazilian groups, female soloists and jazz. The restaurant is open lunchtime and evening Wednesdays to Sundays with Sunday lunch starting at 2pm.
Beaumesnil	Baraba's Club, 3 route de la Ferrière ☎ 02 32 44 45 02 (between Conches and Bernay) Club/disco that holds regular themed evenings.
Bernay	le France, le Bois d'Alençon ☎ 02 32 43 44 70 Disco with cocktail bar open Fridays and Saturdays.

Evreux	**le 8ième Art, 67 rue Josèphine** ☎ 02 32 38 27 06 Pool room, cocktails and late bar Mondays to Saturdays 7pm to 1am, Sundays 3pm to 1am.

le 8ième Art, 67 rue Josèphine ☎ 02 32 38 27 06
Pool room, cocktails and late bar Mondays to Saturdays
7pm to 1am, Sundays 3pm to 1am.

la Dolce Vita, 55 boulevard Gambetta ☎ 02 32 39 13 40
Brasserie with karaoke on Friday and Saturday evenings.

**the New World, Palais des Congrès,
boulevard de Normandie** ☎ 02 32 62 36 43
This club has two discos: '80s and techno. Open
Thursdays 10.30pm to 4am and free entry, Fridays and
Saturdays 10.30pm to 5am. Entry €5, or €8 including
one drink.

**le Parvis Bowling, 2 rue Franklin
D. Roosevelt** ☎ 02 32 62 42 33
(south-east of the town centre)
Bowling and bar open Mondays 7.30pm to midnight,
Tuesdays to Thursdays 2pm to 2am, Fridays and
Saturdays 2pm to 4am, Sundays 2.30pm to 1am. The
restaurant is open Tuesdays to Saturdays.

London Pub, 8 rue Borville Dupuis ☎ 02 32 38 07 00
(just to the side of the Hôtel de Ville)
This bar is open every day until 1am with a brasserie open
lunchtimes and evenings, karaoke Tuesdays and
Thursdays from 10pm and frequent concerts.

le P'tit Paris, 22 rue Chartraine ☎ 02 32 33 21 26
Dinner and cabaret/concerts followed by dancing.

le Victoria, 4 rue Edouard Feray ☎ 02 32 31 61 46
This bar/brasserie is open every day until 1am with live acts
Wednesdays to Saturdays. Food lunchtimes and evenings.

Jouy sur Eure   **la Guinguette, 49 rue de l'Ancienne
Abbaye** ☎ 02 32 36 18 99
(just to the east of Evreux)
Tea dances on Thursdays and Sundays 3 to 7pm and
dinner dances on Saturdays at 8pm.

Pont Audemer   **le Grand Moulin, 36 place Louis
Gillain** ☎ 02 32 41 12 70
This bar is open until around 11pm Mondays to Fridays

Vernon   **le Paris Plage, 6 place de Paris** ☎ 02 32 51 48 54
💻 *www.le-paris-plage.com*
(directly south of Les Andelys, east of the A13, junction 16)

Karaoke, theme evenings, cocktails and take-aways with a
restaurant open 11am to 12.30am.

Pets

Farriers

General   Cheval Services, 8 rue de la Chète,
                       Le Fidelaire   ☎ 02 32 30 10 25
                       Farrier and horse dentist.

                       Didier Portzert, 18 chemin Loges,
                       Courbépine   ☎ 02 32 43 48 35

Horse Dentists

General   Cheval Services, 8 rue de la Chète,
                       Le Fidelaire   ☎ 02 32 30 10 25
                       Horse dentist and farrier.

Pet Parlours

See page 79.

Riding Equipment

Vernon   Sellerie Allard, 3 rue Cendrier   ☎ 02 32 21 95 56
                       💻 *www.sellerie-allard.com*
                       (east of Evreux on the eastern border of the department)

SPA

Evreux   17 chemin Huest   ☎ 02 32 39 07 17

Veterinary Clinics

See page 80.

Places to Visit

This section isn't intended to be a definitive guide but gives a wide range
of ideas for the department. Prices and opening hours were correct at the
time of writing, but it's best to check before travelling long distances.

Beaches & Leisure Parks

Brionne   Base de Loisirs   ☎ 02 32 43 66 11

This lake offers pedalos, kayaks, windsurfing, water bikes and supervised bathing plus table tennis, *boules*, fishing crazy golf, barbeques and a picnic area. Open July and August all day Mondays to Fridays 9am to 6pm, afternoons only at weekends; September to May Mondays to Fridays 9am to noon, 1.30 to 5.30pm.

Poses   Base Régionale de Plein Air et de Loisirs
                      de Léry Poses   ☎ 02 32 59 13 13
                      The centre comprises two areas, one a lake and one part of the river Seine, both open all year from 10am to 7pm. Waterskiing, crazy golf, pedalos, kayaks, windsurfing and a beach with supervised bathing, weekends in June, every day in July and August. There's also fishing, football pitches, volleyball and tennis courts, picnic areas and a snack bar.

                      Lac du Mesnil   ☎ 02 32 59 13 13
                      Courses all year for archery, mountain biking, climbing, potholing, kayak, windsurfing and rowing. Accommodation on site at the sports centre or at a campsite.

Boat, Train & Wagon Rides

Boat Trips

Poses   Rives Seine Croisières   ☎ 02 35 78 31 70
                      🖳 *www.rives-seine-croisieres.fr*
                      Based at Poses this company operates various trips departing from Rouen, Poses, Les Andelys and Elbeuf. Two- or four-hour cruises. From €15 for the cruise only; €59 or €85 including lunch or dinner depending on menu chosen (both menus include all drinks). Booking required.

Vernon   Fleuves Réceptions   ☎ 01 30 74 43 39
                      🖳 *www.fleuves.receptions.fr*
                      Cruises along the river Seine operating on Sundays May to September (Wednesdays to Sundays July and August) at 3.30pm. Lunch cruises at 12.30pm from May to September; booking required. Themed evening dinner cruises also available.

Train Rides

Pacy sur Eure   Chemin de Fer de la Vallée d'Eure, place
                      de la Gare   ☎ 02 32 36 04 63
                      Tourist train that runs along the Eure valley with two different routes. Departures from Easter to the first weekend in October, Sundays and bank holidays at 3pm (July and August Wednesdays and Saturdays 3pm, Sundays 2pm and 4.30pm). Various theme trips throughout

the year including a Halloween and Father Christmas train. Adults €8, under 16s €5. Dogs allowed if on a lead.

Pont Audemer   Train Touristique   ☎ 06 08 42 90 81
💻 *www.pontaurail.com*
This train travels between Honfleur and Pont Audemer weekends and bank holidays, taking just under an hour. There are certain theme trips, including *train et vélo*, where you cycle one way, have a meal and then return by train.

Wagon Rides

Jouy sur Eure   les Attelages du Jouy   ☎ 02 32 36 68 90
See the Eure valley from a horse and carriage with driver and commentary.

St Aubin le   les Attelages du Pays d'Ouche   ☎ 02 32 43 16 24
Vertueux   Tours by horse-drawn caravan, covered wagon or on horseback.

Chateaux

Les Andelys   Château Gaillard, Le Petit Andely   ☎ 02 32 54 04 16
Built in 1297 by Richard the Lionheart, the chateau is now in ruins. High up above the town they give a panoramic view over the river Seine, Les Andelys and the surrounding area. Open from 8.30am to noon and 2 to 6pm, closed Tuesday and Wednesday mornings. Guided tours available.

Beaumesnil   Château de Beaumesnil   ☎ 02 32 44 40 09
An impressive Louis 13th chateau built in 1633 and surrounded by water. The interior is furnished and houses a museum of ancient book bindings. Open July and August 2 to 6pm (closed Tuesdays), April to June and September Fridays to Mondays 2 to 6pm.

Fleury la Forêt   Château Fleury la Forêt   ☎ 02 32 49 63 91
💻 *www.chateau-fleury-la-foret.com*
A 17th century furnished chateau with a collection of French dolls inside and formal French gardens outside. Open all year round at weekends and bank holidays 2 to 6pm (mid-June to mid-September every day 2 to 6pm). Adults €6, children €5, under four-year-olds free.

Harcourt   Domaine d'Harcourt   ☎ 02 32 46 29 70
A large and impressive chateau, a masterpiece of medieval architecture, with integrated towers either side of the corner entrance and still the home of the Harcourt family. Open from mid-June to mid-September every day from 10.30am to 6.30pm; March to mid-June and mid-September to mid-

November Wednesdays to Mondays 2 to 6pm. Adults €4,
children €1.50.

Vernon   Château de Bizy   ☎ 02 32 51 00 82
Built around 1740 this chateau is famous for its vast
stables, the great courtyard and the ornamental water
features scattered throughout the gardens. The formal
rooms inside the chateau are decorated with 18th century
tapestries and furniture. Open March weekends 2 to 5pm;
April to October Tuesdays to Sundays 10am to noon and 2
to 6pm. Adults €6, children €3.50.

Miscellaneous

Radepont   Fontaine Guérard, Château de
                        Radepont   ☎ 02 32 49 03 82
On the banks of the river Andelle stands the abbey of
Fontaine Guérard, the remains of the abbey church,
chapter house, parlour, early Gothic workroom of the nuns
and St Michael's chapel. Open Tuesdays to Sundays from
April to October 2 to 6pm.

St Amand des   Moulin Amour, 16 route de Tourville   ☎ 02 32 35 80 27
Hautes Terres   🖳 www.avpn.asso.fr
A 15th century water mill in full working order with a bucket-
wheel mechanism producing millstone ground flour. Open
May, June and September Sundays and bank holidays 2.30
to 6.30pm; July and August Tuesdays to Sundays 2.30 to
6.30pm. Under 12s free, over 12s €4.

Museums, Memorials & Galleries

Les Andelys   Musée Normandie-Niemen, rue Raymond
                       Phelip   ☎ 02 32 54 49 76
This museum recalls the 96 pilots who made up the
Normandie-Niemen fighters' group, which flew 5,000
missions. A collection of documents, photographs and other
memorabilia, including a Mirage F1 aircraft at the entrance.
Open June to mid-September Wednesdays to Mondays
from 10am to noon and 2 to 6pm; mid-September to the
end of May 2 to 6pm.

                       Musée Municipal Nicolas Poussin, rue
                       Sainte Clotilde   ☎ 02 32 54 31 78
Housed in a 17th century building this museum has an
exhibition of Norman and Andelysien paintings from the
19th and 20th centuries, statues and religious artefacts, as
well as paintings by Poussin, a native of Les Andelys.

Bernay   Musée des Beaux Arts, place Guillaume
                       de Volpiano   ☎ 02 32 46 63 23

An extensive collection of Rouen porcelain and French,
Italian and Dutch paintings from the 16th to 20th centuries.
Open mid-September to mid-June Tuesdays to Sundays 2
to 5.30pm; mid-June to mid-September 10am to noon and
2 to 7pm. Adults €3.20, under 16s free.

Tosny

Musée de Tosny, route de Louviers ☎ 02 32 54 30 30
The only private museum in France to possess two
previously secret weapons, the V1 and Goliath, as well as a
collection of wartime posters and newspapers and life-size
models of soldiers belonging to the seven main warring
nations in the 1939 to 1945 period. Open April to June and
September weekends and bank holidays 2.30 to 7pm; July
and August Wednesdays to Mondays 2.30 to 7pm. Adults
€4, children €1.50.

Tolysland Parc d'Attractions, route de
Louviers ☎ 02 32 54 00 19
💻 www.tolysland.fr
A huge playground for children from 1 to 13 years old,
based around themed bouncy castles. Inflatable climbing
walls and a rodeo plus crazy golf, giant slides and a
traditional playground. Open mid-April to the end of August,
every day in July and August from 11am to 7pm.

Giverny

Musée d'Art Américain, 99 rue Claude
Monet ☎ 02 32 51 93 99
American artists working in the impressionist style gathered
in Giverny, home to Claude Monet, where this museum
houses a collection of American art from the 1750s to
present day. Open April to October Tuesdays to Sundays
10am to 6pm (open Mondays if a bank holiday). Adults
€5.50, 12 to 18-year-olds €3.

Musée Claude Monet, 84 rue Claude
Monet ☎ 02 32 51 28 21
💻 www.fondation-monet.com
This was the home of the impressionist painter Claude
Monet, which has been restored to its former glory. The
gardens have been replanted and the water lily ponds, with
their archways, weeping willows and Japanese bridge,
make it worth the visit alone. Open Tuesdays to Sundays
May to October 9.30am to 6pm, (open Mondays if a bank
holiday). Adults €5.50 for entry into both the house and
gardens. Allow around two hours for the visit.

Parks, Gardens & Forests

Acquigny

Château d'Acquigny ☎ 02 32 50 23 31
(north of Evreux)

The large gardens that surround this chateau offer great variety with a newly restored orangery, walled former kitchen garden, waterfalls, pools, a stone passage and large park. Open May to mid-October weekends and bank holidays (July and August every day) 2 to 7pm. Guided tours available in English. Adults €5.50, 8 to 16-year-olds €4.

Evreux

Parc François Mitterrand, rue de Pannette
A public garden with greenhouses and orangery, a cave, waterfall and open summer house.

Forêt d'Evreux   ☎ 02 32 24 04 43
(south-west side of the town)
This forest covers over 45ha (120 acres) and offers marked trails (maps available from the tourist office). The Parc du Château de Trangis is to the side of the forest and has a cycle/running path, playground and picnic areas.

Miserey

Jardins et la Roseraie de Miserey   ☎ 02 32 67 00 21
A traditional French garden, an English garden and a themed garden, Hell, Purgatory and Eden, which includes a collection of thorny bushes and thornless roses. There's an observation tower and greenhouses. Open May to mid-August Sundays, Mondays and bank holidays 2.30 to 6pm; mid-September to the first week in October Sundays 2.30 to 6pm. Guided tours Sundays at 3.30pm.

Le Neubourg

Château du Champ de Bataille   ☎ 02 32 34 84 34
🖥 www.chateauduchampdebataille.com
Spectacular formal gardens laid out in front of the chateau with water features and intricate designs replicated from the 17th century. The gardens are open from Easter to October weekends and bank holidays (May to September every day) 2 to 6pm. The chateau is open Easter weekend 3.30 to 5.30pm, May to August Sundays and bank holidays 3.30 to 5.30pm.

Le Vieil Evreux

Jardin Archéologique, Therms du Vieil Evreux   ☎ 02 32 31 93 70
The Gallo-Roman baths were part of a vast complex around 2,000 years ago, combining town and religious centre. Archaeological research on this 250ha (750-acre) site enables you to follow a route, with information boards along the way, describing the history of these ancient baths. Open weekends from mid-March to the end of October Saturdays 2 to 6.30pm, Sundays 10.30am to 12.30pm and 2 to 6.30pm.

Regional Produce

Amfreville sur Iton   Les Ducks de la Mare Hermier, 24 rue
de la Métairie   ☎ 02 32 50 42 13
Duck breeding and the production of duck-related foods
including *foie gras* and dried sausage. Open March to
October 9am to 7pm.

Cormeilles   Distillerie Busnel, Maison de Pays
d'Auge et des Calvados   ☎ 02 32 57 80 08
The largest distillery in Normandy with an exhibition centre
recalling the history of calvados and showing
manufacturing techniques past and present, tasting room
and distillery. Open April to October every day 10am to
12.30pm and 2.30 to 7pm. Under 12s free, over 12s €2.

Damville   Chocolatrium Cluizel, avenue de
Conches   ☎ 02 32 35 20 75
Various information boards describe the history and
manufacture of chocolate, there's a video display on the
company and the manufacturing process and a tour of a
chocolate maker's workshop. Open Tuesdays to Saturdays
10am to 6pm, closed for one week April/May and for four
weeks July/August.

Gauciel   le Clos Cérisey, 12 rue de Reuilly   ☎ 02 32 67 02 23
Cider, apple juice and various local aperitifs produced here.
Open all year by appointment.

Professional Services

The following offices have an English-speaking professional.

Accountants

Evreux   Thieulloy et Associés, 58 rue Victor
Hugo   ☎ 02 32 31 39 09
M. Thieulloy speaks English.

Solicitors & Notaires

Pont Audemer   Natal & Meyer, 14 boulevard Pasteur ☎ 02 32 41 15 08
Maître Meyer speaks English.

Religion

Catholic Churches

These churches aren't always unlocked, but are open normal shop hours.

Les Andelys	Eglise Notre Dame	
	Presbytère, 10 rue de Fontanges	☎ 02 32 54 12 70
	Services generally 10.30am Sundays, but check on the notice board inside.	

| Bernay | Eglise Sainte Croix | |
| | Presbytère, 12 rue Alexandre | ☎ 02 32 43 06 82 |

Evreux	Eglise Notre Dame	
	Parish Notre Dame-St Taurin	☎ 02 32 33 06 57
	Service Sundays at 11am.	

| Pont Audemer | Eglise St Ouen | |
| | Presbytère, 9 impasse St Ouen | ☎ 02 32 41 12 88 |

Protestant Churches

Selected churches are listed below.

Bernay	Eglise Evangéliste, 10 rue Louis Gillain	☎ 02 35 75 08 46
	Eglise Réformée du Pays d'Auge	☎ 02 31 87 13 95
Evreux	Eglise Evangélique, 46 rue Georges Bernard	☎ 02 32 33 56 89
	Eglise Reformée d'Evreux, 5 rue Chantier	☎ 02 32 33 02 16

Restaurants

See page 87.

Rubbish & Recycling

See page 88.

Shopping

When available, the opening hours of various shops have been included, but these are liable to change and so it's advisable to check before travelling long distances to any specific shop.

Architectural Antiques

Boissy   Lamberville Matériaux Anciens,
                      Bretagne   ☎ 02 32 44 78 37
                      (north-east of Bernay)

Department Stores

Evreux   Printemps, 1 rue Chartraine   ☎ 02 32 33 02 49
                      🖥 *www.printemps.fr*
                      Open Mondays 2 to 7pm, Tuesdays to Saturdays 9.30am to
                      7pm.

DIY

See page 95.

Frozen Food

Evreux   Picard, boulevard du 14 Juillet   ☎ 02 32 23 22 78
                      🖥 *www.picard.fr*
                      (part of the Carrefour hypermarket complex)
                      Open Mondays to Thursdays 10am to 12.30pm and 2.30 to
                      7pm, Fridays 10am to 1pm and 2.30 to 7pm, Saturdays
                      9.30am to 7pm.

Garden Centres

See page 95.

Hypermarkets

See **Retail Parks** on page 197.

Kitchens & Bathrooms

See page 96.

Markets

Les Andelys   All-day market Saturdays in Place Nicolas Poussin
                     and a local produce market Sunday mornings.

Bernay   Saturday mornings and a small market Wednesday
                     mornings.

Etrépagny   All-day market Wednesdays

Evreux   Saturday morning market at rue du Duc de Bouillon,
                     by the multi-storey car park and a smaller market on
                     Wednesday mornings.

Gaillon	Tuesday mornings
Gisors	All-day market Mondays
Louviers	Wednesday and Saturday mornings
Pont Audemer	All-day market Mondays and morning market Fridays.
Vernon	Wednesday and Saturday mornings.

Organic Produce

Bernay	Bio-Forme, 4 bis rue Albert Parissot ☎ 02 32 45 85 17 🖥 *www.bio-forme.fr* Open Tuesdays to Saturdays.
Evreux	Bio-coop, 2 rue St Léger ☎ 02 32 31 13 72

Retail Parks

Evreux   Carrefour Complex, boulevard du
14 Juillet   ☎ 02 32 23 64 00
🖥 *www.carrefour.fr*
(on the south-east side of Evreux in the direction of Paris)
This hypermarket complex has a photo booth, photocopier
and business card machine as well as restaurant,
newsagent's, shoe and key bar, computer and console
games shop, dry cleaner's, France Télécom shop, cash
machines and photo developing service. Open Mondays
to Saturdays 8.30am to 9pm, 9.30pm Fridays. Main
shops include:
- Aubert – baby goods;
- Bricorama – DIY;
- BUT – furniture;
- Carrefour – hypermarket;
- Conforama – furniture, household appliances
  and accessories;
- Darty – electrical goods;
- Décathlon – sports goods;
- Gémo – clothes;
- Mondial Moquette – carpets;
- Picard – frozen food;
- Pier Import – household accessories and gifts.

Second-hand Goods

See page 97.

Wines & Spirits

See page 98.

Sports & Outdoor Activities

The following is just a selection of the activities available, large towns having a wide range of sports facilities. Full details are available from the tourist office or the *mairie*.

Aerial Sports

Bernay
Club Aéronautique de l'Arrondissement de Bernay, Aérodrome de Bernay St Martin ☎ 02 32 43 15 62
There's someone at the club Wednesday and Saturday afternoons and all day Sundays and bank holidays.

Evreux
Aéroclub d'Evreux les Authieux, route Damville, Les Authieux ☎ 02 32 37 52 80
✉ *aeroclub.evreux@wanadoo.fr*
Introductory flights and flying school for planes and microlights.

Eure en Ciel, MJC d'Evreux, 1 avenue Aristide Briand ☎ 06 11 77 81 03
Hang-gliding.

St Pierre Champs
les Montgolfières du Pays de Bray ☎ 03 44 82 62 74
Ballooning.

Archery

Les Andelys
Compagnie d'Arc des Andelys, Gymnase D. Houssays, rue du 3ième Bataillon de Normandie ☎ 02 32 71 04 75
Equipment available to hire, open to all ages from nine years.

Evreux
Gymnase Joliot Curie, 1 rue Joliot Curie ☎ 06 81 51 39 12
Instruction on Wednesday evenings 4.45 to 6.30pm, open sessions Tuesday to Friday evenings and Sundays 9am to noon if the school isn't otherwise occupied.

Pont Audemer
Arc Club Rislois, contact M. Marcon ☎ 02 32 41 17 86

Badminton

Evreux
la Maison de Quartier, Gymnase Jean Jaurès ☎ 02 32 38 39 37
Monday evenings from 6.30pm.

Pont Audemer   Club Rislois, M. Farineaux   ☎ 02 32 42 15 37

Boules/Pétanque

Les Andelys   Boulodrome, avenue de la République
                   Two groups, under 17-year-olds and adults. Meetings every
                   day from 4.30pm.

Evreux   Pétanque, ALSM, 34 chemin de
                   Sacquenville   ☎ 02 32 33 24 25
                   Leisure and competitions, Tuesdays and Fridays 2 to 8pm,
                   Thursdays 3.30 to 8pm.

Pont Audemer   Boulodrome, rue du Pré Baron

Bowling

Louviers   le Kolyse, 23 avenue François
                   Mitterrand   ☎ 02 32 25 33 80
                   💻 www.kolyse.com
                   (south of Rouen)
                   Eight bowling alleys, a bar/brasserie, pool tables and
                   electronic games. At the same complex there's also a
                   restaurant, sauna, squash courts, cyber café and gym.
                   Bowling open Tuesdays to Sundays. Adults €4.50 to €6,
                   under 18s €3.50 to €4.50 (price dependent on time of day).
                   Entry before 7pm includes shoe hire; after 7pm there's a €1
                   shoe hire charge for all ages. Sunday and Wednesday
                   mornings and Tuesdays, Thursdays and Fridays noon to
                   2pm €2 for everyone.

Canoeing & Kayaking

Autheuil   le Randonn'Eure, route d'Evreux   ☎ 02 32 49 02 83
Authouillet   (just north-east of Evreux)
                   Canoes and kayaks to hire for descents down the river
                   Eure. Open May to September 9.30am to 6pm.
                   Accompanied descents possible for groups and a bus back
                   to base.

Pont Audemer   allée Pierre de Coubertin   ☎ 02 32 56 04 15
                   Canoes and kayaks for hire from May to September.
                   Descents from 7km to 14km or just paddle around by the
                   canoe centre. For descents down the river there's mini-bus
                   transport back to the starting point.

Climbing

Bernay   Vertical'Cité, contact M. Le Maho   ☎ 02 32 44 35 82

| Pont Audemer | ASPA Escalade, Gymnase J. Prévert,
Président Georges Pompidou ☎ 02 32 56 81 39
Various sessions throughout the week for children and
adults. |

Cycling

Les Andelys
CSA Cyclisme ☎ 02 32 71 04 75
Children's training at Ecole Marcel Lefèvre on Wednesdays
at 2.30pm, adults at Place St Sauveur Saturdays at 2pm.

Bernay
Vélo Club, Mairie de Bernay, place
Gustave Héon ☎ 06 83 09 66 50
Contact Pascal Didtsch for details of training and meetings.

Berville sur Mer
l'Entre-Ponts, Parc de Loisirs ☎ 02 32 41 07 81
Traditional and mountain bikes for hire.

Evreux
Cycles Chasserez, 63 rue Isambard ☎ 02 32 33 32 17
Traditional and mountain bikes for hire. €12 per day, €18
for a weekend. Open Tuesdays to Saturdays 9am to noon
and 2 to 7pm.

Cyclisme, Parc de Trangis ☎ 06 85 11 92 49
(south of the town by Château Trangis)
Cycle rides depart from the car park at Parc de Trangis
every Sunday at 8.30am, 9pm in winter, open to everyone
over 15. Distance covered depends on the season. Contact
Jacques Bourthourault for more information.

Cyclo Loisirs, ALSM, 34 chemin de
Sacquenville ☎ 02 32 33 24 25
Leisurely rides on Thursday mornings and rides for the
more serious cyclist on Sunday mornings 9 to 11.30am.

Pont Audemer
Cyclotourisme, ACPA ☎ 02 32 57 04 67
Contact M. Georges for departure points and dates.

St Georges du
Vièvre
Office de Tourisme, route Lieurey ☎ 02 32 56 34 29
Bicycle hire.

Vernon
Cyclo News, 7 cours Marché aux
Chevaux ☎ 02 32 51 10 59
Bicycle hire.

Fencing

Les Andelys
CSA Escrime, Gymnase D. Houssays, rue
du 3ième Bataillon de Normandie ☎ 02 32 71 04 75

(east of the town near the supermarket)
Various sessions Wednesdays and Fridays for different
ages and levels.

Bernay   Escrime de Bernay   ☎ 02 32 43 37 99
                     Contact M. Bouquet

Evreux   Association Jeanne d'Arc d'Evreux,
                     45 rue St Germain   ☎ 02 32 33 05 14
                     Child and adult groups, Monday, Wednesday and Friday
                     evenings.

Fishing

Maps are available from fishing shops and tourist offices showing local
fishing waters, prices of fishing permits and dates of the fishing season. If
there's a lake locally, permits will be on sale in nearby *tabacs* and fishing
shops and at the *mairie*.

Les Andelys   la Seine et ses Poissons   ☎ 02 32 71 04 75
                     This club fishes locally in the river Seine and lakes in the
                     surrounding area.

Bernay   Association de Pêche et de Pisciculture,
                     58 rue du Général Leclerc   ☎ 02 32 43 55 38

                     Etang de Pêche, route de St Quentin
                     des Isles   ☎ 02 32 46 44 61
                     Fly fishing and snack bar on site. €11 half day, €19
                     full day.

Cailly sur Eure   Two trout lakes and four carp lakes. ☎ 06 81 95 75 18

Ecardenville sur   les Buissonnets   ☎ 02 32 67 27 79
Eure   🖥 *www.giteauxbuissonnets.free.fr*
                     Two private lakes with picnic area, barbecue and bikes to
                     hire.

Football

Les Andelys   Stage Tomasini, allée du Roi
                     de Rome   ☎ 02 32 54 44 77
                     Training sessions Wednesday afternoons and Thursday
                     evenings, including a ladies team. Contact M. Quesnot.

Evreux   Stade de la Madeleine, boulevard du
                     14 Juillet   ☎ 02 32 28 32 51
                     Teams for all ages from five-year-olds to adults.

Golf

Evreux	Golf d'Evreux, chemin de Valème ☎ 02 32 39 66 22
	🖥 *www.golfevreux.com*
	18-hole course, par 72, 6,350m. Practice area, six-hole pitch and putt, lessons, courses, equipment hire and gastronomic restaurant. Green fees: 18 holes €35 midweek, €45 weekends.

Le Neubourg	Golf du Champ de Bataille, route Ste Opportune du Bosc ☎ 02 32 35 03 72
	🖥 *www.champdebataille.com*
	18-hole course, par 72, 5,950m. Pro shop, golf trolleys and buggies for hire. Restaurant, driving range and putting green. Green fees €40 mid-week, €60 weekends, €25 Wednesdays.

Horse Riding

Bernay	Ecurie de Bernay, 35 place du Lait de Mai, Hameau Champeaux ☎ 02 32 44 56 18
	(in the direction of Champeaux, west of Bernay)
	Lessons, courses, hacks, cross-country and stabling.

Gisors	Poney Club du Mont de l'Aigle ☎ 02 32 55 14 11

Le Neubourg	Centre Equestre du Neubourg ☎ 02 32 35 03 95
	🖥 *www.club-hippique-neubourg.fr*

Tourneville	le Retour aux Sources, 1 rue des Jardins ☎ 02 32 34 77 76
	Hacks from one hour to several days and courses for children, including accommodation. Open every day from 8am to 8pm.

Judo

Les Andelys	CSA Judo, Gymnase Henri Boyer, rue Maurice Delance ☎ 02 32 71 04 75

Bernay	Judo de Bernay ☎ 02 32 45 13 15
	Contact M. Duchemin for details of training sessions.

Evreux	Dojo de la Galerie St André, la Madeleine, boulevard du 14 Juillet ☎ 02 32 28 22 86
	Classes Tuesdays, Wednesdays and Fridays for children and adults.

Pont Audemer	Judo Club PA, contact M. Gougeon ☎ 02 32 41 31 45

Motorsports

Motorbikes

Les Andelys   CSA Motor Club, Circuit du Trou
de Renard   ☎ 02 32 71 04 75
(by the river Seine to the west of the town)

Evreux   Moto, Salle d'Activité, boulevard du
14 Juillet   ☎ 02 32 33 35 52
(within the grounds of the football stadium)
This club meets the second and fourth Friday of each
month at 8.30pm. Everyone welcome with or without a
motorbike.

Pont Audemer   Moto Club de Pont Audemer   ☎ 06 07 39 29 09
Contact Benoît Pierre.

Quad Bikes

Prey   Quad'Prey, 2 rue de Grossœuvre   ☎ 02 32 30 69 68
🖥 *www.quadprey.com.fr*
(6km from Evreux)
Trips out in the countryside from one hour to all day all year
round. Booking required.

Paintball

Aizier   Viking Aventure Park   ☎ 06 73 04 51 54
(from the D89 take the road to Aizier and it's signposted
before you arrive in the village)
Paintball, mountain bike hire and orienteering.

Potholing

Poses   Lac du Mesnil   ☎ 02 32 59 13 13
Courses all year for archery, mountain biking, climbing,
potholing, kayaking, windsurfing and rowing.
Accommodation on site at the sports centre or a campsite.

Rollerskating

Evreux   Roller, ALSM, 34 chemin de
Sacquenville   ☎ 02 32 33 24 25
Instruction, beginners' and outdoor skating sessions held
throughout the week. An introduction to roller hockey on
Saturdays from noon to 1pm.

Rowing

Les Andelys   Aviron Club Andelys Tosny, Etang de

Tosny, Chemin de la Haguette　☎ 02 32 71 04 75
(south-west of the town)

Poses　　　　　　　Lac du Mesnil　　　　　　　☎ 02 32 59 13 13
(midway between Rouen and Les Andelys)
Rowing on the lake and on the (adjoining) river Seine.

Shooting

Les Andelys　　　　CSA Tir, Stand de Tir de Port Mort　☎ 02 32 71 04 75
Training Mondays, Wednesdays and weekends 9am to
noon, 2 to 5pm.

Bernay　　　　　　Tir de Bernay　　　　　　　☎ 02 32 44 30 00
Contact M. Hucheloup.

Swimming

Les Andelys　　　　rue Gilles Nicolle　　　　　☎ 02 32 43 10 82
(in the west of the town by the river and tennis courts.

Bernay　　　　　　Centre Nautique André Pérée, rue
du Stade　　　　　　　　☎ 02 32 43 10 82
Indoor pool open all year, closed Mondays, hours vary
according to school holidays.

Evreux　　　　　　Piscine Jean Bouin, rue Jean Bouin　☎ 02 32 31 42 50

Piscine de la Madeleine, rue de
Rüsselsheim　　　　　　☎ 02 32 31 52 36
Both of the above are indoor pools and open all year round.

Pont Audemer　　　Piscine les 3 Ilets, avenue de l'Europe　☎ 02 32 41 02 20

Tennis

Les Andelys　　　　CSA Tennis, Gymnase Houssays, rue du
3ième Bataillon de Normandie　☎ 02 32 71 04 75
Outdoor courts at rue Gilles. Training sessions held
throughout the week.

Bernay　　　　　　Tennis club, rue du Stade　　　☎ 02 32 43 38 85
Clubhouse and five courts, including one indoors.

Evreux　　　　　　ALSM, 34 chemin de Sacquenville　☎ 02 32 33 24 25
Courses at various venues across the town Wednesday
and Saturday afternoons and in the evenings during the
week from 5pm.

Tennis Club d'Evreux, boulevard du
14 Juillet　　　　　　　☎ 02 32 28 16 67

Open to adults every day from 6 to 8pm. Children's courses.

Pont Audemer   Tennis Club, 14 rue du Pré Baron   ☎ 02 32 41 16 97
💻 *www.tcpont-audemer.com*
Tennis for all from four years old including courses and competitions.

Tree Climbing

Aizier   Viking Aventure Park   ☎ 06 73 04 51 54
(from the D89 take the road to Aizier and it's marked before you arrive in the village)
Adventure course through the tree tops with rope ladders and aerial runways. Full safety equipment supplied; bring your own head for heights. Open weekends April to May and every day June to mid-September.

Walking

Bernay   Bernay-Sentiers   ☎ 02 32 44 44 81
Contact the Mairie at Bernay for details of forthcoming walks and departure points.

Evreux   la Maison de Quartier, 5 rue Pierre et
Marie Curie   ☎ 02 32 38 39 37
Organised walks one Sunday a month – see the notice board at la Maison de Quartier for departure times and venues.

Pont Audemer   les Risles Pattes   ☎ 02 32 57 54 91
✉ *bretincatherine@aol.com*
Contact Catherine Bretin for the calendar of walks and departure points.

Watersports

Sailing

Les Andelys   Yacht Club des Andelys, Club House,
Port des Andelys   ☎ 02 32 71 04 75
Sailing on the river and local lakes.

Vernon   Yacht Club, Base des Tourelles   ☎ 02 32 21 51 26
💻 *www.asso.ffv.fr/yc-vernon*
Sailing for all levels including courses at the training centre and trips out on the river Seine.

Windsurfing

Poses   Lac du Mesnil   ☎ 02 32 59 13 13

Courses all year for windsurfing, plus archery, mountain
biking, climbing, potholing, kayak and rowing.
Accommodation on site at the sports centre or a campsite.

Tourist Offices

General   Comité Régional du Tourisme d'Eure, 3 rue
                 du Commandant Letellier, Evreux   ☎ 02 32 62 04 27
                 🖥 www.cdt-eure.fr

Les Andelys   rue Philippe Auguste   ☎ 02 32 54 41 93
                 🖥 www.ville-andelys.fr
                 Open May to September Mondays to Saturdays 10am to
                 noon and 2 to 6pm; October to April Mondays to Saturdays
                 2 to 6pm (in December and January hours may be shorter).

Bernay   29 rue Thiers   ☎ 02 32 43 32 08
                 🖥 www.bernay27.fr
                 Mid-May to mid-September Mondays to Saturdays 9.30am
                 to 12.30pm and 2 to 7pm, Sundays and bank holidays
                 10am to 1pm. Mid-September to mid-May Mondays to
                 Saturdays 9.30am to 12.30pm and 2 to 6pm.

Evreux   1 ter place du Général de Gaulle   ☎ 02 32 24 04 43
                 🖥 www.ot-pays-evreux.fr
                 🖥 www.evreux.fr
                 Open all year round Mondays to Saturdays 9.30am to
                 12.30pm and 1.30 to 6.15pm, June to September also
                 Sundays 10am to 12.30pm.

Pont Audemer   place Maubert   ☎ 02 32 41 08 21
                 🖥 www.cc-pont-audemer.fr
                 🖥 www.ville-pont-audemer.fr
                 Open May to September Mondays to Saturdays 9am to
                 12.30pm and 1.30 to 7pm, Sundays 10am to noon; October
                 to April Mondays to Saturdays 9.30am to 12.30pm and 2 to
                 5.30pm (bank holidays 10am to noon), closed Sundays.

Tradesmen

Architects & Project Managers

Evreux   Constructions Porte Normande, 25 rue
                 de Grenoble   ☎ 02 32 62 68 77
                 Project management of new building and renovation. Some
                 English spoken.

Laurent Bellevin, 1 rue du Pont de Fer ☎ 02 32 33 31 12
Project manager.

Pont Audemer   H. Yazdanpanah, 75 rue de la
République   ☎ 02 32 57 84 00
Architect.

Builders

Les Andelys   Langlet, 6 rue Egalité   ☎ 02 32 54 09 81

Bernay   J. Leroy, rue de la Tour, Hameau
Camfleur, Fontaine l'Abbé   ☎ 02 32 44 12 29
General building, renovation and restoration work.

Evreux   Normandie Bati Services, 5 rue Victor
Hugo   ☎ 02 32 33 71 71

Pont Audemer   Maçonnerie de l'Ouest, 5 rue de
la Seule   ☎ 02 32 56 72 91

These companies specialise in new construction.

Brionne   Habitat Concept, 32 rue du Maréchal
Foch   ☎ 02 32 43 07 93
💻 *www.habitatconcept-fr.com*

Evreux   Constructions Porte Normande, 25 rue
de Grenoble   ☎ 02 32 62 68 77
Some English is spoken here.

Louviers   Pierres et Traditions Normandes, 15 rue
du Maréchal Foch   ☎ 02 32 40 16 08

Carpenters

Many carpentry firms that make wooden windows and doors also work in
aluminium.

Les Andelys   Vignon, rue Marcel Lefèvre   ☎ 02 32 54 72 22

Bernay   C. Dulong, rue St Michel   ☎ 02 32 43 42 76
General carpentry including staircases.

Evreux   ABMC, 7 rue des Marguerites   ☎ 02 32 62 71 37
Gates, stairs, kitchens and windows.

| Pont Audemer | Atelier Artisanal, 53 route de Rouen ☎ 02 32 57 93 04 |

General carpentry including roofing and some stonework.

Chimney Sweeps

Les Andelys	Alain Quesnot, 3 rue Hamelin	☎ 02 32 54 44 77
Bernay	Philippe Mocquereau, 44 bis Louis Gillain	☎ 02 32 46 34 40
Evreux	Baye, 28 rue Harrouard	☎ 02 32 62 91 78
Pont Audemer	Au Petit Ramoneur, 9 rue Doult Vitran	☎ 02 32 41 02 03

Electricians

Les Andelys	Littée Samson, 85 rue Lavoisier	☎ 02 32 54 07 67
Bernay	Tabur Electricité, ZA du Grande Malouve	☎ 02 32 43 77 88
Evreux	Lesens Normandie, 41 rue de Cocherel	☎ 02 32 39 18 19
Pont Audemer	Bellois, rue du Général Koenig	☎ 02 32 41 04 24

Painters & Decorators

| Bernay | JL Hardouin, 351 rue Chouquet, La Grande Malouve | ☎ 02 32 43 04 17 |

Interiors and exteriors plus parquet flooring.

| Evreux | Brico Décor, 65 boulevard Gambetta ☎ 02 32 38 02 31 |

Plumbers

| Les Andelys | Assistance Habitation, ZAC de la Marguerite, route de Paix | ☎ 02 32 54 06 76 |

Plumbing and heating.

| Bernay | Snipac, 23 rue du 11 Novembre | ☎ 02 32 45 87 48 |

Plumbing and heating.

| Evreux | ADP, 31 rue Maillot | ☎ 06 15 31 72 20 |

Plumbing and heating.

| Pont Audemer | ELT Services, 13 rue du Maquis |

Surcouf   ☎ 02 32 41 04 00
Plumbing, heating and electrics.

Utilities

Electricity & Gas

General   EDF/GDF Services Normandie Eure,
                           2 boulevard Pasteur, Evreux   ☎ 0810 02 70 28
                           💻 *www.edf.fr*
                           💻 *www.gazdefrance.com*

                           EDF/GDF local offices are listed below (there are no
                           direct telephone numbers for these offices).

Les Andelys   13 rue de Lavoisier

Bernay   13 rue Gabriel Dumoulin

Brionne   rue Martyrs le Lieu

Evreux   rue Chartraine
                           This office is in the centre of town and is open Mondays to
                           Fridays 9.45am to 12.30pm and 1.30 to 7pm, Saturdays
                           8.45am to 1pm and 2 to 6pm.

Pont Audemer   19 quai de la Ruelle

Heating Oil

Les Andelys   Worex SNC, 27 rue Hamelin   ☎ 08 10 62 17 17

Evreux   Combustibles de Normandie, 31 rue
                           d'Hardencourt   ☎ 02 32 33 00 22

Pont Audemer   Combustibles de Normandie, 3 rue
                           Stanislas Delaquaize   ☎ 02 32 41 03 32

Water

The main water supply companies are listed below. If you aren't covered
by one of these, your *mairie* will have details of your water supplier.

General   Générale des Eaux
                           6 rue de Penthièvre, Les Andelys ☎ 08 10 33 31 11
                           4 rue Guillaume Cousin, Pont

	Audemer	☎ 08 10 33 31 11
	1 rue Mecanique, Louviers	☎ 08 10 33 31 11
	Lyonnaise des Eaux *emergencies*	☎ 08 10 87 98 79
	4 avenue Victor Hugo, Vernon	☎ 08 10 37 93 79
	1 rue Chemin Vert, St Marcel	☎ 02 32 51 28 86
	SAUR, 203 rue Peupliers, Bourg Achard	☎ 02 32 56 71 90
	Service des Eaux	
	6 rue Thomas Lindet, Bernay	☎ 02 32 43 08 48
	7 rue Industrie, Vernon	☎ 02 32 64 38 48

Wood

Gasny	TNT, 27 rue Industrie	☎ 02 32 52 72 73
Perriers sur Andelle	Folliot Fils, 55 rue Valette	☎ 02 32 49 18 38
Les Ventes	Patrick Leu, 4 rue Breteuil	☎ 02 32 34 82 00
Bezu St Eloi	Emmanuel Robert, 27 rue Briqueterie	☎ 02 32 55 27 51

Le Mont-St-Michel

5

Manche

This chapter provides details of facilities and services in the department of Manche (50). General information about each subject can be found in **Chapter 2**. All entries are arranged alphabetically by town, except where a service applies over a wide area, in which case it's listed at the beginning of the relevant section under 'General'. A map of Manche is shown below.

══════ Motorways and dual carriageway roads

────── Other main roads

Accommodation

Chateaux

Le Rozel · Château du Rozel · ☎ 02 33 52 95 08
(on the coast north of Barneville)
This chateau was originally owned by a companion of
William the Conqueror and was extended considerably in
the 18th century. From the towers in the gardens you have
a panoramic view over the sea and the Channel Islands.
There's a suite for three or four people costing €76
including breakfast for two people, €31 each additional
person. English spoken.

Picauville · Château de l'Isle-Marie · ☎ 02 33 21 37 25
🖥 *www.islemarie.com*
(north-west of Carentan)
A tree-lined avenue leads you to the front of this attractive
castle, surrounded by a 40ha (100-acre) estate with rivers,
meadows and woodland. The chateau has been in the
same family for over a thousand years and now offers
luxurious guest rooms from €145 for two people per night,
including breakfast. Open 1st March to 1st November, out
of season on request. English spoken.

Sartilly · Manoir de Brion, Dragey · ☎ 02 33 70 82 36
✉ *manoirdebrion@wanadoo.fr*
(on the coast, east of Avranches)
Although not a chateau, this is an attractive manor house
that was once a Benedictine priory. English is spoken
fluently and bedrooms are available from €46 to €110 per
night for two people, breakfast €6.

Gîtes and Bed & Breakfast

General · Gîtes de France, 98 route de Candol,
Saint Lô · ☎ 02 33 56 28 80
🖥 *www.manche-locationvacances.com/gites-de-france.htm*
This is a joint website with Clévacances specifically for this
area.

Clévacances, Maison du Département,
Saint Lô · ☎ 02 33 05 98 70
🖥 *www.clevacances.com*

Hotels

Various tourist office websites have details of hotel accommodation in
Manche, including the following:
🖥 *www.normandy-tourism.org*

🖥 *www.ot-cherbourg-cotentin.fr*
🖥 *www.manchetourisme.com*

Business Services

Computer Services

Avranches	Médd Ware, 80 rue de la Constitution ☎ 02 33 60 66 60 Standard and made-to-measure computers sold, home installation, spares, software and accessories.
Cherbourg	Labo 144, 7 rue du Général de Gaulle ☎ 02 33 10 07 97 ✉ *labo144@wanadoo.fr* Sales, repairs, spares and computers made-to-measure.
Coutances	Desk Info, 4 rue de la Poissonnerie ☎ 02 33 19 14 14
Saint Lô	A2G Informatique, 55 rue Havin ☎ 02 33 72 23 04 🖥 *www.a2ginformatique.fr* Advice and training, maintenance, software, sales and telephone support.

Employment Agencies

The main offices of the national employment agency, ANPE, are as follows:

Avranches	3 bis rue St Martin	☎ 02 33 79 06 50
Cherbourg	24 rue François La Vieille	☎ 02 33 87 54 54
Coutances	103 rue Geoffroy de Montbray	☎ 02 33 19 16 00
Saint Lô	place Georges Pompidou	☎ 02 33 77 44 00

Communications

France Télécom

General	Dial ☎ 1014 or go to 🖥 *www.francetelecom.fr* Local France Télécom shops are listed below.
Avranches	11 rue Valhubert Tuesdays to Saturdays 9am to 12.15pm and 2 to 6.30pm (opens at 10.30am on Wednesdays).

Cherbourg	11 rue Albert Mahieu

Cherbourg
11 rue Albert Mahieu
Open Tuesdays 9.30am to 12.30pm and 2 to 6.30pm, Wednesdays to Saturdays 9am to 12.30pm and 2 to 6.30pm.

Coutances
8 place Parvis Notre Dame
(tucked away in the far right corner of the square opposite the Hôtel de Ville)
Open Tuesdays to Fridays 9.30am to 12.15pm and 2 to 6.30pm, Saturdays 9.30am to 12.15pm and 2 to 6pm.

Saint Lô
23 rue Torteron
(below the ramparts)
Open Mondays 2 to 6.30pm, Tuesdays to Fridays 9.30am to 12.15pm and 2 to 6.30pm, Saturdays 9.30am to 1pm and 2 to 6pm. Closed some Saturday afternoons.

Internet Access

Avranches
Cyber Espace du PIJ, 24 place du Marché ☎ 02 33 79 39 41

Barneville
Médiathèque, 3 rue Jeanne Provost, Le Bourg ☎ 02 33 04 92 73
Open Tuesdays 2 to 6pm, Wednesdays 10am to 12.30pm and 2 to 6pm, Fridays 2 to 6pm and Saturdays 9.30am to 12.30pm.

Cherbourg
la Poste, rue de l'Ancien Quai ☎ 02 33 08 87 01
Open Mondays to Fridays 8am to 7pm, Saturdays 8.30am to noon.

Archesys Cybercafé, 16 rue de l'Union ☎ 02 33 53 04 93
Open Tuesdays to Fridays 11.30am to 10pm, Saturdays until midnight, Sundays 2 to 10pm.

Saint Lô
Planet R, 2 rue Maréchal Leclerc ☎ 02 33 77 17 77
(50m from the tourist office, down on the main road, the entrance is recessed from the pavement)
Open Mondays to Saturdays 9am to 7.30pm.

la Passerelle, place de la Gare ☎ 02 33 56 79 35
(by the railway station)
Open Mondays to Fridays 11.30am to 1am, 4pm to 1am at weekends.

Mobile Telephones

See page 62.

Domestic Services

Clock Repair & Restoration

Coutances   la Tocante, 41 rue Gambetta   ☎ 02 33 17 02 31
                         Specialising in the restoration of old clocks and repairs on
                         timepieces of all ages and styles. Tuesdays to
                         Saturdays 10am to 12.30pm and 2.30 to 7pm,
                         closed Thursdays.

Clothes Alterations

Avranches   le Dé à Coudre, rue de la Constitution ☎ 02 33 48 10 75
                         Mondays 3 to 6.30pm, Tuesdays to Saturdays 9.30am to
                         noon and 2 to 7pm.

Cherbourg   Atelier de Couture, 7 bis rue Paul
                         Doumer   ☎ 02 33 94 55 67
                         (behind the post office)

Coutances   Edith Couture, 6 rue Georges
                         Clémenceau   ☎ 02 33 45 47 20
                         Repairs, alterations and clothes made to measure. Open
                         Mondays 2 to 6pm, Tuesdays to Fridays 9am to noon and 2
                         to 7pm, Saturdays 9am to noon.

Saint Lô   Martine Retouche, 29 rue de Villedieu ☎ 02 33 06 91 65
                         Curtains made and clothes repaired and altered.

Crèches & Nurseries

Avranches   le Cerf Volant, 4 rue d'Orléans   ☎ 02 33 58 66 66

Cherbourg   Halte-Garderie de l'Amont-Quentin,
                         3 rue Strasbourg   ☎ 02 33 88 55 31

Coutances   les Lutins, rue Paul le Tarouilly   ☎ 02 33 19 17 90
                         This crèche is open Mondays to Fridays 7.45am to
                         6.30pm with prior booking, Mondays 8.30am to
                         12.30pm and Wednesday 9am to 1pm without
                         booking.

                         Babysitting, Centre d'Animation, les
                         Unelles, rue St Maur   ☎ 02 33 76 78 50

| Saint Lô | Halte-Garderie, rue Fontaine Venise | ☎ 02 33 57 04 05 |

Equipment & Tool Hire

| Beaumont Hague | Laho Equipement, ZI Digulleville 🖳 *www.laho.fr* (west of Cherbourg, off the D901) | ☎ 02 33 52 71 14 |

| Coutances | Régis Location, Auberge de la Mare 🖳 *www.regis-location.fr* | ☎ 02 33 07 28 28 |

| Martinvast | Cotentin Location, ZI Le Pont 🖳 *www.cotentin-location.com* (on the D900 south of Cherbourg) | ☎ 02 33 01 31 10 |

| Saint Lô | Loxam, ZA Chevalerie, rue Jules Vallés 🖳 *www.loxam.fr* (south of the town, on the south side of the ring road) | ☎ 02 33 57 48 66 |

Garden Services

| General | Ker Breizh Services, Le Plessis l'Epine 🖳 *www.kerbreizh.com* (just over the south-west border of the department, south-west of Avranches) Garden design and maintenance including the installation of terraces, fencing and walls. English spoken. | ☎ 02 99 73 34 93 |

| Avranches | Y. Asseline, Bréhal Garden design and maintenance. | ☎ 02 33 91 68 29 |

| Benoîtville | Jardin Vert, 6 la Maison (south-west of Cherbourg along the D904) Garden design and maintenance, ground clearance and tree surgery. | ☎ 02 33 52 44 89 |

| Les Chambres | Dal'Espace, la Mahonnière (north of Avranches) Garden design and maintenance, tree surgery and garden-related building work. | ☎ 02 33 58 85 82 |

| Quettreville sur Sienne | la Lande, Gardin-Thuillet (south of Coutances) Design and garden maintenance. | ☎ 02 33 07 43 46 |

Septic Tank Services

Remilly sur Lozon   Patrick Poisson, Le Colombier   ☎ 02 33 56 29 74
(north-west of Saint Lô, north-east of Coutances)

Cherbourg   Lehoux, La Maison Bertrand,
                     la Glacerie   ☎ 02 33 43 50 50
(on the south-east outskirts of the town)

La Ronde Haye   Fatout Gervais, l'Hôtel Félix   ☎ 02 33 07 61 63
(just north of Coutances)

Saint Gilles   Assainit Vite, 1 les Maisons Neuves ☎ 02 33 55 03 99
(just west of Saint Lô)

Entertainment

This section isn't intended to be a definitive guide but gives a wide range
of ideas for the department. Prices and opening hours were correct at the
time of writing, but it's best to check before travelling long distances.

Cinemas

Avranches   Cinéma Star, 49 rue de la Constitution ☎ 02 33 58 07 55
                     🖥 www.allocine.fr

Barneville   Cinéma de la Plage, 4 avenue de
                     la République, Carteret   ☎ 02 33 53 85 67
Tickets aren't available in advance, so the traditional
queuing method applies.

Cherbourg   Odeon Club 6, 20 rue de la Paix   ☎ 02 33 93 88 55
(facing the marina)

Coutances   Drakkars Cinéma, rue Paul Mandrell ☎ 02 33 07 57 09
                     🖥 www.cinefil.com

Saint Lô   Drakkars Cinéma , rue Alsace
                     Lorraine   ☎ 02 33 05 16 60
                     🖥 www.cinefil.com

Festivals

June   Avranches
                     Triathlon de la Baie du Mont
                     St Michel   ☎ 06 60 82 26 67

The first weekend in June. On Saturday the event is open to everyone; on Sunday it's for the top athletes from the previous day.

Avranches
Fête de la Musique ☎ 02 33 58 00 22
An evening when the streets of Avranches are full of musical shows and concerts.

Cherbourg
Festival du Livre de Jeunesse et de la
Bande Dessinée ☎ 02 33 93 52 02
2005 will be the 18th Cartoon and Children's Book Festival.

Mont St Michel
Marathon de Cancale ☎ 02 99 89 54 54
🖥 *www.mont-saint-michel-marathon.com*

July
Cherbourg
Tall Ships' Race ☎ 02 33 93 52 02
Four days of festivities, shows, concerts and street performers, all centred around the Tall Ships' Race.

August
Avranches ☎ 02 33 58 00 22
Marché du Terroir et de l'Artisanant
Regional produce and craftsmen meet at place Littré.

Barneville
Fête de la Mer ☎ 02 33 04 90 58
Held at Port de Carteret

Barneville
Festival du Cerf-Volant ☎ 02 33 04 90 58
Kite festival on the beach.

September
Avranches
Fête des 3 Quartiers ☎ 02 33 58 00 22
A weekend festival and funfair at place d'Estouteville with fireworks on the Saturday evening.

Barneville
Challenge de la Déroute ☎ 02 33 04 90 58
Regatta at the yacht club.

Saint Lô
Foire aux Croûtes et à la Brocante ☎ 02 33 77 60 35

A major art fair with over 70 painters and sculptors in front of the Centre Culturel. At place du Champ de Mars and in the surrounding streets there's a flea market and car boot sale.

October   Cherbourg
Foire de Cherbourg   ☎ 02 33 93 52 02
A large fair on the last weekend of October.

Saint Lô
Concours de Sauts d'Obstacles
International   ☎ 02 33 77 60 35
International show jumping event.

November   Cherbourg
Fête des Produits de la Mer et
du Terroir   ☎ 02 33 93 52 02
A celebration of local produce.

Libraries

All the following libraries have a selection of books in English.

Avranches   place St Gervais   ☎ 02 33 68 33 18
Open Tuesdays, Wednesdays and Fridays 10am to noon and 1.30 to 6pm, Saturdays 9.30am to 1pm and 2 to 5pm.

Barneville   rue Jeanne Provost, Le Bourg   ☎ 02 33 04 92 73
Open Tuesdays and Fridays 2 to 6pm, Wednesdays 10am to 12.30pm and 2 to 6pm, Saturdays 9.30am to 12.30pm.

Cherbourg   rue Vastel   ☎ 02 33 23 39 40
Open Tuesdays, Thursdays and Fridays 1 to 6pm, Wednesdays and Saturdays 9 to 5pm.

Coutances   l'Esplanade des Unelles, rue St Maur   ☎ 02 33 19 05 70
Tuesdays and Fridays 1.30 to 6pm, Wednesdays and Saturdays 10am to 12.15pm and 1.30 to 5pm, Thursdays 11am to 2pm and 4 to 6pm.

Mrs Brooke, Guéhébert   ☎ 02 33 46 44 86
In the centre of the village Mrs Brooke runs an English library with a large volume of books. There are no time limits and no limit on the number of books borrowed, so you can take enough to keep you going for a few months. There's also a small selection of English videos; donations always welcome. Both services are free.

Saint Lô	Bibliothèque Municipale, place Champ de Mars ☎ 02 33 72 52 53
	(inside the Centre Cultural Jean Lurcat)
	Open Tuesdays 2 to 6pm, Wednesdays 10am to 6pm,
	Thursdays 1 to 5pm, Fridays 1 to 6pm and Saturdays 10am
	to 5pm.

Theatres

| Avranches | Théâtre Municipal d'Avranches, boulevard Léon Jozeau Marigné ☎ 02 33 68 33 27 |
| | 🖳 *www.ville-avranches.fr* |

| Cherbourg | le Trident, Théâtre à l'Italienne, place du Général de Gaulle ☎ 02 33 88 55 55 |

| | Théâtre de l'Arlequin, 39 rue de la Polle ☎ 02 33 08 08 43 |

| Saint Lô | Théâtre Roger Ferdinand, rue Octave Feuillet ☎ 02 33 57 11 49 |

Video & DVD Hire

See page 67.

French Teachers & Courses

| Avranches | Greta, 2 place Patton ☎ 02 33 79 02 79 |
| | Government-run organisation. |

| Barneville | Portbail Formation Internationale, Mairie de Portbail, 9 rue Lechevalier ☎ 02 33 10 04 80 |
| | (just south of the town) |

Cherbourg	Greta, 4 avenue L. Lumière ☎ 02 33 88 60 40
	✉ *greta.cotentin@ac-caen.fr*
	Government-run organisation.

| Saint Lô | Greta, 3 rue Léon Déries ☎ 02 33 05 62 39 |
| | Government-run organisation. |

St Sauveur	Maison Familiale Rurale d'Education, la Salmonerie ☎ 02 33 07 72 61
	(directly north of Coutances)
	French courses. Ask for Mme Chable.

Leisure Activities

This section isn't intended to be a definitive guide but gives a wide range of ideas for the department. Prices and opening hours were correct at the time of writing, but it's best to check before travelling long distances.

Arts & Crafts

Avranches	Ecole Municipale d'Arts Plastiques, Centre Culturel, boulevard Jozeau Marigné ☎ 02 33 68 33 44 Over 16 different courses to cover all ages and all media.
Barneville	Patchwork, 8 rue des Ecoles, Le Bourg ☎ 02 33 04 06 16 This group meets 2.30 to 5.30pm on Wednesdays.
Cherbourg	Ecole Régional des Beaux-Arts, 19 avenue de Paris ☎ 02 33 43 33 74
Coutances	Ecole Municipale de Dessin, les Unelles, rue St Maur ☎ 02 33 47 86 15 Courses for all levels including drawing, painting, modelling and pottery.

Astronomy

Coutances	Groupe Astronomique du Coutançais, Les Unelles, rue St Maur ☎ 02 33 45 65 12 The group meets the first Friday of each month at 8.30pm.

Bridge

Avranches	Avranches Bridge Club ☎ 02 33 58 23 38 Training and tournaments. Contact Mme Doublet.
Barneville	Bridge, 8 rue des Ecoles, Le Bourg ☎ 02 33 04 06 26 Tournaments Mondays 8pm, Thursdays 2pm and 6pm.
Carentan	Carentan Bridge Club, 13 rue St Germain ☎ 02 33 71 06 74
Cherbourg	Bridge Cherbourgeois, rue Roger Glinel Querqueville ☎ 02 33 03 25 65
Coutances	Bridge Club Coutances, avenue Tennis, Agon Coutainville ☎ 02 33 47 24 76

| Saint Lô | Bridge Club Briovère, passage Queillé |
| | Chopin | ☎ 02 33 05 50 20 |

Children's Activity Clubs

| Avranches | Gym Oxygène, Salle de Sport Parisy, rue |
| | de la Liberté | ☎ 02 33 51 86 85 |

Baby gym and junior gym classes for three to ten-year-olds.

| Cherbourg | MJC, 20 rue de l'Abbaye | ☎ 02 33 53 31 72 |

Activities for children of all ages.

| Coutances | Centre d'Animation, les Unelles, rue |
| | St Maur | ☎ 02 33 76 78 50 |

Activities on Wednesdays in term time and all week in the school holidays.

| Saint Lô | Maison de Quartier de la Dollée, 243 |
| | rue des Clos | ☎ 02 33 57 46 67 |

Sporting, educational and cultural activities.

Choral Singing

| Avranches | Sée Rénade, Espace Ponty, Théâtre |
| | Municipal | ☎ 02 33 68 14 92 |

💻 *www.seerenade.org*
Everyone welcome Tuesdays at 8.15pm.

Atelier de Chant, Ecole Maternelle, rue
de Verdun   ☎ 02 33 48 20 68

| Cherbourg | la Clé des Chants, Espace Dolto, |
| | Equeurdreville-Hainneville | ☎ 02 33 03 47 05 |

Classic and contemporary songs. Rehearsals Tuesdays at 8.30pm.

Circus Skills

| Cherbourg | Ecole du Cirque-Sol'Air, 844 rue Aristide |
| | Briand, Tourlaville | ☎ 02 33 22 06 69 |

Courses run by M. & Mme Valogne.

| Saint Lô | Les Saltimbrés, 165 rue du |
| | Mesnilcroc | ☎ 02 33 55 29 51 |

Workshops for all ages including juggling, acrobatics and balancing.

Computer Training

Cherbourg   MJC Centre, 20 rue de l'Abbaye   ☎ 02 33 53 31 72
Training in pairs at various times throughout the week.

Coutances   Salle Multimédia, Centre d'Animation, les
Unelles, rue St Maur   ☎ 02 33 76 78 50
Courses at all levels, including introductory sessions.

Dancing

Avranches   Gymnastes Volontaires d'Avranches ☎ 02 33 58 17 95
Children and adult classes, including a jazz class.

American Country Club, Salle Polyvalente
de Ponts-sous-Avranches   ☎ 06 61 17 51 25
Line dancing, Tuesdays at 8pm for beginners and at
9.15pm for those with at least one year's experience.

Tina Picker Danse, 82 rue de la
Constitution   ☎ 02 33 61 52 41
Children's ballet, jazz and tap.

Barneville   Salle des Douits, avenue des Drouits,
Carteret   ☎ 02 33 94 62 44
Various classes including ballet and jazz.

Salle des Douits, avenue des Drouits,
Carteret   ☎ 02 33 04 61 28
Ballroom dancing Tuesdays from 7.30pm.

Cherbourg   Association Culturelle de la Polle, 167 rue
de la Polle   ☎ 02 33 10 07 07
Ballet classes for children and adults.

Ecole de Danse Avenel, 18 rue de
la Marine   ☎ 02 33 22 15 20
🖳 www.danse-avenel.com
Ballroom and Latin American, rock, jazz, salsa and more,
all ages.

Danse de Salon, MJC Centre, 20 rue de
l'Abbaye   ☎ 02 33 53 31 72
Classes on Wednesday evenings for ballroom and Latin
American dancing.

Coutances   Salle de Danse, Centre d'Animation, les
Unelles, rue St Maur   ☎ 02 33 76 78 50

Ballet and modern dance classes held on Wednesdays and Saturdays, jazz for adults Tuesdays and Thursdays, ballroom dancing Monday and Tuesday evenings.

Saint Lô   Cha Cha Rock Club   ☎ 02 33 22 15 20
Contact Daniel Avenel for current classes, including rock, tango and ballroom dancing.

Drama

Cherbourg   Atelier Théâtre, MJC la Grange, allée Marguerite   ☎ 02 33 44 35 58
Drama workshops for 8 to 15-year-olds.

MJC Centre, 20 rue de l'Abbaye   ☎ 02 33 53 31 72
Adult workshops Tuesday 8.45 to 10.45pm.

Saint Lô   Troupe Les Embruns   ☎ 02 33 50 18 32
Workshops for children, youngsters and adults on Mondays, Tuesdays and Saturday mornings. Contact Fabrice Hervé for current groups.

Flower Arranging

Avranches   Club Art et Bouquets, 13 rue des Grèves   ☎ 02 33 51 09 76

Coutances   Centre d'Animation, les Unelles, rue St Maur   ☎ 02 33 76 78 50
Groups for various levels, each meeting once a month.

Gardening

Avranches   Société d'Horticulture d'Avranches, Salle de Réunion, 1 rue St Martin   ☎ 02 33 58 12 70

Saint Lô   Société d'Horticulture du Pays Saint Lois   ☎ 02 33 06 08 74
✉ *sim.l.phil@wanadoo.fr*
For amateur gardeners. Contact Louis Philippe for forthcoming events.

Gym

Avranches   Gymnaste Volontaires d'Avranches   ☎ 02 33 58 17 95
A wide range of classes for all ages at various venues.

Barneville   Gymnastique Volontaire, Salle Omnisports, rue Jean Jaurès, Le Bourg   ☎ 02 33 53 86 54
Classes on Tuesdays at 10am, Thursdays at 8.30pm.

Gymnastique Volontaire, Salle Omnisports,
rue Jean Jaurès, Le Bourg   ☎ 02 33 04 90 61
Classes for older people on Thursdays 3pm.

Cherbourg   Fitness Form, MJC Centre, 20 rue de
l'Abbaye   ☎ 02 33 53 31 72
Various classes including cardio and fitness.

Coutances   Gymnastique Volontaire Coutançaise ☎ 02 33 07 58 49
Various classes held throughout the week.

Saint Lô   Gymnastique Volontaire, Centre Sportif Fernand
Beaufils, place du Champ de Mars   ☎ 02 33 57 10 25

Gyms & Health Clubs

Cherbourg   Club Super Forme, 3 rue Noël   ☎ 02 33 94 43 39
Weights, aerobics, gym and various exercise classes.

Coutances   Physic Center, 1a rue de
Normandie   ☎ 02 33 07 80 85
Free weights area and more than 30 cardio machines.
Open all year, Mondays to Fridays 10am to 9pm, Saturdays
10am to 1pm.

Ice Skating

Cherbourg   Patinoire Chantereyne, port
de Plaisance   ☎ 02 33 53 60 50
(by the marina)

Coutances   le Yéti, route de Granville   ☎ 02 33 45 02 02
This ice rink is open all year, with disco evenings, ice
karting and a bar.

Music

Avranches   Ecole de Musique, boulevard Léon Jozeau
Marigné   ☎ 02 33 60 39 98

Barneville   8 rue des Ecoles, Le Bourg   ☎ 02 33 04 88 16
Piano, accordion and guitar lessons.

Cherbourg   MJC la Grange, allée Marguerite   ☎ 02 33 44 35 58
Guitar lessons (acoustic and electric), and orchestral
workshops.

Ecole Municipale de Musique,
rue Gibert   ☎ 02 33 94 22 77

| Coutances | Ecole de Musique de Coutances, les |
| | Unelles, rue St Maur ☎ 02 33 07 46 01 |

Lessons in guitar, violin, piano, keyboard and wind instruments plus vocal classes.

| Saint Lô | Atelier Musical, 2 bis rue des 80ième |
| | et 136ième Territorial ☎ 02 33 56 15 90 |

(behind the medical centre)
Individual and group lessons, a wide range of instruments from piano to drums, saxophone to synthesiser.

Photography

| Avranches | Photo Vidéo Club ☎ 02 33 58 70 30 |

Contact M. Germain

| Cherbourg | Atelier Photo, MJC Centre, 20 rue de |
| | l'Abbaye ☎ 02 33 53 31 72 |

Tuesday and Wednesday evenings and outside photography every other Saturday.

| Coutances | Atelier Photo, Salle 513, Centre d'Animation, les |
| | Unelles, rue St Maur ☎ 02 33 76 78 50 |

| Saint Lô | Essor Philatélique Saint Lois ☎ 02 33 57 19 60 |

Contact M. Poupart.

Pottery

| Coutances | Salle de Poterie, Centre d'Animation, les |
| | Unelles, rue St Maur ☎ 02 33 76 78 50 |

Scouts & Guides

| Avranches | Scouts de France ☎ 02 33 48 74 58 |

Contact M. Lallement.

| Cherbourg | Guides de France ☎ 02 33 78 92 16 |

Contact Mlle Revert.

Scouts de France ☎ 02 33 52 87 02
Contact M. Stéphan.

Sea Scouts ☎ 02 33 93 53 91
Contact M. Petitet.

| Saint Lô | Scouts de France, 61 rue du |
| | Bois Ardent ☎ 02 33 05 56 36 |

🖳 *www.scouts-france.fr*

Social Groups

General

Anglophones Association   ☎ 02 33 46 44 86
✉ *jeanandjeff@wanadoo.fr*
This group has been going around 13 years and was
started by two French ladies who wanted to help the
British integrate into the area. Currently run by Mr Brooke
and based around Coutances the association publishes
a bi-monthly newsletter giving details of the monthly
activities and runs a gardening group, computer club
and craft group.

Rotary Club

Avranches

Rotary Club   ☎ 02 33 60 63 76
Contact M. Lemaux.

Cherbourg

Rotary Club Cherbourg   ☎ 02 33 53 38 36
Contact M. Véron.

Coutances

Rotary Club   ☎ 02 33 46 73 33
Contact M. Aubert for current venue.

Saint Lô

Rotary Club 'Servir'   ☎ 02 33 55 13 28
Contact Patrick Paul.

Town Twinning

Avranches

Hôtel de Ville, place Littré   ☎ 02 33 89 29 40
Twinned with Crediton in England.

Barneville

Comité de Jumelage   ☎ 02 33 08 31 18
Twinned with Guernsey and Jersey. Contact M. Blancheton
for further details.

Cherbourg

Hôtel de Ville   ☎ 02 33 87 88 89
Twinned with Poole in Dorset.

Coutances

Comité de Jumelage   ☎ 02 33 45 40 31
Twinned with Ilkley in Yorkshire. Contact Mme Vaquer for
details.

Coutances is also twinned with St Ouen in Jersey.
Contact M. Lesauvage.   ☎ 02 33 45 57 14

Saint Lô

Comité de Jumelage Saint
Lô-Christchurch   ☎ 02 33 55 70 61
Informal gathering the first Tuesday of each month at Bar le
Scottish, 45 rue Torteron, from 8.30pm. Contact Isabelle
Lestrelin for current details.

Welcome Groups

General
Accueil des Villes Françaises (AVF)
🖳 *www.avf.asso.fr*
Some towns have a branch of this organisation, which is specifically to help newcomers settle into the town. The site is available in English.

Avranches
Avranches Bienvenue, place des Halles
☎ 02 33 58 70 83
Contact Lucile Claveau.

Cherbourg
AVF Cherbourg, 41 rue Au Blé (sq Phélippot le Cat)
☎ 02 33 94 97 12
🖳 *www.site.voila.fr/avf.cherbourg*

Spas

Granville
Institut Prévithal, 3 rue Jules Michelet ☎ 02 33 90 31 10
🖳 *www.previthal.com*
The Prévithal Institute of Thalassotherapy offers a variety of packages for relaxation or to cure various health problems. Accommodation is in a three-star hotel with unspoilt views over the sea.

le Jardin du Bien Être, 104 rue de la Parfonterie
☎ 02 33 69 22 77
Anti-stress centre, Indian massage, aromatherapy, slimming and tanning centre.

Stamp Collecting

Avranches
Amicale Philatélique de la Baie
☎ 02 33 58 05 33
Contact Michel Beust.

Cherbourg
Cercle Philatélique et Cartophile du Cotentin
☎ 02 33 94 51 18
Contact M. Cauchebrais.

Coutances
Union Philatélique Manchoise ☎ 02 33 45 13 43
Meets the second Sunday of each month at 9.30am at the Mairie in Coutances.

Yoga

Avranches
Denis Blondel, le Théâtre
☎ 02 33 58 86 49

Barneville
Hatha Yoga, 8 rue des Ecoles, Le Bourg
☎ 02 33 53 78 81
Various classes held on Tuesdays.

Cherbourg	Association Cherbourgeoise de Yoga, Salle de la Fraternelle, rue Gambetta ☎ 02 33 54 70 12

Contact Mme Corbel for details of current sessions.

Coutances	Association Coutançaise de Yoga, les Unelles, rue St Maur ☎ 02 33 07 24 56

Three different classes held on Wednesday nights. Contact Mme Martin for further details.

Saint Lô	Association Saint Lois de Yoga, Centre Sportif, place du Champ de Mars ☎ 02 33 54 70 12

Classes every Thursday.

Medical Facilities & Emergency Services

Ambulances

See page 68.

Doctors

English-speakers may like to contact the following doctors:

Avranches	Cabinet Pouderoux & David, 20 place Littré ☎ 02 33 58 67 15

Barneville	Cabinet Haquet & Picot, 27 rue Guillaume le Conquérant, Le Bourg ☎ 02 33 52 61 36

Cherbourg	Cabinet Médical, 52 rue Ancien Quai ☎ 02 33 10 00 50
	duty doctor out of hours ☎ 02 33 01 58 58

Coutances	Cabinet Médical, 60 rue Geoffroy de Montbray ☎ 02 33 19 18 00

Saint Lô	Cabinet Médical, 2 bis rue 80ième & 136ième Territorial ☎ 02 33 57 85 30

Gendarmeries

Avranches	26 rue du Docteur Béchet	☎ 02 33 79 48 10
Barneville	37 rue Pic Mallet, Le Bourg	☎ 02 33 53 80 17
Cherbourg	4 rue du Val de Saire	☎ 02 33 88 74 10

| Coutances | 8 boulevard Alsace Lorraine | ☎ 02 33 76 12 70 |
| Saint Lô | 367 rue Tessy | ☎ 02 33 75 50 00 |

Health Authority

| General | Caisse Régional Assurance Maladie de Normandie, Montée Bois André, Saint Lô ☎ 02 33 06 58 90 This is the main office for the department. Other offices are listed below. | |

Avranches	61 boulevard Amiral Gauchet	☎ 08 20 90 41 78
Cherbourg	33 rue Grande Vallée	☎ 08 20 90 41 78
Coutances	103 rue Geoffroy de Montbray	☎ 08 20 90 14 78

Hospitals

All the following hospitals have emergency departments.

Avranches	Centre Hospitalier d'Avranches-Granville, 59 rue de la Liberté	☎ 02 33 89 40 00
Cherbourg	Centre Hospitalier Louis Pasteur, 46 rue du Val de Saire	☎ 02 33 20 70 00
Coutances	Centre Hospitalier de Coutances, rue de la Gare	☎ 02 33 47 40 00
Saint Lô	Hôpital Mémorial, 715 rue Dunant	☎ 02 33 06 33 33

Nightlife

This section isn't intended to be a definitive guide but gives a wide range of ideas for the department. Prices and opening hours were correct at the time of writing, but it's best to check before travelling long distances.

Agon Coutainville   Casino de Coutainville, avenue Président Roosevelt   ☎ 02 33 47 06 88
🖥 *www.partouche.com*
(on the coast directly west of Coutances)
Casino with games machines, piano bar and a restaurant. Open every day from 10am to 3am (4am on Saturdays and bank holidays).

Avranches	**Aaron's Café, 22 rue des Chapeliers** ☎ 02 33 58 58 59 Bar open every day with karaoke on Sundays.

le Big Ben, 18 place Littré   ☎ 02 33 60 55 90
This pool club has karaoke from 10pm every Thursday.

Chrisly, 16 place Estouteville   ☎ 02 33 58 10 01
Late night bar, open until 2am on Saturdays.

Barneville

le Barnevill's, 33 boulevard Ecrehou,
la Plage   ☎ 02 33 04 46 46
💻 *www.barnevills.fr.st*
This pub/disco is open every evening with free entry during
the week.

le Kissing, 3 route Barneville Portbail, St Jean
de la Rivière   ☎ 02 33 04 63 27
(south-east of the town towards Portbail)
This club is open all year round, every evening in the
summer with a terrace and outside bar. Free entry for ladies
before midnight on Wednesdays and
Thursdays.

Cherbourg

l'Amiraute, 18 quai Alexandre III   ☎ 02 33 43 00 56
(in the town centre, facing the fishing port)
This nightclub is part of the casino.

Bowling, port Chantereyne   ☎ 02 33 78 17 20
Bowling and pool tables, open every day 2pm to 2am.

Casino de Cherbourg, 18 quai
Alexandre III   ☎ 02 33 43 00 56
(in the town centre, facing the fishing port)
Disco, '50s diner, bar, brasserie, casino and disco.

Fifty's Diner, 18 quai Alexandre III   ☎ 02 33 43 58 20
(facing the fishing port and part of the casino)
This bar/brasserie has concerts Thursday evenings and
karaoke on Fridays.

Modern Café, 15 place du Général
de Gaulle   ☎ 02 33 43 03 94
Open 10am to 2am every day, karaoke Saturdays from
9pm.

le Quartier Latin Café, 20 rue des
Fossés   ☎ 02 33 94 07 76
A late night bar on a pedestrian side street.

le Scuba, 19 rue de la Marine   ☎ 02 33 22 10 32
(just up from the marina)
Late night club/bar open Mondays to Thursdays 3pm to
2am, Fridays 3pm to 3am, Saturdays 4pm to 3am.

Tam Tam Café, 5 rue Christine   ☎ 02 33 93 55 55
Late night cocktail bar.

Coutances   le Shadow, 58 rue St Nicolas   ☎ 02 33 45 95 95
(entrance is recessed between a lingerie shop and a ladies'
clothes shop, on the left as you go up the hill)
This is a bar/pub with table football, pool and snooker.
Open Mondays to Fridays from noon to 1am, Saturdays
2.30pm to 1am, closed Sundays.

le Triskell, 10 rue Louis Beuve   ☎ 02 33 45 01 01
Bar that has a happy hour every day from 8 to 9pm. Similar
atmosphere to a British wine bar.

le Yeti, route de Granville   ☎ 02 33 45 02 02
Bar and pool tables plus ice rink open all year round with
discos and karting on ice.

Granville   Casino, place Maréchal Foch   ☎ 02 33 50 00 79
🖳 *www.casino-granville.com*
Gaming machines open from 10am to 4am, plus a
restaurant, blackjack, poker, etc.

Gratot   la Soifferie   ☎ 02 33 47 88 34
(just north-west of Coutances)
This disco is open from 11pm to 5am Fridays, Saturdays
and bank holidays, plus Thursdays in the
summer.

Poilly   Moulin de Quincampoix   ☎ 02 33 48 53 91
(south of Avranches, near Ducey)
Pub/club with themed evenings.

Saint Lô   le Macao, 2 rue Maréchal Leclerc   ☎ 02 33 57 40 00
Bowling, brasserie, pool tables and bar. Open Mondays to
Fridays 11am to 1am, Saturdays from 11.30am, Sundays 2
to 8pm.

le Scottish, 45 rue Torteron   ☎ 02 33 05 47 47
Late night bar open until midnight Tuesdays to Saturdays.

Sunset Club, 2 rue des Fossés   ☎ 02 33 05 13 60
🖳 *www.sunsetclub.fr*
(below the ramparts, by the Majestic cinema)

This disco is open Wednesdays and Thursdays 11.30pm to 4am, Fridays and Saturdays until 5am, with a happy 'hour' from 11.30pm to 1am. Various themed evenings

le Weekend, rue Maréchal Leclerc   ☎ 02 33 57 08 14
Late night bar open until 1am Fridays and Saturdays.

St Pair sur Mer   Casino de St Pair, 2 rue Plage   ☎ 02 33 91 34 00
(on the coast north-west of Avranches)
Casino, disco, bars, gaming machines and restaurant.

Tanis   la Bodega, Brée   ☎ 02 33 48 17 94
💻 www.bodegaclub.fr.st
(on the N175 between Avranches and Pontorson)
This club is open Fridays and Saturdays with free entry for women before 1am.

Torigni sur Vire   l'Echo du Lac   ☎ 02 33 55 89 46
💻 www.echodulac.com
(south-east of Saint Lô, going towards the N175)
The largest disco in Normandy with four areas, swimming pool and grill.

Pets

Farriers

General   Lypca Pietro, 51 rue Corderie, la Plage,
Barneville   ☎ 02 33 53 86 83

Christophe Gobé, 9 route Brûlé,
Juilley   ☎ 02 33 60 66 25
(directly south of Avranches)

Eric Laville, le Bisson, Tirepied   ☎ 02 33 68 12 21
(just north-east of Avranches)

Horse Dentists

Vets don't generally deal with teeth rasping and there are specialist equine dentists. You need to phone in order to be booked onto their next circuit.

Coutances   Clinique Vétérinaire de la République, 38 avenue
de la République   ☎ 02 33 07 67 47
One of the vets at this surgery carries out teeth rasping.

Pet Parlours

See page 79.

Riding Equipment

Coutances	Dogon Frères, Zac Auberge de la Mare, route de Périers	☎ 02 33 07 57 30
	Saddles, harnesses and all horse-related equipment.	

St Jean de Savigny   'Galop', les Mesnil   ☎ 02 33 05 87 57
(north-east of Saint Lô, on the border with Calvados)

Villedieu les Poêles 'A Cheval', les Hauts Vents,
la Trinité   ☎ 02 33 58 98 45
(between Saint Lô and Avranches, on the A84)

SPA

Cherbourg   Avenue Amiral Lemonnier   ☎ 02 33 20 49 74

Veterinary Clinics

See page 80.

Places to Visit

This section isn't intended to be a definitive guide but gives a wide range of ideas for the department. Prices and opening hours were correct at the time of writing, but it's best to check before travelling long distances.

Animal Parks & Aquariums

Beauvoir   Reptilarium du Mont St-Michel,
route Pontorson   ☎ 02 33 68 11 18
💻 *www.le-reptilarium.com*
(4km/2.5mi from Mont St Michel, south-west of Avranches)
Alligators, caimans and other crocodiles plus a large garden holding over 300 tortoises and a display area with viewing tunnels, suspension bridges and glass towers from which to observe over 200 lizards and snakes. Open every day February to December, January weekends and school holidays only. 1st April to 30 September 10am to 7pm, the rest of the year 2 to 6pm. Adults €7, 13 to 18-year-olds €6, 4 to 12-year-olds €5.

Cherbourg   Cité de la Mer, Gare Maritime
Transatlantique   ☎ 08 25 00 25 50

⌨ *www.citedelamer.com*
The world's largest submarine that is open to the
public, along with the control deck of a virtual submarine
that you can steer in an interactive dive. There's an
exhibition showing all the submarines that have been
invented, along with an open pool for touching sea life and
a 'bottomless' aquarium, the deepest in Europe. Allow
around three hours for the visit. June to August 9.30am to
7pm; September to May 10am to 6pm (2 to 6pm from
3rd to 28th January inclusive and closed Mondays from
mid-November to mid-December and December 25th and
1st January). Adults €11.50/€13, 6 to 17-year-olds
€8.50/€9.50 (higher prices from 1st May to 30th
September).

Montaigu la Brisette

Parc Animalier St Martin ☎ 02 33 40 40 98
An animal park of 2.5ha (6 acres) with many animals
from Asia and Africa including lamas, zebra and camels.
Open weekends and bank holidays in May 2 to 7pm; 1st
June to the school summer holidays Mondays to
Fridays 11am to 5pm, weekends and bank holidays
2 to 7pm; during the summer holidays Mondays to
Fridays, 11am to 7pm, weekends and bank
holidays 2 to 7.30pm; remainder of the year
Sundays and bank holidays only from 2pm.

Villedieu les Poêles

Zoo Champrepus ☎ 02 33 61 30 74
⌨ *www.zoo-champrepus.com*
Wild animals set in 7ha (17 acres) of parkland, which you
explore by moving amongst the animals, passing over them
on rope bridges or looking through viewing windows.
There's also a children's zoo, parrot section and play
area with ball pond and giant inflatables and in the
summer there are opportunities to get closer to various
animals such as lemurs, camels and yaks. Picnic area and
snack bar/*crêperie*. Open February, October and
November daily from 1.30 to 6pm; March weekends only
1.30 to 6pm; April to June and September daily from
10am to 6pm; July and August to 7pm; closed mid-
November to mid-February. Adults €10,
children €5.50.

Beaches & Leisure Parks

Agon Coutainville

Plage du Centre ☎ 02 33 76 67 30
⌨ *www.ot-agoncoutainville.com*
Fine sandy beaches with a beach club for 4 to 12-year-
olds.

Barneville

Barneville has two beaches, both with fine sand, which have
won awards for cleanliness.

Carolles	Between Granville and Avranches, Carolles has long, fine sandy beaches.
Granville	Granville is known as a 'health resort', having beaches, promenades and beachfront shops. Popular for surfing and sailing, but has some of the strongest tides in Europe.
Jullouville	St Michel des Loups Long sandy beaches, promenades, sailing, swimming and a general holiday resort. The beaches offer a wide variety of sand- and surf-based sports. There are lifeguards in the summer, a playground, picnic tables and a *boules* court.
St Martin de Landelles	Parc de Loisirs, l'Ange Michel ☎ 02 33 49 04 74 🖥 *www.ange-michel-loisirs.com* (south-east of Avranches) An activity park with quad bikes, mini-karting, a variety of chutes, a water park, snack bar, pool and gym. Open April and May weekends from 1.30pm; June to August every day from 11am; September weekends only from 11am. Adults €9, children under 12 €7.

Boat, Train & Wagon Rides

Boat Trips

Cherbourg	Mettez les Voiles! ☎ 06 83 52 57 10 🖥 *www.grand-depart.fr.st* Sail from Cherbourg or Carteret on a 13m vessel to discover the Channel Islands for a day, weekend or week.
Carentan	la Rosée du Soleil, 601 la Cour, Tribehou ☎ 02 33 55 18 07 Discover the waterways of the Marais on this boat trip. It lasts two and a half hours and departs from Carentan on the river Taute. Adults €7.50, children €6.
Granville	Gare Maritime ☎ 02 33 61 08 88 Operated by Hugo Express, boats cross from Granville to Jersey, Guernsey and Sark.
	Iles Chausey, Gare Maritime ☎ 02 33 50 16 36 🖥 *www.compagniecorsaire.com* Boat trips operated by Corsaire to the Chausey islands. The Chausey Archipelago consists of 365 tiny islands, 17km (10mi) out to sea. Operates all year.
Saint Lô	Saint Loise, place Général de Gaulle ☎ 02 33 77 06 35 This boat trip takes you through Saint Lô with a commentary on the history of the town and on the boat

traffic on the Vire river in the 19th and early 20th century
(available in English during the summer). The number
above is that of the tourist office, from which you can obtain
further information and make bookings.

Train Rides

Cherbourg

Promenades Petit Train, place du
Général de Gaulle   ☎ 02 99 88 47 07
(departs from in front of the theatre)
This 'train' takes you through the old town and past the
Cité de la Mer and the botanical gardens with
commentaries in French and English. Operates from
Easter to the end of September, Mondays to Saturdays
from 10am to 6pm.

Marchésieux

Marshlands Miniature Railway, Base
Touristique Centre Manche   ☎ 02 33 05 15 54
🖳 www.minitrain.fr
(just off the D900 to the east of Périers)
A miniature train running on a real train tracks through
woods, marshland and over bridges, based in an 1830s
village. April to June, September and October weekends
and bank holidays from 2.30pm; July and August daily.
Adults €2.50, children €1.70.

Chateaux

Gratot

Château de Gratot   ☎ 02 33 45 18 49
(just north-west of Coutances)
The chateau and its four towers are surrounded by a moat
and have a permanent exhibition offering an insight into the
architecture and history of the site from its ruin to its
renaissance. Garden festival at the beginning of August.
Open all year round from 10am to 7pm. Adults €3, children
from 10 to 18 €1.50.

Pirou

Château de Pirou   ☎ 02 33 46 34 71
(near the coast, north of Coutances)
A fortified castle built on the shores of a lake, with historical
connections with England and a tapestry relating to the
conquest of southern Italy and Sicily by the Normans. Open
from the February school holidays to the end of November
10am to noon and 2 to 6.30pm (October, November,
February and March 10am to noon and 2 to 5pm, July and
August 10am to 6.30pm). Closed Tuesdays all year. Adults
€4, children €2.30, guided tours €4.60.

St Sauveur

Grand Taute   ☎ 02 33 19 19 24
A manor house built at the end of the 16th century by Jean
le Coq, a police officer. There's an elaborate defence
system that protected the house from enemy attack, and,

grouped around a courtyard in front of the manor, a bakery, cider press, barns and stables. Open July and August daily from 2 to 6pm, free of charge.

| Torigni sur Vire | Château des Matignons   ☎ 02 33 56 71 44 |

(south of Saint Lô, on the D174)
This chateau enjoyed its heyday at the end of the 17th century. It was damaged during the Revolution but restored after the Second World War. It's now the Hôtel de Ville and houses a collection of 17th century tapestries, a display of sculptures, paintings and other items, with temporary exhibitions in the summer.

Urville Nacqueville Château et Parc de Nacqueville   ☎ 02 33 03 21 12
(just west of Cherbourg)
Construction of this chateau started in 1510. Originally a fortified manor, it's now a picturesque chateau with a turreted gate house and formal gardens, created in the 18th century. Guided tours only, from Easter to the end of September every day except Tuesdays and Fridays, hourly from 2 to 5pm inclusive.

Churches & Abbeys

Mont St Michel   Abbaye du Mont Saint Michel   ☎ 02 33 89 80 00
(west of Avranches)
This abbey appears to be balanced on the rock that rises out of a landscape smoothed flat by the wind. Built in 708AD, it includes a crypt of huge pillars, refectory, cloister, monks' walkway and a great wheel. Open May to August 9am to 7pm, September to April 9.30am to 6pm. Night time tours Mondays to Saturdays 9pm to 12.30am, last admission one hour before closing. Adults €7, under 25's €4.50, under 18's free. Night time tour €10 for adults. **The roads and parking around the bay of Mont St Michel can become extremely congested and you're strongly advised to arrive early in the day to avoid long queues and having to park some distance away.**

Coutances   Cathédrale de Coutances   ☎ 02 33 19 08 10
A magnificent cathedral reconstructed during the 13th century after the original was burnt down. There are stained glass windows from the Middle Ages and towers and turrets that are visible high over the surrounding area. Located in the centre of the town, it's open to visitors all year from 9am to 7pm; guided tours are available Mondays to Fridays and Sunday afternoons from the end of May to late September – allow an hour and a half. Guided tour €5.50.

Saint Lô   Eglise Sainte-Croix   ☎ 02 33 77 60 35
Dedicated in 1204, this Romanesque church is the oldest in Saint Lô.

Coutances	**Eglise St Nicolas** This old parish church dates from the 16th and 17th centuries and is a beautiful example of the late gothic styles. Open every day in the summer from 10am to 6pm.
Saint Lô	**Eglise Notre-Dame** ☎ 02 33 77 60 35 This cathedral sustained a lot of damage in 1944, some of which has been left intentionally. As you approach the church from rue Carnot you can see a shell embedded in the corner of one of the buttresses.
La Forêt	**Abbaye de Cerisy** ☎ 02 33 57 34 63 This abbey was built between 1035 and 1110 and now has a permanent exhibition of Norman Art. Open Easter to June and September Tuesdays to Sundays 9am to 6.30pm; July and August every day 9am to 6.30pm; October weekends and bank holidays 9am to 6.30pm. Guided tours at 10.30am.

Miscellaneous

Bellefontaine	**Village Enchanté** ☎ 02 33 59 01 93 🖳 *www.village-enchante.fr* In a natural park of wells and brooks you enter a child's imaginary world with a 'valley of fairy tales', fountain gardens and 'enchanted' waterfalls, and ride upon a miniature railway. Open daily from Easter to the end of September 10am to 6pm (weekends in July and August open until 7pm). Adults €6, 3 to 12-year-olds €4.50.
Bricquebec	**le Labyrinthe Végétal, route de Valonges (D902)** ☎ 02 33 40 23 40 A maze made out of six-foot high corn. Open mid-July to the end of September. Adults €4.50, children under 14 €3.50.
Fierville les Mines	**Moulin à Vent du Cotentin, la Lande** ☎ 02 33 53 38 04 🖳 *www.moulin-du-cotentin.com* (a few km east of Barneville) This two-storey windmill dates back to 1744, was renovated in 1997 and now produces flour alongside a bread/flour shop and restaurant. Open to the public July and August 10am to noon and 2 to 7pm.
Flottemanville Hague	**Ludiver, route du Haras** ☎ 02 33 78 13 80 🖳 *www.ludiver.com* (directly west of Cherbourg)

Planetarium, observatory and space museum. Open July
and August 10am to 7pm every day; September to June
Mondays to Fridays 9am to 1pm and 2 to 5.30pm,
Saturdays and Sundays 2 to 6pm (closed Saturdays from
1st November to Easter). You can buy tickets for the
museum, museum and planetarium or just the
observatory at night. Adults €3.50 to €7, children
€2 to €4.50.

Gatteville   Phare de Gatteville   ☎ 02 33 23 17 97
(north-east tip of the Cherbourg peninsular)
At 75m (250ft) high, this is the second-highest lighthouse in
France. After climbing 365 steps you will have a
magnificent view over the Channel and Val de Saire.
Open mornings from 10am to noon and afternoons in
February, November and December 2 to 4pm, March
and October 2 to 5pm, April 2 to 6pm, May and August
2 to 7pm. Closed January and from mid-November to
mid December, plus 25th December and
1st May.

Le Hutrel
(going south out of Saint Lô town centre on the route de
Tessy take the last turning on the right before the bridge
under the bypass)
This village is one of the rare places that has been kept
intact since the Second World War, in memory of the
exodus from the Saint Lô area during the bombings of
June 1944. Every year on the Thursday of Ascension
an open-air mass is celebrated in front of the Holy
Virgin in remembrance of those traumatic
days.

Marchésieux   Miniature 1930s Village, Base Touristique
Centre Manche   ☎ 02 33 46 74 98
🖥 *www.villageminiature.fr.fm*
(off the D900 Périers to Saint Lô road)
This village is built to a scale of 1:10 using official plans of
the period. The village is fully animated and includes a farm
and a collection of horse-drawn carriages plus an exhibition
of crafts no longer practised. Open April, May and mid-
September to the end of October, Sundays from 2.30pm;
June and the first two weeks of September, Saturdays and
Sundays from 2.30pm; July and August open every day
from 2.30pm.

Remilly sur Lozon l'Art du Bois, Château de Montfort   ☎ 02 33 55 30 11
🖥 *www.vanibois.fr*
(north-west of Saint Lô)
An amazing exhibition with all the exhibits made entirely of
wood including full-size cars, motorbikes and tractors.

Open July and August every day 2.30 to 7pm; April to the end of October weekends only 2.30 to 6pm. Adults €3.50, children €2.

Sourdeval

Moulin de la Sée, 2 le Moulin de Brouains   ☎ 02 33 59 20 50

💻 *www.moulin-de-la-see.com*
(in the south-east of the department, directly east of Avranches)
This mill shows the life of the salmon born in one of France's finest salmon rivers, La Sée, as well as the paper mills and the story of cutlery making in the Sourdeval area. Open September to June Mondays to Fridays 9am to 12.30pm and 2 to 6pm, weekends and bank holidays 2 to 6pm; July and August Mondays to Saturdays 9am to 7pm, Sundays and bank holidays 11am to 7pm. Closed Saturdays in November and December and from mid-December to the end of February. Adults €4, children €2.30.

Saint Lô

Haras National, avenue du Maréchal Juin   ☎ 02 33 55 29 09

💻 *www.haras-nationaux.fr*
This stud (there are several 'national' studs in France!) currently has around 70 stallions and specialises in the Norman Cob horse and the French Saddle horse – an outstanding sports breed. Various exhibitions are held throughout the year and a display of horses and carriages takes place at 3pm every Thursday in August (*les jeudis du Haras*). The stud is open every afternoon from June to September for guided tours at 2.30pm, 3.30pm and 4.30pm, with an additional tour at 11am in July and August.

Liberation Route
A leaflet available from the tourist office traces a route around Saint Lô taking you to 15 places connected with the battles of 1944.

Mémorial de la Madeleine, avenue de Paris
Located opposite number 1028 avenue de Paris, these are the remains of an old leper house dating from the 14th century. The chapel was classified as a historic monument in 1974 with restoration work completed in 1994. Open from the first weekend of July to the Heritage Days in mid-September.

Villedieu les Poêles

Atelier du Cuivre, 54 rue Général Huard   ☎ 02 33 90 20 92
This workshop keeps alive the great traditions of copperware and French gastronomy. You will see the skilful

art of embossers, tinsmiths, polishers and beaters while a
film explains the purpose of their every gesture. They will
also make to order any item out of copper, brass or silver.
Open from the end of March to mid-November 10am to
12.30pm and 2 to 6.30pm. Adults €3.50, children over
ten €2.

Fonderie des Cloches, rue du Pont
Chignon ☎ 02 33 61 00 56
🖳 *www.cornille-havard.com*
An active bell foundry. A 20-minute guided tour takes you
through the workshops, an exhibition of antique bells and a
commentary on works in progress; available in English.
There's also a shop with various copper and bronze
products. Adults €4, 6 to 12-year-olds €3.20. The workshop
is open from mid-February to mid-November Tuesdays to
Saturdays 10am to 12.30pm and 2 to 5.30pm (July and
August open every day from 9am to 6pm).

Museums, Memorials & Galleries

Cherbourg   Musée de la Glacerie, Hameau Luce,
la Glacerie ☎ 02 33 20 33 33
A museum commemorating the royal glass factory founded
here in 1667. There's also a large exhibition of lace and
headdresses and various temporary exhibitions. Open
Easter to the end of June Sundays and bank holidays 2.30
to 6pm; July to mid-September Wednesdays to Mondays
2.30 to 6pm.

Granville   Musée Christian Dior, Villa les
Rhumbs ☎ 02 33 61 48 21
This museum is in the designer's childhood house and has
various exhibitions relating to his life and work. Open daily
from the end of May to the end of September 10am to
12.30pm and 2 to 6.30pm.

Barenton   Maison de la Pomme et de la Poire,
La Logeraie ☎ 02 33 59 56 22
Discover a Normandy tradition – the production of apple-
based products such as cider and calvados – and sample
local products. Open from 1st April to 30th September daily
9.30am to 12.30pm and 2 to 7pm.

Hauteville la   Musée Tancrède de Hauteville ☎ 02 33 47 88 86
Guichard   🖳 *www.bons-plans-tourisme.com*
(west of Saint Lô)
In a village that was the home of the Norman kings of Sicily,
this exhibition gives an insight into the Norman rule of Italy
and the Mediterranean and covers Norman art in Sicily. The
medieval gardens have been restored and are open to

visitors. Open July and August Tuesdays to Sundays 2 to 6.30pm; the rest of the year only the last Sunday of the month from 2 to 6pm and the first two Sundays of September. Adults €4, children €1.50.

Coutances

Quesnel Morinière Museum, 2 rue
Quesnel Morinière   ☎ 02 33 45 11 92
This museum is housed in a late 17th century town house at the entrance to the town park. It has a collection of 17th to 20th century paintings, 14th to 19th century sculptures and an important collection of Norman ceramics. Open April to October Mondays and Wednesdays to Saturdays 10am to noon and 2 to 5pm, Sundays 10am to noon; July and August until 6pm during the week, Sundays and bank holidays 10am to noon and 2 to 6pm. Adults €2.50, under 18s free.

Périers

Musée du Vélo   ☎ 02 33 76 54 80
This bicycle museum has a large collection of bicycles and pedal-operated toys recounting the history of the bicycle from 1817 to the present day. In addition to admiring the exhibits you're able to try out some of the bikes. Open May to June and September Sundays 2 to 6pm; July and August Tuesdays to Fridays 2 to 6pm, Saturdays 10am to noon and 2 to 6pm, Sundays 2 to 6pm. Adults €3.

St Mère Eglise

Musée Airborne, 14 rue Eisenhower ☎ 02 33 41 41 35
🖥 *www.airborne-museum.org*
St Mère-Eglise claims to be the first town to have been liberated on the night of 5th/6th June 1944 This air museum houses a genuine Waco glider along with vintage documents, weapons, munitions and a liberty torch, with a film relating the events of the 5th/6th June 1944. There's also a C-47 Dakota plane, uniforms and personal objects offered by American war veterans. Open daily from February to November. Adults €5, 6 to 14-year-olds €2.

Saint Lô

Musée des Beaux-Arts, place du Champ
de Mars   ☎ 02 33 72 52 55
This fine arts museum has a collection of tapestries and paintings and an exhibition on the history of Saint Lô. Open Wednesdays to Mondays 10am to noon and 2 to 6pm (closed bank holidays). Adults €1.50.

Parks, Gardens & Forests

Cérisy la Forêt

This national forest has majestic beech woods, footpaths and a parking area.

Cherbourg

Parc & Château des Ravalet,
Tourlaville   ☎ 02 33 22 01 35

An Italian Renaissance building situated in a beautiful park with lakes, greenhouse and children's play area. Open all year.

Coutances	Jardin des Plantes de Coutances ☎ 02 33 19 08 10

This botanical garden is in the grounds of the Quesnel Morinière Mansion museum. A combination of landscaped and formal gardens containing rare trees and flowering shrubs. Open April to September 9am to 8pm (July to mid-September to 11.30pm – with illuminations); October to March 9am to 5pm. Free entry.

Saussey	Jardins d'Argences ☎ 02 33 07 92 04

The 17th century Argences Manor is surrounded by eight prize-winning gardens. Open 1st June to mid-October every day from 2 to 6pm. €5 entry.

Vauville	Jardin Botanique du Château de Vauville ☎ 02 33 10 00 00

(in the north-west corner of the Cherbourg peninsula)
These exceptional botanical gardens were created in 1947 and cover more than 4ha (10 acres). Open Easter weekend, May, June and September Tuesdays, Fridays to Sundays and bank holidays 2 to 6pm; July and August every day 2 to 6pm.

Regional Produce

La Haye du Puits	Jambons du Cotentin, ZA route de Lessay ☎ 02 33 46 47 67

(between Lessay and Cherbourg)
A small production unit of smoked ham and other smoked products. You can discover the different methods of salting, smoking, drying and boning, as well as how to cut and cook ham and, of course, have the opportunity to taste it. July to mid-September Mondays to Fridays 10.30am and 3pm; all other days of the year by appointment.

Lessay	Laiterie du Val d'Ay, 1 rue des Planquettes ☎ 02 33 46 41 33

🖥 *www.reaux.fr*
This dairy makes camembert using traditional methods, unpasteurised milk and moulding using a scoop. Visits of the drying rooms and packaging line plus a video and free tasting. July to September visits at 3pm Mondays to Fridays (during the summer holidays weekdays 10am to noon and 2 to 4pm); other school holidays Fridays only at 2pm.

St Jean des Champs	Ferme de l'Hermitière ☎ 02 33 61 31 51

🖥 *www.ferme-hermitiere.com*
(between Granville and Villedieu)

In an old Normandy farm, see the traditional methods for producing cider, calvados, apple juice and the regional drink *pommeau*. A film shows you the work of the farm throughout the year and you can visit the press room, cellars and stills. Free tasting session and guided tours. Easter to June and September Mondays to Fridays 2 to 6pm; July and August Mondays to Saturdays 10am to noon and 1.30 to 6pm.

Professional Services

The following offices have an English-speaking professional.

Accountants

Saint Lô   KPMG, ZI La Chevalerie   ☎ 02 33 77 14 14

Solicitors & Notaires

Carentan   Maître Lemaître, rue Bassin à Flot   ☎ 02 33 71 40 40

Religion

Anglican Services in English

Coutances   Chapel, Lycée Collège Germaine, 73
                      rue d'Ilkley   ☎ 02 33 46 44 86
                      (north-east side of the town, just south of the bypass)
                      English-language services are held here at 11am on the
                      last Sunday of every month. All Christian denominations
                      welcome. For further details contact Mike Brooke on the
                      number above.

Catholic Churches

Avranches   Église St Gervais
                      Presbytère   ☎ 02 33 48 14 14
                      Services on Saturdays at 6.30pm, Sundays at 10.30am.

Barneville   St Thérèse
                      Services on Saturdays at 7pm and Sundays at 11am.

Cherbourg   Notre Dame du Vœu
                      Presbytère, 32 Prés Loubet   ☎ 02 33 53 35 60

Coutances   Cathédrale Notre Dame
                      Services on Saturdays at 6.30pm, Sundays at 11am.

Saint Lô	Église Sainte Croix	
	Presbytère, 4 place Sainte Croix	☎ 02 33 57 04 89
	Services on Sundays 10.45am.	

Protestant Churches

Selected churches are listed below.

Avranches	Centre Evangélique Protestant, 23 rue Chapeliers	☎ 02 33 68 14 13
Cherbourg	Eglise Evangélique, 24 rue Sennecey	☎ 02 33 44 07 89
	Eglise Réformée de France, 11 rue Paul Doumer	☎ 02 33 53 04 04
Coutances	Centre Evangélique, 5a boulevard Alsace Lorraine	☎ 02 33 47 35 70
Saint Lô	Eglise Réformée de France, 6 rue Fontaine Venise	☎ 02 33 55 15 00
	Centre Evangélique, 43 rue Alsace Lorraine	☎ 02 33 55 09 87

Restaurants

See page 87.

Rubbish & Recycling

See page 88.

Shopping

When available, the opening hours of various shops have been included, but these are liable to change and so it's advisable to check before travelling long distances to any specific shop.

Architectural Antiques

Morville	Gilles Moncuit	☎ 02 33 95 08 01
	🖥 *www.moncuit.com*	
	(just to the south-west of Valonges)	

Period stone work, marble, restoration and stone cutting to any design or style. The website is available in English.

Building Materials

Avranches	Big Mat, la Gare, Val St Père	☎ 02 33 89 69 00
Barneville	Gedimat Hochet, 46 avenue Douits, Le Bourg 🖳 *www.gedimat.fr*	☎ 02 33 04 88 00
Cherbourg	Point P, 14 rue Baptiste Marcet, Tourlaville 🖳 *www.pointp.fr*	☎ 02 33 23 37 00
Coutances	Larivière, 6 rue Pasteur 🖳 *www.lariviere-sa.fr*	☎ 02 33 45 50 68
Saint Lô	Reseau Pro, ZI la Capelle, rue Léon Jouhaux	☎ 02 33 57 41 31

Department Stores

Avranches	Nouvelles Galeries, 26 rue Constitution	☎ 02 33 58 04 23

DIY

See page 95.

Frozen Food

Avranches	Eismann Gélor, ZI Mottet	☎ 02 33 68 34 09
Saint Lô	Picard, 127 rue Maréchal de Lattre de Tassigny 🖳 *www.picard.fr*	☎ 02 33 72 09 45
Cherbourg	Thiriet, Les Marettes, la Glacerie 🖳 *www.thiriet.com* (on the retail park in the south-east of the town)	☎ 02 33 88 73 70

Garden Centres

See page 95.

Hypermarkets

See **Retail Parks** on page 252.

Kitchens & Bathrooms

See page 96.

Markets

Avranches	Tuesdays and Saturdays, place du Marché.
Barneville	Thursdays at Carteret, Saturdays at Barneville and Sundays at La Plage during July and August.
Carentan	Monday mornings.
Cherbourg	Tuesdays, Thursdays and Saturday mornings in the town centre.
	Wednesday mornings at avenue de Bremerhaven and Tourlaville.
	Friday mornings at Equeurdreville.
	The first Saturday of the month there's a flea market at place des Moulins.
	Sunday mornings at Octeville.
Coutances	Thursday mornings.
Granville	Saturday mornings.
Hauteville sur Mer	Sunday market all year round and in the summer additional markets on Tuesdays to Saturdays.
Portbail	Tuesday mornings.
St Hilaire du Harcouët	Wednesday and Friday mornings.
Saint Lô	Main market on Saturdays and a small local produce market on Friday mornings.
Valognes	Friday mornings.
Villedieu les Poêles	Tuesday mornings.

Organic Produce

Cherbourg	Bio Coop, ZA la Pont, Martinvast ☎ 02 33 93 93 03 (on the south-west side of the town)

Coutances	Bio Coop Coutances, 12 rue Paul Letarouilly ☎ 02 33 46 86 46

Coutances

Bio Coop Coutances, 12 rue Paul
Letarouilly   ☎ 02 33 46 86 46
(on a small road accessed via an archway off the
roundabout from rue Gambetta or rue Tourville if coming
away from the town centre)
Open Tuesdays to Saturdays 10am to 12.30pm and 3 to
7pm, Saturdays 6pm.

Saint Lô

Chante la Vie, 14 rue des Noyes   ☎ 02 33 57 08 17
(on a small parade of shops below the ramparts on the
north side)
Open Mondays to Fridays 2.30 to 7.30pm.

Retail Parks

Cherbourg

Centre Commercial Cotentin,
la Glacerie   ☎ 02 33 88 13 13
🖳 *www.auchan.fr*
(on the south-east side of Cherbourg)
There's a crèche for three to ten-year-olds, mobile phone
shops, hairdresser's, computer games shop, clothes shops,
bar/brasserie, key and shoe bar, France Télécom shop,
photo booth and business card machine. The hypermarket
is open Mondays to Saturdays 8.30am to 10pm while shops
in the complex are generally open 9.30am to 8pm. Main
shops include:
● Auchan – hypermarket;
● Buffalo Grill – steak house restaurant;
● Darty – electrical goods;
● Décathlon – sports goods;
● Jardiland – garden centre;
● La Peyre – DIY, kitchens & bathrooms;
● Pier Import – gifts and household accessories;
● Thiriet – frozen food .

Saint Lô

Retail park.
(on the southern outskirts, along the D972 ring road)
Shops include:
● Aubert – baby superstore;
● BUT – furniture and furnishings;
● Casa and Gifi – furnishing and gifts;
● Décathlon – sports goods;
● Gémo – clothes;
● Hygena – kitchens;
● Mobilier de France – furniture;
● Point P – building materials;
● Schmidt – kitchens;
● La Trocante – second-hand goods.

Second-hand Goods

See page 97.

Stamps

Cherbourg   Philatélie 50, 9 rue Albert Mahieu   ☎ 02 33 93 55 91

Wines & Spirits

See page 98.

Sports & Outdoor Activities

The following is just a selection of the activities available, large towns having a wide range of sports facilities. Full details are available from the tourist office or the *mairie*.

Aerial Sports

Flying

Avranches   Aéro Club des Grèves, Aérodrome de
                          Bouillé, Le Val St Père   ☎ 02 33 58 02 91

Cherbourg   Aéro Club J. Picquenot, Aéroport Cherbourg-
                          Maupertus   ☎ 02 33 53 19 73
                          Flying school with five aircraft and eight instructors.

Lessay   Centre de Vol à Voile, Aérodrome Charles
                          Lindbergh   ☎ 02 33 46 44 22
                          Microlights and hang-gliding.

Parachuting & Paragliding

Lessay   Para-Club Manche, Aérodrome Charles
                          Lindbergh   ☎ 02 33 61 30 87
                          Parachuting.

Orglandes   Para Club de la Manche 'B. Boulanger' ☎ 02 33 41 07 41
                          (directly south of Valonges)
                          Parachuting.

Vauville   Cotentin Vol Libre, Ecole de
                          Parapente   ☎ 02 33 94 03 27
                          Paragliding.

Archery

Avranches   Gymnastes Volontaires d'Avranches,
                          Salle René Fenouillère   ☎ 02 33 58 17 95
                          Wednesdays and Fridays from 8.30pm.

| Cherbourg | ASAM, 60 avenue de Cessart | ☎ 02 33 92 56 28 |

| Coutances | les Archers de la Rose aux Bouais, Salle Marcel Hélie
Contact M. Levavasseur. | ☎ 02 33 45 01 71 |

| Saint Lô | Arc Club Saint Lois
Contact M. Leconte. | ☎ 02 33 05 38 13 |

Badminton

| Barneville | Salle Omnisports, rue Jean Jaurès, Le Bourg
Tuesdays and Fridays at 6pm. | ☎ 02 33 53 86 54 |

| Cherbourg | CSAM Cherbourg, Foyer du Marin, rue de l'Abbaye | ☎ 02 33 92 69 25 |

| Coutances | Club de Badminton Coutançais   ☎ 02 33 45 91 62
Training throughout the week at the Gymnase de Claires Fontaines and the gymnasium of the École Normale. | |

| Saint Lô | Badminton Saint Lois, Salle St Ghislain
Contact Mme Tourainne for current training sessions. | ☎ 02 33 57 52 83 |

Ballooning

| Carentan | les Vents d'Ouest, 34 rue de Beuzeville, Les Veys
🖳 *www.normandie-montgolfiere.com*
Flights available all year, weather permitting. | ☎ 02 33 42 49 08 |

Boules/Pétanque

| Barneville | Avenue de la Mer, La Plage
Fridays in July and August at 2.30pm.

Place de la Gare, Carteret.
2pm every day, all year round. | |

| Cherbourg | Pétanque-Boules Lyonnaises | ☎ 02 33 44 33 22 |

| Coutances | Club Pétanque-Coutances, place du Vaudon
Lessons and training on Wednesdays from 5pm. | ☎ 02 33 45 58 04 |

Canoeing & Kayaking

Agon Coutainville — Club Nautique de Coutainville, avenue
des Dunes ☎ 02 33 47 14 81
Open all year round for canoe hire.

Avranches — Canoë Club d'Avranches, 83 rue de
la Liberté ☎ 02 33 68 19 15
Descents down the rivers Sée and Sélune, full days, half
days or just canoe hire.

Climbing

Avranches — Club d'Escalade ☎ 02 33 58 02 26
Indoor climbing wall and outdoor sites, for youngsters and
adults. Contact M. Lemoigne.

Cherbourg — Club Alpin Français, section Cotentin ☎ 02 33 93 59 96
Plateau Baquesne, quartier des Provinces,
An artificial climbing wall with open access.

Montmartin sur Mer — Centre Régional d'Escalade ☎ 02 33 47 92 93
(on the coast, south-west of Coutances)
Climbing wall with 42 routes plus outdoor climbs at an old
quarry.

Saint Lô — Club Alpin Français ☎ 02 33 05 57 81
🖳 *www.clubalpin.saintlo.free.fr*
Climbing wall and outdoor climbs including mountain
activities. Contact M. Bonnet for details of forthcoming events.

Cycling

General — A (French) guide containing details of 50 signposted
mountain bike circuits ranging from 11 to 45km (6 to
25mi) is available from bookshops or La Manche
Tourist Board for €12.

Avranches — Cyclotouristes d'Avranches ☎ 02 33 58 13 27
Road cycling and mountain bike instruction.

Barneville — Vélosport, le Petit Port, Carteret ☎ 02 33 93 20 73
Bike hire.

Cherbourg — Cycles Peugeot Kehrir, 31 boulevard
Robert Schumann ☎ 02 33 53 04 38

Cherbourg — Amicale Cycliste Octevillaise ☎ 02 33 52 33 50
Cycling on roads, tracks and for leisure, for everyone over 13.

	Club Alpin Français	☎ 02 33 93 59 96

Mountain biking.

Coutances	AG Orval Coutances Cyclisme	☎ 02 33 45 30 69

This club runs a cycle school on Saturdays from 10am
to noon, meeting at the Stade, rue de
Saint Malo.

	VTT 'Bekanabou'	☎ 02 33 46 86 48

Mountain bike rides on the third Sunday of each month
from September to April. Contact M. Lavieille for
details.

Saint Lô	Vélo Club Saint Lô, Pont Hébert	☎ 02 33 57 37 47

Road racing and mountain biking, plus a road safety school
and mountain bike courses on Wednesday afternoons for 8
to 18-year-olds.

Fencing

Coutances	Cercle d'Escrime de Coutances	☎ 02 33 45 86 76

Held at the Gymnase des Courtilles. Competitive and
leisure fencing; equipment available. Open to all ages from
seven years old.

Cherbourg	CSAM Cherbourg, Foyer du Marin, rue	
	de l'Abbaye	☎ 02 33 92 69 25

Saint Lô	Cercle d'Escrime de Saint Lô	☎ 02 33 57 40 51

Contact M. Danino.

Fishing

Maps are available from fishing shops and tourist offices showing local
fishing waters. If there's a lake locally, permits will be on sale in nearby
tabacs and fishing shops and at the *mairie*.

Avranches	Amicale des Pêcheurs à la Ligne de	
	l'Avranchin	☎ 02 33 58 31 95

The river Sée is the best salmon river in France. There's
also fishing at the Etang René Forget.

Barneville	

Fishing on the river Gerfleur. Permits for sale at Bar des
Sports, place du Docteur Auvret, Le Bourg (☎ 02 33 52 01 57)

Cherbourg	la Truite Cherbourgeoise	☎ 02 33 43 18 72

Local fishing group.

Football

Barneville	Stade, rue Hauvet, le Bourg	☎ 02 33 04 90 99

Various training sessions for all ages from five years old.

Coutances	Entente Sportive Coutançaise, Stade, rue de Saint Malo	☎ 02 33 45 35 23

Saint Lô	Football Club Saint Lô Manche	☎ 02 33 57 00 94

Training at the Centre d'Entraînement des Ronchettes, route de Torigni.

Golf

Agon Coutainville	Golf de Coutainville, 6 avenue du Golf	☎ 02 33 47 03 31

💻 *www.golfdecoutainville.free.fr*
18 holes, 5025m, par 68. Links course on the coast, lessons available, courses, pro shop, bar and putting green, golf equipment and caddies for hire. Open every day, 9am to 5pm in the winter, 8am to 7pm in the summer.

Bréhal	Municipal Golf Course	☎ 02 33 51 58 88

9 holes, 2086m, par 31. Driving range and putting greens, open all year, courses for beginners and amateurs and a golf school on Saturday mornings.

Cherbourg	Golf Club, rue des Verriers, la Glacerie	☎ 02 33 44 45 48

9 holes, 2831m, par 36. Covered and outdoor driving range, lessons, and bar, equipment and caddies for hire.

Granville	Golf de Granville, Bréville sur Mer	☎ 02 33 50 23 06

18 holes, 5834, par 71 plus another 9 holes along the sea front, 2186, par 33. Covered driving range, putting green, pro shop, bar and restaurant. Open all year.

Hockey

Cherbourg	Nord Cotentin Hockey Plus, 57 rue Gambetta	☎ 02 33 94 00 94

Ice hockey.

	les Aigles d'Or	☎ 02 33 43 15 07

Roller hockey.

Horse Riding

Agon Coutainville	Centre Equestre, Charrière du Commerce	☎ 02 33 47 00 42

(on the coast directly west of Coutances)
Indoor riding school for all levels and rides by the sea.

| Avranches | Centre Equestre de l'Avranchin, 22 les Landelles, Le Val St Père | ☎ 02 33 58 10 23 |

| Barneville | A Cheval, rue de la Corderie, La Plage | ☎ 02 33 04 93 63 |

Hacking, dressage, jumping and polo. Lessons indoors and outdoors.

| Cherbourg | l'Etrier Cherbourgeois, Haras de Siva, Tollevast | ☎ 02 33 44 69 30 |

| Coutances | Poney Club la Galaisière, La Galaisière | ☎ 02 33 47 91 28 |

| Saint Lô | Poney Club de la Ticquerie, La Ticquerie | ☎ 02 33 57 67 52 |

Judo

| Avranches | Judo Club, Salle de la Chaussonnière, rue Division Leclerc | ☎ 06 67 98 11 17 |

| Barneville | Salle Omnisports, rue Jean Jaurès, Barneville | ☎ 02 33 04 73 13 |

Various groups for all ages and levels.

| Cherbourg | Salle Arts Martiaux, Complexe Sportif Chantereyne | ☎ 02 33 53 31 72 |

🖳 *www.mjc-cherbourg.com*

| Coutances | Coutances Judo, rue Eléonor Daubrée | ☎ 06 72 36 92 79 |

Classes for all levels for children and adults.

| Saint Lô | Judo Club Saint Lois, Dojo, place du Pompidou | ☎ 02 33 56 59 38 |

Contact Alain Crépieux.

Kite Flying

| Cherbourg | Cerf-Volant Club de Cherbourg | ☎ 02 33 43 34 54 |

Motorsports

| Cherbourg | Automobile Club de l'Ouest, 2 quai Alexandre III | ☎ 02 33 93 97 95 |

Cars and motorbikes. Courses for young drivers.

Karting

Gréville-Hague	Karting du Circuit de la Hague	☎ 02 33 03 35 82

(in the north-west corner of the Cherbourg peninsula)

Montmartin en Graignes	Montmartin Karting	☎ 02 33 56 58 83

🖳 *www.montmartin-karting.fr*
(north of Saint Lô)

Le Neufbourg	Karting du Mortannais, la Tête à la Femme	☎ 02 33 59 60 33

(south of Vire, on the outskirts of Mortain)

Sainte Pience	Circuit Karting Bois du Parc	☎ 02 33 58 50 34

(off the N175 between Villedieu and Avranches)
Open July and September daily 10am to 10pm; March to
June weekdays 2 to 8pm; October to June weekends, bank
holidays and school holidays 10am to 8pm.

Motorbikes

Avranches	Avranches Moto Club	☎ 02 33 68 25 26

Contact M. Mérille.

Saint Lô	Moto Club Saint Lois	☎ 02 33 57 64 85

Competitive and leisure plus a driving school for 4 to 12-
year-olds. Contact M. Joubin for details of forthcoming
meetings.

Quad Bikes

Tourville sur Sienne	Natur'Quad Randonnée	☎ 02 33 45 52 13

(signposted from the D44 Coutances to Agon Coutainville, to
the right just before the village of Tourville sur Sienne)
Open April to June weekends and bank holidays 1.30 to
7pm; daily from July to September.

Rollerskating

Avranches	Gymnastes Volontaires d'Avranches, Salle de la Chaussonnière, rue Division Leclerc ☎ 02 33 58 17 95

Wednesdays 5 to 6pm and 6 to 7pm, adults Saturdays
noon to 1pm and Thursdays 9 to 10pm.

Cherbourg	Roll Training, Terrain Sainte Anne, Equeurdreville

(on the sea front, 5km west of Cherbourg railway station)
Indoor area for everyone to learn roller skating,
skates for hire, free entry, lessons for all levels €5.
Open mid-May to the end of September
in 2005.

Cycle Roller Skate ☎ 02 33 94 34 11
Rollerskating, skateboarding and BMX. M. Ford is the
current president.

There are outdoor skate parks next to the statue of
Napoleon by 'Plage Verte', at la Fauconnière (near the
water tower) and at Plaine de Jeux de Pontmarais,
Tourlaville.

Coutances Gymnastique Volontaire
Coutançaise ☎ 02 33 07 58 49
Exercise and fitness sessions a week for adults, either in
the Salle Marcel-Hélie or outside: Tuesdays at 7pm for
experienced skaters, Wednesdays at 7pm for beginners.
Sessions for children from 6 to 11 on Wednesdays at 11am.
Booking advisable for all sessions.

There's a skate park by the swimming pool on rue de Saint
Malo, with organised sessions for 11 to 17-year-olds the
first Wednesday of each month from 2 to 5pm.

Saint Lô Club Roller Saint Lois ☎ 06 61 49 46 50
Contact Nathalie Lemeulais.

Section Raymonde Skate Club ☎ 06 85 55 39 25
Contact Gary Leclerc.

Shooting

Cherbourg ASAM, 60 avenue de Cessart ☎ 02 33 92 55 09

Coutances la Cible Coutançaise, Stand de Tir ☎ 02 33 61 71 25
Saturdays 9am to noon and 2 to 7pm, Sundays 9am to
noon.

Saint Lô Tir Sportif Saint Lois ☎ 02 33 05 45 04

Swimming

Avranches Aqua Baie, rue Guy de Maupassant ☎ 02 33 58 07 20
Indoor heated pool with sauna, paddling pools and water
slides. Swimming lessons for children and adults.

Barneville Piscine, 32 avenue de la Mer, La Plage ☎ 02 33 04 60 28
Open July and August only.

Cherbourg Centre Aquatique, Rond-point de
la Saline, Equeurdreville ☎ 02 33 01 86 20
(to the west of the Cherbourg)

Water chutes, outdoor 'lazy river', aqua-aerobics and swimming lessons. Hours vary according to school holidays.

Piscine Municipale, place Napoléon,
Port Chantereyne   ☎ 02 33 53 18 42

Coutances   Piscine Municipale, rue de Saint Malo ☎ 02 33 45 55 41
A selection of pools, water chute and sauna, plus scuba diving and water polo clubs.

Saint Lô   Piscine St Ghislain, rue de l'Exode   ☎ 02 33 05 53 62

Tennis

Avranches   Tennis Club d'Avranches, rue des
Ecoles   ☎ 02 33 68 29 31
Tennis for all levels and all ages from three.

Barneville   avenue des Douits, Carteret   ☎ 02 33 04 90 16
Four all-weather courts. Clubhouse open July and August every day 9am to 7pm; May, June and September weekends 2 to 7pm. Courts to hire by the hour; out of season book at the grocery shop Epi-Service, La Plage (☎ 02 33 53 66 28).

avenue de la Sablière, La Plage
One all-weather court.

Cherbourg   Tennis Club du Blanc Ruisseau, 61 rue
Henri Barbusse   ☎ 02 33 93 17 85

Tennis Couvert de Bagatelle, rue du
Grand Pré   ☎ 02 33 22 48 10
Indoor courts.

Coutances   Tennis Club, rue de Saint Malo   ☎ 02 33 07 50 31
(by the stadium in the north-west of the town)
The club is open to all ages with lessons, courses, competitions and 'short tennis' for younger children.

Walking

General   Association du Tourisme Pedestre de
la Manche   ☎ 02 33 45 04 30
Two walks are organised each month, usually day long walks on Sundays.

Avranches   Gymnastes Volontaires d'Avranches ☎ 02 33 58 17 95

A walk is arranged once a month on a Sunday, date and venue published in the local press.

Barneville   Every Monday (except bank holidays) at 2pm there's a walk of 5 to 8km (3 to 5mi) from the car park behind the church at Le Bourg.

les Randonneurs des Dunes et du
Bocage   ☎ 02 33 45 98 64
Walks around the area take place every Tuesday afternoon, leaving at 2.15pm. Contact M. Hue for details of meeting places.

Watersports

Rowing

Barneville   Club d'Aviron en Mer, promenade Abbé
Lebouteiller, Carteret   ☎ 02 33 93 13 97
🖳 *www.aviron.barneville-carteret.net*
Rowing on the sea.

Cherbourg   Cherbourg Club Aviron de Mer, place
Napoléon   ☎ 02 33 01 77 39
Rowing on the sea.

Sailing

Agon Coutainville Club Nautique de Coutainville, avenue
des Dunes   ☎ 02 33 47 14 81
Introductory sessions available and all levels welcome from complete beginners to experienced sailors. Open all year round for catamaran, windsurfing, land yachting and canoe hire.

Barneville   Ecole de Voile, rue de Paris, Carteret ☎ 02 33 04 83 54
Courses dependent on the school holidays.

Cherbourg   Ecole de Voile, place Napoléon   ☎ 02 33 94 99 00
✉ *ecdevoilecherbourg@free.fr*

Scuba Diving

Avranches   Club Subaquatique de la Baie   ☎ 02 33 68 20 75
Contact M. Petit.

Coutances   Club Subaquatique de Coutances   ☎ 02 33 47 27 05
Training on Tuesdays, Wednesdays and Thursdays dependent on level, at the indoor pool on rue de Saint Malo.

Saint Lô	Club Subaquatique Le Barracuda	☎ 02 33 05 42 59
	Contact Mme Ratti.	

Windsurfing

Agon Coutainville	Club Nautique de Coutainville, avenue des Dunes	☎ 02 33 47 14 81
	Introductory sessions and courses, open all year round.	

Tourist Offices

General	Comité Départemental de Tourisme de la Manche, Maison du Département, route de Villedieu, Saint Lô	☎ 02 33 05 98 70
	💻 *www.manchetourisme.com*	
Avranches	2 rue du Général de Gaulle	☎ 02 33 58 00 22
	💻 *www.ville-avranches.fr*	
	Open Mondays to Saturdays 9.30am to 12.30pm and 2 to 6pm, and Sundays in July and August.	
Barneville 90 58	10 rue des Ecoles, Le Bourg	☎ 02 33 04
	💻 *www.barneville-carteret.net*	
	Open Mondays to Fridays 9am to 12.30pm and 2 to 6pm, Saturdays 9am to 12.30pm; closed bank holidays.	
Cherbourg	2 quai Alexandre III	☎ 02 33 93 52 02
	💻 *www.ot-cherbourg-cotentin.fr*	
	Open July and August Mondays to Saturdays 9am to 6.30pm, Sundays 10am to 12.30pm; September to June Mondays to Saturdays 9am to 12.30pm and 2 to 6pm (June until 6.30pm).	
Coutances	place Georges Leclerc	☎ 02 33 19 08 10
	✉ *tourisme-coutances.@wanadoo.fr*	
	Open Mondays to Wednesdays and Fridays 9.30am to 12.30pm and 2 to 6pm, Thursdays 9.30am to 6pm, Saturdays 10am to 12.30pm and 2 to 5pm (slightly longer opening hours in the summer).	
Saint Lô	place du Général de Gaulle	☎ 02 33 77 60 35
	💻 *www.saint-lo.fr*	
	Open September to June Mondays 2 to 6pm, Tuesdays to Fridays 10am to 12.30pm and 2 to 6pm, Saturdays 9.30am to 6pm; July and August Mondays to Saturdays 9.30am to 6pm.	

Tradesmen

Architects & Project Managers

General	DADA Designs, Barbey d'Aurévilly, Le Bourg, Barneville ☎ 02 33 94 74 00 💻 *www.dada-projects.com* David Ackers is an English-speaking architect and interior designer who specialises in the restoration of old properties including the use of reclaimed materials.
Agon Coutainville	RCM, 4 bis rue Alexis Lemoine ☎ 02 33 45 76 43 Project management, renovation and construction work undertaken.
Carentan	Maître d'Oeuvre en Bâtiment, 2 rue Sivard de Beaulieu ☎ 02 33 42 37 72 All aspects of project management including planning permission.
Coutances	Stéphane Bellée, 8 place de la Poissonnerie ☎ 02 33 46 59 04 This company specialises in project management. Some English is spoken.
	Denis Lamare, 9 rue Paul Letarouilly ☎ 02 33 45 15 68 (on a small road accessed via an archway off the roundabout from rue Gambetta or rue Tourville if coming away from the town centre) Architect.

Builders

Avranches	Corebat, rue des Chapeliers ☎ 02 33 68 22 64 New building and renovation.
Barneville	Maisons Delacour, 21 place de l'Eglise, Le Bourg ☎ 02 33 04 90 23 House builders and general builders.
Cherbourg	Claude Leterrier, 1645 les Rouges Terres, la Glacerie ☎ 02 33 43 16 74 General builder.
	Bernard SARL, 37 rue de l'Alma ☎ 02 33 04 41 38 Tiling and plastering.
Coutances	Danton Charton, ZA les Landelles,

| Blainville sur Mer | ☎ 02 33 45 70 78 |

General builder and carpenter, new and renovation work.

| Saint Lô | Zenone Construction, 769 rue Jules Vallés | ☎ 02 33 77 29 00 |

Carpenters

Many carpentry firms that make wooden windows and doors also work in aluminium.

| Avranches | Paul Leboux, le Pont Corbety, Marcy les Grèves | ☎ 02 33 48 72 27 |

| Barneville | Stéphane Pesnel, Le Bourg | ☎ 02 33 05 47 82 |

🖳 *www.pesnel-couverture.com*
General carpentry and roofing.

| Cherbourg | Entreprise Foucher, 111 rue de la Saline, Tourlaville | ☎ 02 33 22 43 90 |

(east of the town)
General carpentry and roofing.

| Coutances | C. Delalaine, 8 rue Normandie | ☎ 02 33 07 49 36 |

| Saint Lô | Raymond Valette, 85 rue Louis Armand | ☎ 02 33 05 25 81 |

Chimney Sweeps

| Avranches | SOS Gaz, 10 rue Docteur Gilbert | ☎ 02 33 60 46 64 |

| Cherbourg | Clin Combustibles, 14 route Lande Tibère, Tourlaville | ☎ 02 33 22 42 15 |

| Coutances | Jacques Josseaume, 87 avenue de la République | ☎ 02 33 45 12 85 |

(near the Renault garage on the road to Saint Lô)

| Saint Lô | Villemer SARL, 45 rue Yser | ☎ 02 33 05 14 52 |

Electricians

| General | Craig Hutchinson, 158 rue Henri-Veniard, St Georges des Groseillers | ☎ 06 73 11 40 89 |

✉ *craighutchinson@aol.com*
English-speaking tradesman who undertakes all electrical work from small jobs to full re-wiring.

| Avranches | Denis Couenne, 25 rue du Soleil Levant | ☎ 02 33 58 42 44 |

| Barneville | Sogelect 50, 10 rue Guillaume le Conquérant, Le Bourg | ☎ 02 33 53 81 48 |

Cherbourg — Petitpierre, 7 rue Victor Grignard   ☎ 02 33 53 24 90
General electrical work and a shop open Mondays to
Fridays 8.30am to noon and 2 to 6pm
(Fridays to 5pm).

Coutances — Harry Leriche, ZA Auberge de la Mare,
rue Glacière   ☎ 02 33 45 26 63
Electrics, plumbing and heating.

Saint Lô — Stevenin, 7 bis rue Bouloir   ☎ 02 33 05 05 80

Painters & Decorators

Avranches — Jean Olivacce, 3 place St Gervais   ☎ 02 33 58 13 22
Painting, decorating and parquet flooring.

Barneville — Fabrice Gauvain, 8 rue Guillaume le
Conquérant, Le Bourg   ☎ 02 33 04 95 64
The office in the high street is open on Saturday mornings
from 10am to noon.

Coutances — JP Langlois, 1 rue de la Mare   ☎ 02 33 45 03 16

Plumbers

General — Chris Williams, Les Hersandières, La
Mancellière, Isigny le Buat   ☎ 02 33 58 64 20
✉ howard.williams@wanadoo.fr
English-speaking plumber and heating engineer.

Avranches — Patrick Bivaud, St Michel des Loups   ☎ 02 33 51 41 09
Plumbing, electrics and heating.

Barneville — SARL Simon, 10 rue de Valnott,
Carteret   ☎ 02 33 04 95 98
Bathrooms and heating.

Cherbourg — Le Roy, 37 rue Ingénieur Cachin   ☎ 02 33 20 43 21
✉ le-roy.cherbourg@wanadoo.fr
Plumbing, electrics and heating.

Coutances — M&J Aunay, 5 rue du Lycée   ☎ 02 33 45 05 60

Heating and plumbing. Office open Tuesdays to Saturdays
8am to noon.

Saint Lô   Stevenin, 7 bis rue du Brouloir   ☎ 02 33 05 05 80
                  Plumbing, heating and electrics.

Utilities

Electricity & Gas

General   EDF/GDF Services Manche, 76 bis boulevard Pierre
                  Mendès France, Cherbourg   ☎ 08 10 50 50 00
                  🖥 www.edf.fr
                  🖥 www.gazdefrance.com

                  EDF/GDF local offices are listed below (there are no
                  direct telephone numbers for these offices).

Avranches   5 rue Général Ruel

Cherbourg   25 avenue de Tourville, Equeurdreville

Saint Lô   ZI la Chevalerie, rue Jules Vallés

Heating Oil

Avranches   Les Combustibles de Normandie, 15 rue
                  Valhubert   ☎ 02 33 79 08 08

Cherbourg   Clin Combustibles, 14 route Lande Tibère,
                  Tourlaville   ☎ 02 33 22 42 15
                  Oil, coal and wood.

Coutances   les Combustibles de Normandie, 87 avenue
                  de la République   ☎ 02 33 45 12 85

Saint Lô   Worex SNC, rue Léon Jouhaux   ☎ 08 10 10 23 45

Water

The main water supply companies are listed below. If you aren't covered
by one of these, your *mairie* will have details of your water supplier.

General   Compagnie Générale des
                  Eaux   *emergencies* ☎ 08 11 90 08 00
                  12 place du Marché, Avranches   ☎ 02 33 58 60 60

rue Vieux Furnichon, Baudre   ☎ 02 33 57 05 11
40 boulevard de l'Atlantique,
Cherbourg   ☎ 08 11 90 08 00
rue Jules Vallés, Saint Lô   ☎ 08 10 33 31 11

Lyonnaise des Eaux, le Pont,
Martinvast   ☎ 08 10 38 43 84
emergencies ☎ 08 10 88 48 84

SAUR
🖳 *www.saurfrance-clients.com*
Zone Artisanale, Bricquebec   ☎ 02 33 52 26 30
17 rue Moulin, St Clair sur l'Elle   ☎ 02 33 05 85 21
6 Zone Artisanale Sienne, Villedieu-
les-Poêles   ☎ 02 33 61 02 39

STGS, 22 rue des Grèves, Avranches   ☎ 02 33 79 46 79
🖳 *www.stgs.fr*

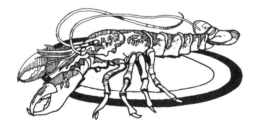

château d'O

6

<u>Orne</u>

This chapter provides details of facilities and services in the department of Orne (61). General information about each subject can be found in **Chapter 2**. All entries are arranged alphabetically by town, except where a service applies over a wide area, in which case it's listed at the beginning of the relevant section under 'General'. A map of Orne is shown below.

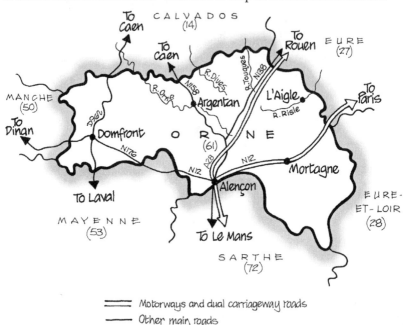

═══ Motorways and dual carriageway roads
─── Other main roads

Accommodation

Chateaux

Alençon   Château de Sarceaux, Valframbert   ☎ 02 33 28 85 11
                 ✉ *sarceaux@wanadoo.fr*
                 (north of the town in the direction of Sées)
                 A former 18th century hunting lodge that offers elegant and
                 comfortable bedrooms with views over the park. Suites and
                 rooms available from €90 to €125 per night for two people,
                 breakfast included.

Domfront   Château de la Maigraire, St Bômer
                 les Forges   ☎ 02 33 38 09 52
                 (north of the town towards Caen)
                 This chateau has been carefully restored to retain its
                 original elegance and offers both suites and a double room.

Prices from €80 to €120 including breakfast and afternoon tea. No smoking in the bedrooms. English spoken.

Mortagne   la Grande Noë   ☎ 02 33 73 63 30
💻 *www.chateaudelagrandenoe.com*
This chateau has been in the same family since its construction in the 15th century and offers bedrooms with en-suite facilities from €90 to €105 per room for two people, including breakfast. Open from Easter to 1st November. English spoken.

Gîtes and Bed & Breakfast

General   Gîtes de France, 90 rue St Blaise,
Alençon   ☎ 02 33 28 07 00
💻 *www.itea2.com/GDF/61*
Bookings can be made by phone or via the internet.

Hotels

Various tourist office websites have details of hotel accommodation in Orne, including the following:

💻 *www.normandy-tourism.org*
💻 *www.paysdelaigle.com*
💻 *www.argentan.fr*

Business Services

Computer Services

L'Aigle   Web Reflex, rue Carnot   ☎ 02 33 84 13 73
💻 *www.web-reflex.com*
Open Mondays to Saturdays 9am to 12.30pm and 2 to 7pm (Mondays till 6.30pm, Saturdays till 6pm).

Alençon   AMI Informatique, rue de Sarthe   ☎ 02 33 80 42 18
Sales, installation, accessories and software. Open Tuesdays to Saturdays 9.30am to noon and 2 to 7pm.

Domfront   Orditop, 23 Grande Rue   ☎ 02 33 14 92 42
✉ *ordi.top@free.fr*
Sales, repairs, made-to-measure computers, internet access and general computer advice. Open Tuesdays to Saturdays 9.30am to noon and 2 to 7pm (Saturdays till 6pm).

Mortagne   Uranus Micro, Les Grands Champs,
Autheuil   ☎ 02 33 83 70 94

(just north of the town)
Made-to-measure computers, demonstrations and
telephone assistance. Open by appointment; telephone
help Mondays to Saturdays 9am to 8pm.

Employment Agencies

The main offices of the national employment agency, ANPE, are as follows:

L'Aigle	2 rue Parc	☎ 02 33 84 14 50
Alençon	37 avenue Quakenbrück	☎ 02 33 82 45 00
Argentan	8 rue Serg Escoffier	☎ 02 33 12 11 11
Mortagne	19 rue Moncacune	☎ 02 33 25 06 40

Communications

France Télécom

General	Dial ☎ 1014 or go to
	🖳 *www.francetelecom.fr*
	Local France Télécom shops are listed below.

L'Aigle — 29 bis rue Bec'ham
Open Tuesdays to Saturdays 9.30am to 12.15pm and 2 to
6.30pm.

Alençon — rue du Jeudi
Open Tuesdays, Wednesdays and Fridays 9.30am to
12.30pm and 2 to 6.30pm, Thursdays 10am to 12.30pm
and 2 to 6.30pm, Saturdays 9.30am to 12.30pm and 2 to
6pm.

Argentan — rue de la Chausée
Open Tuesdays to Saturdays 9.30am to 12.15pm and 2.30
to 6.30pm.

Mortagne — place du Général de Gaulle
Open Tuesdays to Thursdays 9am to 12.15pm and 1.45 to
6pm, Fridays 10am to 12.15pm and 1.45 to 6pm, Saturdays
9am to 12.30pm and 2 to 6pm.

Internet Access

L'Aigle   Rézeau Informatique, 10 rue des
                 Emangeards   ☎ 02 33 24 60 59

High speed internet connection. Open Mondays and Saturdays 2 to 7pm, Tuesdays to Fridays 10am to 12.30pm and 2 to 7pm.

Alençon	Espace Web, Annexe Mairie, la Rotonde, rue des Filles Notre Dame	☎ 02 33 32 40 33

(close to the glass-domed Halle au Blé)
Free internet access Mondays to Saturdays 8.30am to 7pm.

Argentan	Cyber Base, 1 rue Fontaine	☎ 02 33 12 52 11

🖳 *www.cyber-base.org*
Open Mondays to Wednesdays and Fridays 1 to 7pm, Saturdays 3 to 6pm.

Domfront	Orditop, 23 Grande Rue	☎ 02 33 14 92 42

✉ *ordi.top@free.fr*
Open Tuesdays to Saturdays 9.30am to noon and 2 to 7pm, Saturdays 6pm.

Mortagne	Point Information Jeunesse, 48 rue des 15 Fusillés	☎ 02 33 73 15 07

✉ *pij.mortagne@netcourrier.com*
(enter through the door in the right corner of the front building, go through the hallway and down the stairs and the entrance is on the left)
Open Tuesdays and Thursdays 3.30 to 5.30pm, Wednesdays 9am to 12.30pm and 1.30 to 6.30pm.

Mobile Telephones

See page 62.

Domestic Services

Air-Conditioning Installation

Alençon	Leboin Bastien, rue Cazault	☎ 02 33 26 32 86
Domfront	Herry Florent, 17 rue de Godras	☎ 02 33 38 86 07

Clothes Alterations

L'Aigle	Rapid' Couture, 24 rue des Tanneurs	☎ 02 33 24 11 05

Open Tuesdays to Saturdays 9am to noon and 2 to 7pm, Saturdays until 6pm.

Argentan	Yakut Retouches, 21 rue Aristide

Briand   ☎ 02 33 12 55 38
Curtains and clothes made to measure and altered,
including wedding dresses.

Mortagne   l'Atelier, 23 rue des 15 Fusillés   ☎ 02 33 73 36 69
Clothes repairs and alterations. Open Tuesdays to Fridays
9am to noon and 2 to 6.30pm, Saturdays 9am to
12.30pm and 2 to 6pm. Closed Thursday
afternoons.

Crèches & Nurseries

L'Aigle   Halte-Garderie, rue Abreuvoir
St Jean   ☎ 02 33 23 37 01

Alençon   Halte-Garderie Centre Ville, 16 rue
Etoupée   ☎ 02 33 26 18 09
Open Mondays to Fridays 8.45am to noon and 1.45 to
6pm, Saturdays 8.45am to noon.

Argentan   Halte-Garderie, 29 rue de
Champagne   ☎ 02 33 67 02 49
Open Mondays, Thursdays and Fridays 8.45am to noon
and 1.30 to 5.30pm, Tuesdays 8.45am to 5.30pm,
Wednesdays 9.30am to noon and 1.30
to 5.30pm.

Domfront   Halte-Garderie du Domfrontais, 3 rue
de Godras   ☎ 02 33 30 16 40
Open Mondays 2 to 6pm, Tuesdays 8am to noon and 2 to
6pm, Thursdays and Fridays 8am to noon.

Mortagne   Pirouette, 6 rue des Esquisses   ☎ 02 33 83 70 60
Infants from three months to six years old. Open Mondays
to Fridays 7.45am to 6.45pm.

Equipment & Tool Hire

L'Aigle   Régis Location, 47 avenue Mont
St Michel   ☎ 02 33 23 38 38
🖳 *www.regis-location.fr*

Alençon   Loxam, ZI Nord, 1 rue Lazare Carnot   ☎ 02 33 29 53 75
🖳 *www.loxam.fr*

Flers   Groseillers Régis Location, la Poterie,
St Georges des Groseillers   ☎ 02 33 65 64 66
(in the northern outskirts of the town)

Fancy Dress Hire

Alençon   Gag, rue Maréchal de Lattre de
                 Tassigny   ☎ 02 33 32 18 55
                 Helium balloons, fancy dress costumes and everything for
                 parties.
                 Open Tuesdays to Saturdays 10am to noon and 2.30 to
                 7pm.

Garden Services

General   Iain & Anna Geraghy, Chênedouit   ☎ 02 33 36 94 74
                 ✉ *thefrenchgeraghtys@tiscali.fr*
                 Garden design and maintenance service covering the
                 north of the department, run by an English-speaking
                 couple.

Bagnoles de l'Orne JP Bernier, 19 rue Pierre Vivet   ☎ 02 33 37 86 95
                 (east of Domfront)
                 Design and maintenance, including annual
                 contracts.

Bellou sur Huisne Marc Julien, Boisard   ☎ 02 33 73 48 54
                 (south of Mortagne)
                 Design, maintenance, tree cutting and felling.

Mortagne   Sylvanor, ZI la Gare   ☎ 02 33 25 41 45
                 (next to the Point Vert garden centre)
                 Garden design and maintenance.

Sées   Hubert Renaudin, 9 rue de la
                 République   ☎ 02 33 28 87 24
                 (north of Alençon)
                 Design and maintenance, ponds and ground
                 clearance.

Picture Framing & Restoration

Mortagne   Art et Passion, 33 rue de la
                 République   ☎ 02 33 83 91 71
                 Open Tuesdays to Thursdays 10am to 12.15pm, Fridays
                 and Saturdays 10am to 12.15pm and 3 to 6pm.

Septic Tank Services

La Chapelle Viel EP Vidange, Les Champs Ferrés   ☎ 02 33 34 21 97
                 (just south of L'Aigle)

Mortagne   Alain Launay, St Langis lès
                 Mortagne   ☎ 02 33 25 34 90

Entertainment

This section isn't intended to be a definitive guide but gives a wide range of ideas for the department. Prices and opening hours were correct at the time of writing, but it's best to check before travelling long distances.

Cinemas

L'Aigle	Cinéma l'Aiglon, 7 rue du Docteur Rouyer 🖳 *www.allocine.fr*	☎ 08 92 68 05 89
Alençon	les 4 Normandy, 20 Grande Rue	☎ 08 92 68 70 21
Argentan	les 3 Normandy, 13 rue Georges-Méheudin 🖳 *www.maville.com*	☎ 08 92 68 00 31
Mortagne	Cinéma Etoile, Halle aux Grains 🖳 *www.cinefil.com*	☎ 08 92 68 73 38

Libraries

All the libraries below have a selection of books in English.

L'Aigle	place Fulbert de Beina Open Tuesdays 10am to noon, Wednesdays 10am to 6.30pm and Saturdays 10am to 5pm.	☎ 02 33 84 16 19
Alençon	cour Carrée de la Dentelle Open Tuesdays and Thursdays 2 to 6pm, Wednesdays 10am to noon and 1.30 to 6pm, Fridays 2 to 7pm and Saturdays 10am to noon and 2 to 5 pm.	☎ 02 33 82 46 00
Argentan	1 rue des Rédemptoristes Open Tuesdays and Wednesday 10am to 6.30pm, Thursdays and Fridays 1.30 to 6.30pm, Saturdays 10am to 6pm (4pm in July and August).	☎ 02 33 67 02 50
Domfront	36 rue du Docteur Barrabé This library has a selection of English books and bilingual books (with text in two languages on facing pages – a great help if trying to learn French or another language). Open Tuesdays 11am to noon and 2 to 5pm, Wednesdays 10am to noon and 2 to 5.30pm, Fridays 11am to noon and 3 to 6.30pm, Saturdays 10am to 12.30pm and 1.30 to 5pm.	☎ 02 33 30 83 49
Mortagne	Maison des Contes du Perche, 8 rue du Portail St Denis	☎ 02 33 25 25 87

(behind the church and through the small archway)
Open Tuesdays, Thursdays and Fridays 3 to 6pm,
Wednesdays 9.30am to noon and 1.30 to 6pm, Saturdays
10am to noon and 2 to 5pm.

Theatres

Alençon Théâtre d'Alençon, 2 avenue de
Basingstoke ☎ 02 33 29 16 96
🖳 *www.scenenationale61.com*
Box office open Mondays to Fridays 1 to 6.30pm
and Saturdays 5 to 6.30pm when there's a show
that evening.

Bagnoles de l'Orne Centre d'Animation et de Congrès, 1 rue
du P. Louvel ☎ 02 33 30 72 70

Domfront Théâtre Domfront, 5 place de la Petite
Bruyère ☎ 02 33 38 56 66

Flers Scène Nationale, rue du Collège ☎ 02 33 64 21 21

Mortagne Carré du Perche du Mortagne, 23 rue
Ferdinand de Boyères ☎ 02 33 85 23 00
🖳 *www.lecarreduperche.com*

Video & DVD Hire

See page 67.

French Teachers & Courses

L'Aigle Greta, 8 rue René Vivier ☎ 02 33 84 14 30
✉ *greta.sn.laigle@ac-caen.fr*
This branch of the government organisation Greta
runs evening classes for people settling into the area
and to help with French administrative procedures.
Courses can be arranged for groups of at least ten
people. Dorothy Marissiaux
speaks English.

Alençon Greta Sud-Normandie, 30 rue Jean
Henri Fabre ☎ 02 33 27 44 64
Government-run organisation.

Mortagne Maison pour Tous, 12 place du Palais ☎ 02 33 25 02 76
✉ *mpt.mortagne@wanadoo.fr*

Leisure Activities

This section isn't intended to be a definitive guide but gives a wide range of ideas for the department. Prices and opening hours were correct at the time of writing, but it's best to check before travelling long distances.

Arts & Crafts

L'Aigle   l'UIA, Centre Culturel des Tanneurs,
                     rue des Tanneurs   ☎ 02 33 34 41 73
                     Various art classes including painting and
                     patchwork.

Alençon   Centre Culture et Loisirs de Valframbert,
                     Valframbert   ☎ 02 33 31 01 45
                     (north of the town in the direction of Sées)
                     Art, decorating and patchwork.

Argentan   Espace Xavier Rousseau, 4 rue Charles
                     Léandre   ☎ 02 33 67 81 40
                     Courses for adults and children, including pottery for 9 to
                     12-year-olds.

Domfront   Atelier Peinture   ☎ 02 33 38 80 74
                     Painting workshops. Contact M. Gentil.

Mortagne   Maison pour Tous, 12 place du
                     Palais   ☎ 02 33 25 02 76
                     Art classes including oils, embroidery, painting on silk,
                     pottery and patchwork.

Bridge

L'Aigle   L'Aigle Bridge Club, rue Souchey   ☎ 02 32 24 11 05
                     Contact M. Maxime.

Alençon   Club de Bridge d'Alençon, 175 rue
                     d'Argentan   ☎ 02 33 32 28 27
                     Courses and tournaments Monday and Thursday
                     afternoons and Tuesday afternoons and
                     evenings.

Argentan   Club de Bridge, Maison des Associations,
                     43 route d'Urou   ☎ 02 33 36 77 51
                     Meetings on Mondays at 8pm, Wednesdays and Fridays at
                     2pm.

Mortagne   Maison pour Tous, 12 place du Palais   ☎ 02 33 25 02 76
                     Meetings on Mondays from 2 to 6pm.

Choral Singing

L'Aigle	l'UIA, Centre Culturel des Tanneurs, rue des Tanneurs	☎ 02 33 34 41 73
Argentan	Association Musique et Loisirs Contact M. Laigre.	☎ 02 33 67 11 83
Mortagne	Maison pour Tous, 12 place du Palais Choir practice on Wednesdays from 8.30 to 10pm.	☎ 02 33 25 02 76

Circus Skills

Fresnay sur Sarthe	Ecole de Cirque, Gare de Fresnay-sur-Sarthe (south of Alençon, west of the N138) Courses for all ages from six years old to adult.	☎ 02 43 33 69 44
Ste Scolasse sur Sarthe	Ecole des Arts du Cirque Educatif, les Merisiers (north-west of Mortagne)	☎ 02 33 81 92 64

Computer Training

L'Aigle	l'UIA, Centre Culturel des Tanneurs, rue des Tanneurs	☎ 02 33 34 41 73
Argentan	Médiathèque François Mitterrand, 1 rue des Rédemptoristes	☎ 02 33 67 02 50
Mortagne	Maison pour Tous, 12 place du Palais Courses in general computer knowledge (text and tables) and specialist skills (e.g. Excel software).	☎ 02 33 25 02 76

Dancing

L'Aigle	Ecole de Danse, 10 rue du Pont du Moulin Traditional ballet classes as well as tap, aerobic, salsa and jazz.	☎ 02 33 24 57 28
Alençon	Espace 'Free Dance', Galerie du Pont Neuf, rue du Pont Neuf Jazz, salsa, waltz and tango.	☎ 02 33 32 22 44
	Ecole de Danse, 48 rue du Jeudi Tap, ballet and jazz for children and adults.	☎ 02 33 26 23 64
Argentan	Ecole Intercommunale Agréée de Musique,	

Danse et Théâtre du Pays d'Argentan,
1 rue des Anciens Lavoirs   ☎ 02 33 67 28 03
Group courses or individual lessons, including introductory
sessions, in ballet and jazz.

Espace Xavier Rousseau, 4 rue Charles
Léandre   ☎ 02 33 67 81 40
Ballroom and Latin American classes twice a month.

Domfront   Danse Moderne Domfrontaise, Salle
                  Omnisport Maurice Tencé, place du
                  Champ de Foire   ☎ 02 33 38 56 66
                  (the dance hall is up the stairs on the right)

Mortagne   Ecole de Danse, Au Petit Conservatoire,
                  35 rue Aristide Briand   ☎ 02 33 25 22 74

Drama

Alençon   Centre Culture et Loisirs de Valframbert,
                  Valframbert   ☎ 02 33 31 01 45
                  (north of the town in the direction of Sées)

Argentan   Ecole Intercommunale Agréée de Musique,
                  Danse et Théâtre du Pays d'Argentan,
                  1 rue des Anciens Lavoirs   ☎ 02 33 67 28 03

Mortagne   Maison pour Tous, 12 place du Palais ☎ 02 33 25 02 76
                  Theatre workshops for teenagers and adults on Friday
                  evenings from 6 to 7.30pm.

Dress Making

L'Aigle   Centre Social de L'Aigle, rue de la
                  Maladrerie   ☎ 02 33 84 90 28

Argentan   Espace Xavier Rousseau, 4 rue Charles
                  Léandre   ☎ 02 33 67 81 40

Alençon   Cultures Loisirs Ensemble, Espace Pyramide, 2
                  avenue de Basingstoke   ☎ 02 33 29 03 68

Mortagne   Maison pour Tous, 12 place du Palais ☎ 02 33 25 02 76
                  Thursdays 2.15 to 4.15pm.

Flower Arranging

L'Aigle   l'UIA, Centre Culturel des Tanneurs,
                  rue des Tanneurs   ☎ 02 33 34 41 73

| Argentan | Espace Xavier Rousseau, 4 rue Charles Léandre | ☎ 02 33 67 81 40 |

Various groups throughout the afternoon on the first
Thursday of each month.

Gardening

| L'Aigle | Jardins Ouvriers. | ☎ 02 33 24 36 93 |

Contact M. Hunault.

| Domfront | Jardiniers de France – Club de Domfront | ☎ 02 33 38 91 51 |

🖳 *www.perso.wanadoo.fr/cocorico/jardiniers*
Contact Michèle Corvée.

Gym

| L'Aigle | Centre Aquatique, Cap'Orne, avenue du Président Kennedy | ☎ 02 33 24 18 18 |

Aqua-gym and fitness classes.

Centre Culturel des Tanneurs, rue des Tanneurs
Keep fit for seniors in the Grande Salle, Thursdays 10 to
11am.

| Alençon | Relaxe Forme, 30 avenue Wilson | ☎ 02 33 29 82 82 |

A variety of gym classes including stretching, step and hip
and thigh.

| Argentan | ASPTT, 69 rue Hector Berlioz | ☎ 02 33 67 01 27 |

Gentle exercise and step classes.

| Domfront | Maison des Associations, 52 rue Docteur Barrabé | ☎ 02 33 38 56 66 |

Aerobic classes.

| Mortagne | Maison pour Tous, 12 place du Palais | ☎ 02 33 25 02 76 |

Aqua gym classes on Thursday evenings and occasionally
Saturday mornings. Keep fit classes Mondays at 6pm and
Thursdays 4.30pm.

Gyms & Health Clubs

| Mortagne | Club Olympe, route d'Alençon | ☎ 02 33 83 06 38 |

Ice Skating

| Alençon | Patinoire d'Alençon, rue R. Schumann | ☎ 02 33 26 27 90 |

Open from October to April inclusive.

Music

L'Aigle	l'UIA, Centre Culturel des Tanneurs, rue des Tanneurs ☎ 02 33 34 41 73

Alençon   Orchestre d'Harmonie d'Alençon ☎ 02 33 31 79 59
All musicians welcome. Rehearsals on Tuesday and Friday
evenings.

Cultures Loisirs Ensemble, Espace Pyramide,
2 avenue de Basingstoke ☎ 02 33 29 03 68
Individual lessons on a variety of instruments including
drums, guitar and synthesizer.

Argentan   Ecole Intercommunale Agréée de Musique,
Danse et Théâtre du Pays d'Argentan,
1 rue des Anciens Lavoirs ☎ 02 33 67 28 03

Domfront   Ecole de Musique, rue de Godras ☎ 02 33 38 56 66
(next to the Centre de Loisirs)
Including drums, guitar, piano, synthesizer and choral
singing.

Mortagne   Ecole de Musique, 48 rue des 15
Fusillés ☎ 02 33 25 33 55
Including clarinet, drums, guitar, piano, trumpet, violin, and
singing.

Photography

L'Aigle   Photo Club, MJC, le Rond-point ☎ 02 33 34 09 57
Contact M. Gueret.

Argentan   Objectif Image 61, la Salle de l'ASPTT,
rue Hector Berlioz ☎ 02 33 39 18 22
Exhibitions, photography trips and competitions. Meetings
on Wednesdays at 8.30pm. Contact
M. Châtelais.

Domfront   Club Photo ☎ 02 33 37 62 50
Contact Mme Leguet.

Mortagne   Maison pour Tous, 12 place du Palais ☎ 02 33 25 02 76
Wednesday evenings from 8pm, twice a month.

Social Groups

Rotary Club

L'Aigle   Rotary Club de L'Aigle, Hôtel du Dauphin,

	4 place de la Halle	☎ 02 33 84 18 00
	Contact M. Louwagie.	
Argentan	Rotary Club Argentan, Hôtel de la Renaissance, avenue de la 2ème DB	☎ 02 33 67 27 66
	Contact M. Pottemain de Laroque.	
Mortagne	Rotary Club de Mortagne	☎ 02 33 25 12 35
	Contact M. Oblin.	

Town Twinning

L'Aigle	L'Aigle-Dorchester	☎ 02 31 92 10 20
	Meetings and events between the two towns, contact M. Bonnet.	
Alençon	Comité de Jumelage Alençon-Basingstoke	☎ 02 33 26 50 05
	Contact M. Bigot.	
Argentan	Argentan Cercle Jumelage – Europe	☎ 02 33 35 99 21
	Twinned with Abingdon.	
Domfront	les Amis de Taunton	☎ 02 31 31 26 88
	Contact Karin Carel.	
Mortagne	Association de Jumelage Mortagne-Totnes	☎ 02 31 66 60 29

Welcome Groups

Some towns have a branch of Accueil des Villes Françaises (AVF), a nationwide organisation designed to help newcomers settle into French towns and villages.

☎ *www.avf.asso.fr*
The site is available in English.

Alençon	AVF 'la Pyramide', 2 avenue de Basingstoke	☎ 02 33 32 05 00
	Thursdays 10am to noon during term time.	

Spas

Bagnoles de l'Orne	Les Thermes de Bagnoles de l'Orne, rue Prof. Louvel	☎ 02 33 30 38 00
	🖳 *www.ornetourisme.com*	
	This is the nearest thermal spa to Paris and offers over 120 treatments with various packages from one day to six days.	

Stamp Collecting

L'Aigle
Cercle Philatélique, contact
M. Delorme   ☎ 02 33 84 91 07
Meetings once a month at the Centre Culturel des
Tanneurs. A list of forthcoming dates is on the notice board
inside the foyer.

Alençon
Groupement Philatélique
Alençonnais   ☎ 02 33 26 36 79
Contact M. Assier.

Argentan
Société Philatélique Argentanaise, la Maison
des Associations Pierre Curie, route
d'Urou   ☎ 02 33 67 13 99
Meetings the second Sunday of each month from 9.30 to
11.30am.

Yoga

Alençon
Cultures Loisirs Ensemble, Espace Pyramide,
2 avenue de Basingstoke   ☎ 02 33 29 03 68
Classes on Wednesdays and Thursdays.

Argentan
Espace Xavier Rousseau, 4 rue Charles
Léandre   ☎ 02 33 67 81 40
Adult classes, including beginners.

Domfront
Yoga de Domfront   ☎ 02 33 38 52 67
Contact Mme Morello.

Mortagne
Maison pour Tous, 12 place du Palais   ☎ 02 33 25 02 76
Classes on Mondays, Tuesdays and Thursdays.

Medical Facilities & Emergency Services

Ambulances

See page 68.

Doctors

English-speakers may like to contact the following doctors:

L'Aigle
Dr Magnani, 24 rue des Tanneurs   ☎ 02 33 24 47 13

Alençon
Cabinet Médical, 11 rue Marcheries   ☎ 02 33 26 19 59
duty doctor ☎ 02 33 32 78 78

| Argentan | Dr Moisant, 10 rue du Point du Jour | ☎ 02 33 36 19 12 |
| | *duty doctor* | ☎ 02 33 12 14 60 |

Gendarmeries

L'Aigle	61 rue Porte Rabel	☎ 02 33 84 18 10
Alençon	38 boulevard Duchamp	☎ 02 33 32 70 00
Argentan	3 place des Trois Croix	☎ 02 33 67 05 34
Domfront	2 rue Georges Clémenceau	☎ 02 33 14 03 48
Mortagne	route d'Alençon, St Langis lès Mortagne (opposite the Super U supermarket)	☎ 02 33 25 00 17

Health Authority

| L'Aigle | 5 place d'Europe | ☎ 02 33 84 20 50 |

There's a representative here on Tuesdays, Thursdays and Fridays from 8.30am to noon.

| Alençon | 34 place Général Bonet | ☎ 08 20 90 41 61 |

| Argentan | 11 rue du Griffon | ☎ 02 33 36 21 10 |

Open Mondays to Fridays 8.30am to noon and in the afternoons by appointment.

| Domfront | 15 rue de Montgoméry | |

There's a representative here Mondays 9am to noon, the first to fourth Mondays of the month only!

| Mortagne | 48 rue des 15 Fusillés | ☎ 02 33 32 16 47 |

(on the first floor)
There's a representative here the first and third Mondays of the month, 9am to noon and by appointment in the afternoons.

Centre Hospitalier, 9 rue de Longny
There's a representative here every Wednesday from 9am to 12.45pm and 2 to 4pm.

Hospitals

The hospital listed below have an emergency department unless otherwise stated.

| L'Aigle | Centre Hospitalier, rue du Docteur Frinault | ☎ 02 33 24 95 95 |

Alençon	Centre Hospitalier d'Alençon, 25 rue Fresnay	☎ 02 33 32 30 30

Argentan	Centre Hospitalier, 47 rue Aristide Briand	☎ 02 33 12 33 12

Domfront   Centre Hospitalier Intercommunal
                  des Andaines, 28 rue Gare   ☎ 02 33 30 57 57
                  This hospital doesn't have an emergency department.

Flers   Centre Hospitalier Jacques Monod,
                  rue Eugène Garnier   ☎ 02 33 62 62 00
                  This is the nearest hospital to Domfront that has an
                  emergency department.

Mortagne   Centre Hospitalier, 9 rue de Longny ☎ 02 33 83 40 40

Nightlife

This section isn't intended to be a definitive guide but gives a wide range of ideas for the department. Prices and opening hours were correct at the time of writing, but it's best to check before travelling long distances.

L'Aigle   Bowling Cap'Orne, avenue Président
                  Kennedy   ☎ 02 33 24 12 60
                  Tuesdays to Thursdays 2pm to midnight, Fridays 3pm to
                  2am, Saturdays 2.30pm to 2am, Sundays 2.30pm to 8pm.
                  Opening hours change slightly according to school holiday
                  dates.

Alençon   l'Arc en Ciel, 11 rue de la Halle aux
                  Toiles   ☎ 02 33 26 32 15
                  (south of the town)
                  Disco open Wednesdays to Saturdays 10pm to 5am with a
                  themed evening the first Sunday of each month. Free entry
                  for women Wednesdays to Fridays.

                  Bowling d'Arçonnay, le Coudray, 1 rue
                  du Mans   ☎ 02 33 28 94 76
                  Open Tuesdays to Sundays 3pm to 2am, Fridays until 3am,
                  Saturdays until 4am. Open to all from six-year-olds.

                  Le Harpe d'Or, Galerie du Pont Neuf, 24 rue
                  du Pont Neuf   ☎ 02 33 32 98 98
                  Pub with karaoke every Friday and regular concerts.

                  le Lochness, rue de Sarthe   ☎ 02 33 29 01 83

Scottish bar/pub with concerts and shows and pool tables.
Open Tuesdays to Thursdays 5pm to 12.30am, Fridays and
Saturdays until 1.30am.

la Luciole, 171 route de Bretagne   ☎ 02 33 32 83 33
🖳 *www.laluciole.org*
(off the RN12 towards Rennes, east out of the town)
Concert venue open all year round with international acts
from jazz to funk, soul to rock.

le Shetland, 4 rue de la Halle aux
Toiles   ☎ 02 33 26 05 39
This bar is open 4pm to 1am Tuesdays and Wednesdays
and until 2am Thursdays to Saturdays.

le Singe, 5 rue du Général Leclerc, St
Germain-du-Corbeis   ☎ 02 33 26 25 19
(on the south side of the city)
Pub/club.

Argentan   the Garden, 29 rue de la Chausée   ☎ 02 33 39 99 59
                    Pub/brasserie with occasional concerts.

Bagnoles de l'Orne Casino du Lac,6 avenue Robert
                    Cousin   ☎ 02 33 37 84 00
                    Open every day from 11am until the early hours. There's
                    dancing on Thursdays and Sundays and the restaurant is
                    open for lunch and dinner every day.

Domfront   Hamacabar, 1 rue de Flers   ☎ 02 33 37 75 98
                    Concerts and other shows.

Mortagne   le Caribou, rue des Ravenelles   ☎ 02 33 83 78 79
                    (in a wooden building set back between the Peugeot
                    garage and EDF)
                    A Canadian theme bar open every day from 7pm to 2am.

Reveillon   le Réveillon, Le Bourg   ☎ 02 33 25 04 67
                    (just south of Mortagne)
                    Jazz cafe with various shows, including English bands.

Pets

Farriers

General   Julien Barret, le Chêne, St Mard
                    de Réno   ☎ 02 33 25 22 23
                    (based just east of Mortagne)

Michel Dubois, la Fieffe, Perrou   ☎ 02 33 38 16 82
(based a few km east of Domfront)

Horse Dentists

General   Dr Sellier, 24 bis route de Paris, Anglures,
                   L'Aigle   ☎ 02 33 24 12 36
                   This vet deals with horses within 30km of L'Aigle.

Pet Parlours

See page 79.

Riding Equipment

L'Aigle   Cavalissimo, route de Paris, St Sulpice-
                   sur-Risle   ☎ 02 33 34 33 98
                   (on the main road in front of the Leclerc supermarket)
                   A comprehensive shop with equipment for both horse and
                   rider. Open Mondays to Saturdays (except Thursdays)
                   10am to 7pm.

SPA

There's no branch of the SPA in Orne; the nearest, depending on your location in the department, is in Bayeux (see page 129), Evreux (see page 188) or Le Mans in Sarthe (see below).

Le Mans   8 rue Francois Monier, ZI Arnage   ☎ 02 43 84 32 17

Veterinary Clinics

See page 80.

Places to Visit

This section isn't intended to be a definitive guide but gives a wide range of ideas for the department. Prices and opening hours were correct at the time of writing, but it's best to check before travelling long distances.

Animal Parks & Aquariums

Bagnoles de l'Orne la Ferme du Cheval de Trait, la Michaudière,
                    Juvigny-sous-Andaine   ☎ 02 33 38 27 78
                    💻 www.fermeduchevaldetrait.com
                    (north-west of Alençon)
                    This centre specialises in training horses for working,
                    pulling carriages or performance and has a collection of

equipment used by working horses past and present. Open April to October. Adults €8.50, 5 to 13-year-olds €4, under fives free.

Occagnes	Parc de Loisiers d'Occagnes, la Chanteraine	☎ 02 33 67 33 63

(north-west of Argentan off the N158)
A fish centre with an aquarium containing over 4,000 fish, natural lakes with rainbow trout and breeding tanks, as well as a bar, brasserie, crazy golf and a picnic area. Fishing available. Open every day from 7.30am to 7pm.

Le Pin au Haras	Haras National du Pin	☎ 02 33 36 68 68

(on the RN26 directly east of Argentan)
This stud (there are several 'national' studs in France, although this is one of the largest and most important) has 70 stallions with the breeding concentrated on race horses. The saddlery, workshops and forge contain displays explaining the techniques used at this stud over the last three centuries. Open all year; performances in the courtyard every Thursday at around 2.30pm June to September.

Beaches & Leisure Parks

Longny au Perche	Monaco Parc	☎ 02 33 73 59 59

(east of Mortagne)
Camping, swimming (with lifeguards in July and August), pedalos on the river, playground and pony rides.

Vimoutiers	l'Escale du Vitou, route d'Argentan	☎ 02 33 39 12 04

(north-east of Argentan)
Fishing, pedalos, mini-port with electric boats for children, crazy golf, tennis and *boules*. Snack bar, restaurant and children's playground. Open every day in July and August and weekends from April to October.

Boat, Train & Wagon Rides

Putanges	le Val d'Orne, La Forge	☎ 02 33 39 30 30

💻 *www.valdorne.com*
(east of Argentan)
This boat offers a panoramic view of the passing countryside and is equipped with a bar and a restaurant. Standard cruises depart 4pm Wednesdays to Mondays July and August, Sundays only the rest of the year, and cost from €7 for adults and from €3 for 3 to 12-year-olds (prices vary according to length of cruise). Lunch and dinner cruises depart daily at noon and 7.30pm and cost from €39 to €57 according to the menu chosen. Both lunch and dinner cruises must be booked.

Chateaux

Carrouges

Château de Carrouges ☎ 02 33 27 20 32
(between Argentan and Alençon)
This chateau remained in the same family for over 500
years and still contains its Renaissance furniture, portraits
and decor. Open all year. Guided tours available, as well as
regular exhibitions and concerts.

St Christophe le
Jajolet

Château de Sassy ☎ 02 33 35 32 66
(between Argentan and Alençon)
An 18th century chateau that looks down over the terraces
of the formal gardens. The interior is tastefully decorated
and features Aubusson and Gobelins tapestries. The
gardens include an orangery, patterned box hedges and a
moat. Open mid-June to mid-September 10.30am to
12.30pm and 2 to 6pm; Easter and the last two weeks of
September weekends 3 to 6pm. Guided tours €5.

Miscellaneous

Argentan

Eglise St Martin
Built in the 15th and 16th centuries this church has an
octagonal bell tower and superb stained glass windows in
the choir.

Aube

la Grosse Forge d'Aube ☎ 02 33 34 14 93
🖳 *www.forgeaube.fr.st*
One of the best preserved forges in Europe. There have
been iron and copper works on this site for 450 years.
Open from mid-June to the end of September 2 to 6pm,
closed Tuesdays. Guided tours depart at 2.15, 3.15, 4.15
and 5.15pm. Adults €3.85, children €1.55.

Soligny la Trappe

Abbaye de la Trappe ☎ 02 33 84 17 00
This abbey dates from the 13th and 14th centuries. The
church is open every day from 10.30am to 5pm with a
video showing the history of the abbey and the life of the
Trappist monks today.

Museums, Memorials & Galleries

Alençon

Musée des Beaux Arts et de la Dentelle, Cour
Carrée de la Dentelle ☎ 02 33 32 40 07
(in the centre of the town, on the east bank of the river)
This is a museum of fine art and lace, the art museum
including drawings, engravings and paintings. The section
on lacework was added in the 19th century to display
examples of the local craft that has been practised in
Alençon since the 17th century. Open all year Tuesdays to
Sundays 10am to noon and 2 to 6pm (every day in July and
August). €2.80 for adults.

Flers	Musée du Château de Flers ☎ 02 33 64 66 49

Housed in an 18th century chateau, the museum offers an extensive collection of paintings, sculptures and other works. Open from Easter to October Wednesdays to Mondays 10am to noon and 2 to 6pm.

Lignerolles	Musée de l'Epicerie et des Commerces d'Autrefois ☎ 02 33 25 91 07

(just north-east of Mortagne)
This museum has a collection of shops and trades from times gone by, including an old bar and small hairdresser's. Open September to May weekends and bank holidays 2 to 6pm; June to August Thursdays to Sundays 2 to 6pm.

Parks, Gardens & Forests

Crouttes	Jardins du Prieuré St Michel ☎ 02 33 39 15 15

✉ *leprieuresaintmichel@wanadoo.fr*
(north of Avranches on the boundary with Calvados)
Water is a major feature in these gardens, which are made up of several areas including medicinal and aquatic plants. Open Wednesdays to Sundays from May to September 2 to 6pm. €5 entry.

Parc du Perche	A large natural park east of the Mortagne consisting of several forests and many lakes, ideal for walks.

St Céneri le Gérei	Jardins de la Mansonnière ☎ 02 33 26 73 24

(south-west of Alençon)
Nine beautiful gardens that run into each other. Open June to mid-September 2.30 to 6.30pm. €4 entry, free for under 12s.

St Christophe le	Jardins du Château de Sassy ☎ 02 33 35 32 66

(between Argentan and Alençon)
These formal gardens are overlooked by the 18th century chateau and include an orangery, patterned box hedges and a moat. Open Easter to 1st November every day from 3 to 6pm. Guided tours available for groups by appointment. €5 for the gardens and the chateau.

Trun	le Camp de Bierre, Merri ☎ 02 33 36 93 55

(north of Argentan)
This 8ha (20-acre) area is one of the major standing stone sites in the west of France and is open to the public all year round. Guided tours €2.30; tickets on sale at the tourist office in Trun.

Professional Services

The following offices have an English-speaking professional.

Accountants

L'Aigle   Jean-Marc Baron, 18 rue du Général
                          de Gaulle   ☎ 02 33 24 48 55
                          ✉ *socogere-61@wanadoo.fr*

Solicitors & Notaires

L'Aigle   Office Notarial, 13 rue de Bec'Ham   ☎ 02 33 84 26 16
                          Maître Sarthout at this office speaks English.

Religion

Catholic Churches

L'Aigle   St Martin de l'Aigle
                          Prebytère, Parish of St Martin-
                          en-Ouche   ☎ 02 33 24 08 30
                          Services on Sundays at 10.30am.

Alençon   Église St Léonard
                          Services on Sundays at 11am.

                          Église Notre Dame
                          Presbytère de Notre Dame, 27 rue
                          Bercail   ☎ 02 33 26 20 89
                          (in the centre of town)
                          The church is currently undergoing extensive renovation
                          and is due to re-open in 2005.

Argentan   Église St Germain
                          Services on Sundays at 10am.

Domfront   Église St Julien
                          Presbytère   ☎ 02 33 38 65 72
                          🖥 *www.cate-ouest.com*
                          Services on Sundays at 11am.

Mortagne   Église Notre Dame
                          Presbytère, 19 rue du Colonel Guérin ☎ 02 33 25 12 76
                          Services on Saturdays at 6pm and Sundays at 10.30am.

Protestant Churches

L'Aigle   Église Evangélique, 14 rue Jetées   ☎ 02 33 24 03 98

Alençon   Église Evangélique, 35 rue l'Isle   ☎ 02 33 26 70 14

Église Réformée, 26 place Bonet   ☎ 02 33 27 52 03
Services on Sundas at 10.30am

Argentan   Evangélique, 12 bis rue du Croissant ☎ 02 33 36 14 31

Restaurants

See page 87.

Rubbish & Recycling

See page 88.

Shopping

When available, the opening hours of various shops have been included,
but these are liable to change and so it's advisable to check before travelling
long distances to any specific shop.

Architectural Antiques

Chambois   Péristyle, rue Paul Buquet   ☎ 02 33 36 74 97
                    (north-east of Argentan)
                    Buys and sells reclaimed building materials.

Domfront   Brocante du Donjon, rue Mont
                    St Michel   ☎ 02 33 38 98 64
                    To the side of the *brocante* is an outdoor area containing
                    reclaimed materials such as fireplaces, baths and
                    staircases.

Department Stores

Flers   Nouvelles Galeries, 9 rue 6 Juin   ☎ 02 33 64 95 55
                    Open Mondays to Saturdays 9.15am to 12.15pm and 2.15
                    to 7.15pm.

DIY

See page 95.

Garden Centres

See page 95.

Hypermarkets

See **Retail Parks** on page 297.

Kitchens & Bathrooms

See page 96.

Markets

L'Aigle	The Tuesday morning market is one of the largest in France, and there are smaller local produce markets on Saturday evenings and Sunday mornings.
Alençon	There's a market all day on Thursdays, but the food stalls are in the morning only. Further markets on Saturday and Sunday mornings.
Argentan	Sunday mornings at place St Martin, Tuesdays and Fridays at place du Marché.
Carouges	Wednesdays and Saturdays.
Domfront	Friday mornings.
Flers	Wednesdays and Saturdays.
Mortagne	There's an indoor market at the top of rue des 15 Fusillés on Saturday mornings.
Sées	Saturday mornings.

Organic Produce

L'Aigle	Epi-Bio, 7 rue Carnot ☎ 02 33 84 88 05 Open Tuesdays to Saturdays 9am to 12.15pm and 2.30 to 7pm
Alençon	Biotope, 20 rue André Mazeline ☎ 02 33 26 81 48
Argentan	la Vie Bio, 22 rue du Griffon ☎ 02 33 39 52 69 Open Tuesdays to Thursdays 9.30am to 12.30pm and 2.30 to 7pm, Fridays 9.30am to 7pm, Saturdays 9.30am to 12.30pm and 2.30 to 6pm.
Mortagne	l'Aubier, 68 bis Faubourg St Eloi, St Langis lès Mortagne ☎ 02 33 73 49 92

Open Tuesdays to Saturdays 9.30am to 12.15pm and
2.30 to 7pm.

Retail Parks

L'Aigle

There's a small retail park based around the Leclerc
supermarket, including:
- Jouet Club – toys;
- Bébe 9 – baby clothes and equipment;
- Gémo – clothes;
- Gifi – furniture and accessories;
- Intersport – sports goods.

Alençon

There are two retail parks.
Carrefour hypermarket, route
de Rennes   ☎ 02 33 92 49 00
💻 *www.carrefour.fr*
(east of the town)
The complex around the hypermarket has many shops
and services including hairdressers', restaurants,
opticians', jewellers', florist's, dry cleaner's, post office,
heel and key bar, instant photo developing,
photocopiers, photo booth and business card machine.
Hypermarket open Mondays to Saturdays 9am
to 9pm (Fridays until 10pm). Main shops
include:
- Carrefour – hypermarket;
- GP Décor – painting and decorating;
- Mr Bricolage – DIY;
- Super Sport – sports goods.

Leclerc hypermarket, route de Mans ☎ 02 33 81 41 00
💻 *www.e-leclerc.com*
The surrounding complex includes clothes shops, a
jeweller's, concert ticket service, optician's, mobile phone
shops, travel agent's, hairdresser's, heel and key bar,
photo booth, copier and business card machine. Open
Mondays to Saturdays 9am to 8.30pm (till 9pm on
Fridays). Main shops include:
- Aubert – baby clothes and equipment;
- BUT – furniture;
- Casa – household accessories and gifts;
- Darty – electrical goods;
- Décathlon – sports goods;
- La Halle – clothes;
- Halle aux Chaussures – shoes;
- King Jouet – toys;
- Leclerc – hypermarket;
- Mobiclub – furniture;
- Mr Brico – DIY.

Second-hand Goods

See page 97.

Sports Goods

L'Aigle	Intersport, Anglures, St Sulpice-sur-Rille (near Leclerc on the outskirts of town) Open Mondays to Fridays 9.30am to 12.30pm and 2 to 7pm, Saturdays 9.30am to 7pm.	☎ 02 33 84 26 30
Alençon	Décathlon, route de Mans 🖳 *www.decathlon.fr*	☎ 02 33 80 26 50
Argentan	Sport 2000, Centre Commercial Leclerc Open Mondays to Fridays 9.30am to 12.15pm and 2 to 7pm, Saturdays 9.30am to 7pm.	☎ 02 33 12 27 90

Wines & Spirits

See page 98.

Sports & Outdoor Activities

The following is just a selection of the activities available, te large towns having a wide range of sports facilities. Full details are available from the tourist office or the *mairie*.

Aerial Sports

Alençon	Aéro Club d'Alençon, Aérodrome d'Alençon (in the north of the town) 🖳 *www.aeroclub-alencon.org* Flying school, for theory and practical training.	☎ 02 33 29 25 86
Argentan	Phil'Air Aviation, Aérodrome, rue de Mauvaisville Microlights, flying school and introductory flights.	☎ 02 33 39 27 53

Ballooning

Maintenon	M Com Montgolfière, 16, rue d'Arcueil, Gentilly 🖳 *www.mayerhoeffer-montgolfiere.com* (just over the eastern border of the department)	☎ 01 49 69 04 22

One hour flights, weather permitting, departing from
Maintenon on the Eure border.

Archery

L'Aigle	Club des Archers	☎ 02 33 24 45 52
	Contact M. Ferrovecchio.	

Alençon	les Archers des Ducs	☎ 02 33 26 69 76
	Contact Mme Duval.	

Domfront	Compagnie Tir à l'Arc Domfrontaise	☎ 02 33 38 41 77
	Contact M. Bonfardin.	

Badminton

L'Aigle	Badminton CAA	☎ 02 33 24 42 14
	Contact M. Savary.	

Alençon — Club Alençonnais de Badminton — ☎ 02 33 27 10 45
Introduction, training and competitions for youngsters and
adults, held at various gyms in the town. Contact Corinne
Corvée for venues.

Argentan — Bayard Argentanaise, 65 rue de
la République — ☎ 02 33 36 13 54

Domfront — Badminton Domfrontai — ☎ 02 33 37 40 15
Contact Mme Riflet.

Boules/Pétanque

L'Aigle — Pétanque Aiglonne — ☎ 02 33 24 38 44
Contact M. Marc Dutrait.

Alençon — Club Bouliste Alençonnais, Bar du Château,
rue du Château — ☎ 02 33 26 15 89
This club meets at the bar. Contact M. Pillin for further
information.

Argentan — ASPTT Section Pétanque, Boulodrome
du Paty — ☎ 02 33 67 30 66
Courses, competitions and social sessions, lessons
Tuesdays 5.30 to 6.45pm. Contact M. Robillard.

There's a boules court at Centre Louvrier, accessed via rue
Charlotte Cordet.

Domfront — Pétanque Domfrontaise — ☎ 02 33 38 91 72
Contact M. Ruer.

Canoeing & Kayaking

Alençon   Base de Canoë-Kayak, rue de
                   Guéramé   ☎ 02 33 32 14 82
                   Instruction for children and adults or just canoe hire.

Argentan   Vennelle Alexandre   ☎ 06 87 48 55 36
                   (from Place du Général Leclerc, take rue E. Panthou
                   towards the town centre, then immediately right and the
                   club is on the left)
                   Training in a pool. Canoe hire, full or half days. All ages
                   welcome.

Domfront   Centre de Plaine Nature de Torchamp ☎ 02 33 38 70 41
                   Instruction available as well as canoe hire, half day descent
                   from €11 to €15, full day 12km descent from €15 to €27 per
                   boat.

Clay Pigeon Shooting

Alençon   Ball Trap Club Alençonnais, Stand
                   de Tir   ☎ 02 33 29 19 32
                   (the range is by the aerodrome in the north of the town)
                   The club meets every Saturday afternoon at 2pm.

Domfront   Ball Trap   ☎ 02 33 38 91 72
                   Contact M. Ruer.

Climbing

L'Aigle   Club Evad'O
                   Contact M. Leprevost, Résidence 2000, place de Verdun.

Alençon   Club Alençonnais d'Escalade, la Halle aux Sports
                   de Perseigne, rue Abbé Letacq   ☎ 02 43 34 08 07
                   Introduction to the sport and training for all from seven-
                   years old, Tuesdays, Thursdays and Fridays from 6 to 9pm.

Argentan   Espace Xavier Rousseau, 4 rue Charles
                   Léandre   ☎ 02 33 67 81 40
                   Climbing wall with groups for children, youngsters and
                   adults.

Domfront   Site de la Cluse, route de Flers
                   (to the north of the town)
                   This is a natural site with 72 climbing routes from levels 2 to
                   7, alongside the river Varenne.

                   The tourist office in Domfront has guides to other
                   natural climbing sites.

Cycling

L'Aigle
CYSA, Cyclo Sportif Aiglon ☎ 02 33 24 25 91
Contact M. Soret.

Alençon
Association Sportive de l'ASPTT
d'Alençon ☎ 02 33 28 10 83
Open to all, this club meets at 6pm every Wednesday at
rue Eiffel. Contact M. Burel.

Argentan
Union Cycliste du Pays d'Argentan ☎ 02 33 67 08 57
Mountain biking, road riding, BMX and cycle school. Open
to all from nine years old.

Domfront
Camping Municipal, 4 rue du Champ
Passais ☎ 02 33 37 37 66
Bike hire.

Cyclo Domfrontais Clu ☎ 02 33 38 68 81
Contact M. Fermin.

Mortagne
Union Cycliste Percheronne ☎ 02 33 25 06 48
Contact M. Genellé.

Fencing

Alençon
les Ducs d'Alençon, Salle d'Armes, 43 rue
de l'Isle ☎ 02 33 32 91 41
Open to children and adults with various sessions
throughout the week. Contact M. Girot.

Fishing

Maps showing local fishing waters and indicating the dates of the fishing
season are available from fishing shops and tourist offices. If there's a lake
locally, permits will be on sale in nearby *tabacs* and fishing shops and at
the *mairie*.

L'Aigle
les Gaulois ☎ 02 33 24 11 13
M. Anceaume is the contact for this fishing club.

Domfront
Pisciculture de Champsecret, l'Ecluse,
Champsecret ☎ 02 33 38 08 14
Fishing centre with lakes for trout and fly fishing and fish for
sale. Open every day 8am to 6pm, Half day €12, full
day €21.

la Truite Domfrontaise ☎ 02 33 38 65 12
Fishing club. River fishing is possible on the Varenne and
many of its tributaries. Full information from the club or
tourist office.

| Gémages | Moulin de Gémages | ☎ 02 33 25 15 72 |

🖳 *www.moulindegemages.free.fr*
(south of Mortagne and Bêlleme)
Twelve lakes for trout and salmon fishing. Lessons for
beginners.

Football

| L'Aigle | Football Club du Pays Aiglon |

Contact M. Mongiat, 16 rue de la Madeleine.

| Alençon | Union Sportive Alençonnaise, Stade Jacques Fould,
8 rue Pierre de Coubertin | ☎ 02 33 29 59 69 |

| Argentan | ASPTT, 69 rue Hector Berlioz | ☎ 02 33 67 01 27 |

Various training sessions throughout the week, matches on
Saturdays and Sundays.

| Domfront | Stade, rue du Champ Passais | ☎ 02 33 38 07 43 |

Golf

| Mieuxcé | Golf Rustique de la Bichonnière, la
Bichonnière | ☎ 02 33 32 24 16 |

(just south-west of Alençon)
9-hole course. Open every day from 9am to 9pm.
Beginners by appointment.

| Bêlleme | Golf St Martin | ☎ 02 33 73 12 79 |

🖳 *www.golfdebelleme.com*
(south of Mortagne)
18 holes, 5,935m, par 72. Club house and regular
competitions, golf clubs, trolleys and golf buggies to hire.
Green fees from €21 to €30 out of season, €30 to €42 from
mid-March to 2nd November.

| La Selle la Forge | Golf Flers-Le Houlme, le Clos Foucher ☎ 02 33 64 42 83 |

(south-east of Flers)
9-hole course with driving range, putting greens, lessons,
courses and competitions, plus a golfing school for
children.

Horse Riding

| Alençon | Centre Equestre Champ Gallet,
Damigny | ☎ 02 33 29 66 11 |

(north-west side of the town)
Horses, ponies, lessons and courses.

| Argentan | Equitation 82, Domaine de Bellegarde, |

| | Sévigny | ☎ 02 33 67 58 92 |

Lessons and competitions. Open all week 8am to 8pm.

| Domfront | Ranch de la Fosse Arthour, St George de Rouelley | ☎ 02 33 59 44 14 |

(east of the town, off the D907)

Judo

| Alençon | Judo Club Alençon, Dojo Fabien Canu, rue de l'Isle | ☎ 02 33 82 73 81 |

Contact M. Tardé.

| Argentan | Judo Club Argentan | ☎ 02 33 36 95 09 |

Contact M. Legay.

| Domfront | Judo Club Domfrontais, Maison des Assocations, 52 rue Docteur Barrabé | ☎ 02 33 38 56 66 |

| Mortagne | JC Mortagne, Champ de Course | ☎ 02 33 25 94 31 |

A variety of classes held throughout the week.

Motorsports

Cars

| Alencon | Association Automobiles des Ducs | ☎ 02 33 25 33 74 |

Rallies held at Essay. Contact Guy Petit.

| Argentan | Association Sportive Automobile Argentanaise | ☎ 06 81 78 30 14 |

Various competitions, including motocross.

Karting

| Aunay les Bois | Karting 61, Terrain d'Essai | ☎ 02 33 81 97 85 |

🖳 *www.karting61.com*
(off the D31 just outside Essay in the direction of Courtomer)
Leisure karting and many competitions. All equipment supplied.

Motorbikes

| L'Aigle | Moto Club Aiglon | ☎ 02 33 24 33 14 |

Contact M. Poisson.

| Alençon | Moto Club des Sources | ☎ 02 43 00 92 84 |

Contact M. Besch.

Paintball

Fresnaie Fayel	les Guerriers Katangais	☎ 02 33 12 60 84

(north-east of Argentan, off the D979)
Four hectares of forest dedicated to paintball. From €10 to €40.

Rollerskating

L'Aigle   There's a skate park within the grounds of the Centre Culturel des Tanneurs, rue des Tanneurs.

Alençon   Roller Skating Club d'Alençon, piste de Perseigne, rue Abbé Letacq   ☎ 02 33 29 69 55
This club is based at the skate track but skating is held indoors in wet weather. Groups for adults and children.

There's a skate park near the theatre, just north of the town centre.

Argentan   ASPTT, 69 rue Hector Berlioz   ☎ 02 33 35 32 93
Courses for all ages and all levels. Beginners Tuesdays 6.30 to 8pm, intermediates Wednesday 6 to 7pm and advanced Fridays 6 to 10pm.

Shooting

Alençon   Association de Tir Civil de la Police d'Alençon   ☎ 02 33 29 59 69
Held at either Plaine des Sports at Alençon or Stand des Choux at Sées, contact M. Roullée for further information.

Argentan   Société de Tir d'Argentan, Stand de Tir du Réage du Conqueret   ☎ 02 33 67 69 78
Shooting school for all levels including beginners, all ages welcome from nine-years-old.

Swimming

L'Aigle   Centre Aquatique, Cap'Orne, avenue du Président Kennedy   ☎ 02 33 24 18 18
Several pools plus a sauna, weights room, Jacuzzi and aqua gym classes. Open every day; hours vary according to school holidays.

Alençon   Piscine Pierre-Rousseau, route du Mans, Arçonnay   ☎ 02 33 26 00 61
(on the south side of the town)

Alencéa, rue de Villeneuve   ☎ 02 33 26 63 32
💻 www.recrea.fr

Traditional pool plus leisure pools with water chutes and an outdoor pool. Various aqua aerobic classes and a swimming club.

Argentan   Centre Aquatique, rue Paty   ☎ 02 33 30 38 00
Conventional swimming pool plus various leisure pools and a water chute.

Flers   Capfl'O, les Closets   ☎ 02 33 98 49 49
✉ *capflo.flers@wanadoo.fr*
This water park has indoor and outdoor pools, a giant water slide, a lazy river and a wave machine. Open every day, but hours vary according to the school holidays

Mortagne   Piscine, rue de la Poudrière   ☎ 02 33 25 35 57
Indoor heated pool, uncovered in the summer and closed Tuesdays all year.

Tennis

L'Aigle   Tennis Club Aiglon   ☎ 02 33 24 39 75
The tennis courts are in rue des Sports in the south-east of the town. Contact M. Robert.

Alençon   Tennis Club Alençonnaise, rue
de l'Isle   ☎ 02 33 26 20 15
Three indoor and five outdoor courts. Beginners welcome, competitions for adults and children, and various lessons throughout the week.

Argentan   Stade Gérard Saint, 21 avenue de Paris

Domfront   Tennis Club Domfrontais   ☎ 06 08 95 08 40
Indoor and outdoor courts by the gymnasium. Contact Mme Conan.

Mortagne   Tennis Club de Mortagne, Lycée Jean Monnet,
rue Jean Monnet   ☎ 02 33 25 12 68
Contact M. Martinaggi.

Walking

Alençon   Association Sportif de l'ASPTT
d'Alençon   ☎ 02 33 31 99 39
Walks every Wednesday at 2pm and every other Sunday at 8.30am or 2pm, departing from rue la Voisier.

Argentan   Espace Xavier Rousseau, 4 rue Charles
Léandre   ☎ 02 33 67 81 40
Regular walks for adults, including seniors.

Domfront   Association des Randonneurs
                    Pédestres du Domfrontais   ☎ 02 33 38 58 07
                    Contact M. Boisgontier for forthcoming walks.
                    There's also a board by the tourist office marking local
                    routes.

Mortagne   Maison pour Tous, 12 place du Palais ☎ 02 33 25 02 76
                    Walks twice a month on Tuesdays, departing from place du
                    Palais at 2pm. Information on forthcoming walks is
                    displayed in the window of the tourist office.

Watersports

Scuba Diving

Alençon   Scaphandre Club Alençonnaise, Piscine
                    Marguerite de Navarre   ☎ 02 33 29 17 18
                    Training on Wednesday and Friday evenings from 8 to
                    10pm September to mid-June. Minimum age 14.

Argentan   Section Argentanaise Subaquatique ☎ 02 33 36 87 25
                    Training at the Centre Aquatique, rue du Paty, plus sea
                    dives. Contact M. Ribot.

Tourist Offices

General   Comité Départemental de Tourisme de l'Orne,
                    86 rue Saint Blaise, Alençon ☎ 02 33 28 88 71
                    🖥 *www.ornetourisme.com*

L'Aigle   place Fulbert de Beina   ☎ 02 33 24 12 40
                    🖥 *www.paysdelaigle.com*
                    Open Mondays to Saturdays 9am to 12.30pm and 2 to
                    6.30pm.

Alençon   Maison d'Ozé, place de la
                    Magdeleine   ☎ 02 33 80 66 33
                    🖥 *www.paysdalencontourisme.com*
                    Open Mondays to Saturdays 9.30am to noon and 2 to
                    6.30pm (longer hours in the summer, including Sunday
                    opening).

Argentan   place de la Mairie   ☎ 02 33 67 12 48
                    🖥 *www.argentan.fr*
                    Open Mondays to Fridays 9.30am to 12.30pm and 2 to
                    6pm, Saturdays 9.30am to 12.30pm and 1.30 to 5.30pm.
                    Hours increase in the summer months.

| Domfront | 12 place Pellier de la Roirie | ☎ 02 33 38 53 97 |

Open Tuesdays to Saturdays 9.30am to 12.30pm and 2.30
to 6pm (till 6.30pm on Saturdays)

| Mortagne | Halle aux Grains | ☎ 02 33 85 49 60 |

✉ *office-mortagne@wanadoo.fr*
Open Mondays 10am to 12.30pm and 2.30 to
6pm, Tuesdays to Saturdays 9.30am to 12.30pm
and 2.30 to 6pm, Sundays 10am to 12.30pm. Hours
may increase in the summer
months.

Tradesmen

Architects & Project Managers

| Mortagne | Laurent Bousquet, 6 rue de la Comédie | ☎ 02 33 85 26 30 |

Architect.

Builders

| L'Aigle | Stéphane Zeymes, 44 rue Pierre Chabaud | ☎ 02 33 24 43 05 |

| Alençon | GTA, avenue de Basingstoke | ☎ 02 33 29 23 84 |

General building, new and renovation work.

| Argentan | Entreprise Yakut, rue Aristide Briand | ☎ 02 33 12 55 38 |

General building.

| Domfront | Guy Compagnon, 3 rue Eléanor d'Aquitaine | ☎ 02 33 38 40 55 |

| Mortagne | Guibert Frères, 70 rue des Déportés, ZI la Grippe | ☎ 02 33 25 06 02 |

General building including plastering and tiling.

The following companies specialise in new construction.

| Alençon | Clair Logis, 191 avenue du Général Leclerc | ☎ 02 33 27 08 33 |

| Argentan | Maisons France Confort, 96 rue Aristide Briand | ☎ 02 33 36 28 19 |

Carpenters

Many carpentry firms that make wooden windows and doors also work in aluminium.

L'Aigle	Pottier Vavasseur Menuiserie, 15 rue Louis Lethiec	☎ 02 33 84 83 38
Alençon	Audouin, 234 avenue du Général Leclerc	☎ 02 33 27 80 50
	🖳 *www.audouin61.com*	
	Kitchens and bathrooms made to measure, plasterboarding, parquet flooring and staircases.	
Argentan	Entreprise Maudet, Crennes	☎ 02 33 67 52 64
	Roofing and general carpentry.	
Domfront	Daniel Guerin, le Bas Losé	☎ 02 33 30 04 83
Mortagne	Menuiserie Général du Perche, ZI la Grippe	☎ 02 33 25 40 33

Chimney Sweeps

L'Aigle	Chauffage Service, 25 rue Docteur Frinault	☎ 02 33 24 63 74
Alençon	Michel Guéranger, 14 chemin Muriers, Cerisé	☎ 02 33 29 70 25
	(north-east outskirts of the town)	
Mortagne	Bruno Beuzelin, 68 Faubourg St Eloi, St Langis lès Mortagne	☎ 02 33 25 17 61

Electricians

General	Craig Hutchinson, 158 rue Henri-Veniard, St Georges des Groseillers	☎ 06 73 11 40 89
	✉ *craighutchinson@aol.com*	
	English-speaking electrician for small jobs or complete rewiring.	
L'Aigle	Guy Ligot, route de Paris, Anglures	☎ 02 33 24 53 46
	Electrical repairs and installation.	
Alençon	Vonthron, 197 rue d'Argentan	☎ 02 33 29 04 01
	🖳 *www.vonthron.fr*	
Argentan	Pascal Boissière, Moulins sur Orne	☎ 02 33 35 39 18
	General electrician, including alarms and electric gates.	

| Domfront | Michel Troussier, la Claverie, St Fraimbault | ☎ 02 33 38 30 40 |

Heating, electrics and plumbing.

| Mortagne | Jean-Marc Gresteau, Préaux | ☎ 02 33 73 87 73 |

Installation and repairs, including electric gates and alarm systems.

Painters & Decorators

| L'Aigle | la Peinture Rilloise, route de Paris, Anglures | ☎ 02 33 24 09 06 |

| Domfront | Entreprise de Peinture Colin, 26 rue Maréchal Foch | ☎ 02 33 38 95 90 |

| Mortagne | Michel Davaudet, Bellême | ☎ 02 33 25 27 64 |

Plumbers

| L'Aigle | Delavigne Chauffage Plomberie, 15 rue Louis Pasteur | ☎ 02 33 24 22 02 |

Repairs, installation and maintenance including central heating and bathrooms.

| Alençon | Leboin Bastien, rue Cazault | ☎ 02 33 26 32 86 |

Plumbing, heating, electrics and air-conditioning.

| Argentan | Norma Confort, 12 bis chemin Cayenne, Urou et Crennes | ☎ 02 33 67 19 22 |

(on the outskirts of the town)
Plumbing, heating and bathrooms, installation and repair.

| Domfront | Philippe Lebougre, Grande Rue | ☎ 02 33 38 65 83 |

Installation, maintenance and repairs, including solar panels, plumbing and heating. Shop unit open 9.30am to 12.30pm and 2.30 to 7pm.

| Mortagne | Thierry James, ZI la Grippe | ☎ 02 33 25 44 68 |

Heating, plumbing and bathrooms, repairs and installation, including all types of central heating.

Utilities

Electricity & Gas

| General | EDF/GDF Services Orne |

🖳 *www.edf.fr*
🖳 *www.gazdefrance.com*

Local EDF/GDF offices are listed below.

L'Aigle	19 rue Garenne	☎ 02 33 26 50 98
Alençon	7 boulevard Duchamp	☎ 02 33 26 50 98
Argentan	route d'Urou	☎ 02 33 26 50 98
Mortagne	rue des Ravenelles	☎ 02 33 26 56 98

Heating Oil

L'Aigle   Combustibles de l'Ouest, 20 rue du Général
de Gaulle ☎ 02 33 24 13 45
Closed Wednesdays.

Alençon   Combustibles de l'Ouest, rue Nicolas
Appert   ☎ 02 33 29 61 27

Domfront   A. Derouault, route Mont Margantin   ☎ 02 33 38 51 61
Oil and coal.

Water

The main water supply companies are listed below. If you aren't covered by one of these, your *mairie* will have details of your water supplier.

General   Générale des Eaux
Agence de l'Orne, route de Putanges,
Argentan   ☎ 08 11 90 08 00
Open Mondays to Fridays 8am to noon and 1.30 to 4pm.
14 bis rue Surville, Messei   ☎ 02 33 96 76 20

Lyonnaise des Eaux
46 rue St Barthélémy, L'Aigle   ☎ 08 10 38 43 84
                            emergencies ☎ 08 10 88 48 84
154 rue Cerisé, Alençon   ☎ 08 10 38 43 84
55 rue des Déportés, Mortagne   ☎ 02 33 85 20 40
Les Gaillons, St Hilaire le Chatel   ☎ 02 33 85 25 40

SAUR France, 89 avenue Roger
Martin du Gard, Bellême   ☎ 08 10 14 91 49

Wood

Godisson   JF Desnos, le Champ Guimbais   ☎ 02 33 39 55 43
(centrally located in the department, between Argentan and
L'Aigle and north of Alençon)

Firewood delivered to your house cut to 1m, 50cm or
33cm lengths.

St Mard de Réno   Dominique Marmion, les Sablons   ☎ 02 33 25 29 13
(just to the east of Mortagne)

Condeau   Serge Chaboche, le Cornier   ☎ 02 33 73 30 34
(in the south-east corner of the department)

Dieppe quayside

7

Seine-Maritime

This chapter provides details of facilities and services in the department of Seine-Maritime (76). General information about each subject can be found in **Chapter 2**. All entries are arranged alphabetically by town, except where a service applies over a wide area, in which case it's listed at the beginning of the relevant section under 'General'. A map of Seine-Maritime is shown below.

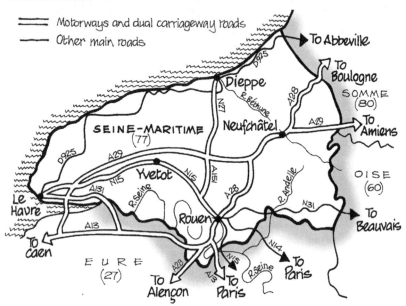

Accommodation

Chateaux

Ermenouville
Château du Mesnil Geoffroy   ☎ 02 35 57 12 77
(west of Dieppe and 6km from the sea)
💻 *www.chateau-mesnil-geoffroy.com*
This 18th century chateau is a listed building and is beautifully furnished. Situated in a park with large rose gardens. Rooms and suites from €65 to €110 per night. Gourmet breakfast €9.20, dinner €42 per person including wine and aperitif. Candlelit dinner by reservation Tuesdays to Saturdays. Bikes to hire. No dogs allowed. English spoken.

St Pierre de Manneville
Manoir de Villers, 30 route de Sahurs   ☎ 02 35 32 07 02
(south-west of Rouen)
This beautiful timbered manor was built in the 16th century and has been in the same family since 1764. The

bedrooms have 18th century furniture and views of the grounds and the river Seine. Open February to mid-December. Rooms from €122 to €155 per night; reduction for two nights or more. No pets allowed. English spoken.

Gîtes and Bed & Breakfast

General   Gîtes de France, SMTR, chemin de la Bretèque, Bois Guillaume   ☎ 02 35 60 73 34
💻 *www.gitesdefrance76.fr*
Bookings can be made by phone or via the internet.

Clévacances Seine-Maritime, 6 rue Couronné, Bihorel   ☎ 02 35 12 10 10
💻 *www.clevacances.com*

The following websites list both *gîte* and bed & breakfast accommodation:
💻 *www.seine-maritime-tourisme.com*
💻 *www.dieppetourisme.com* - in and around Dieppe
💻 *www.lehavretourisme.com*
💻 *www.rouentourisme.com* - in and around Rouen

Hotels

Various tourist office websites have details of hotel accommodation in Seine-Maritime, including those listed above.

Business Services

Computer Services

Dieppe   AGC Informatique, 3 rue Albert Legras, Parc du Talou   ☎ 02 32 90 59 05
💻 *www.agc-informatique.com*
Sale of computers, accessories and software, new and second hand.

Le Havre   Surf Com, 17 rue Amiral Coubet   ☎ 02 35 26 19 70
💻 *www.surfcom.fr*
Sales, repairs, installation and accessories, PC and Mac.

Rouen   Internity, 21 rue Ganterie   ☎ 02 32 10 56 76
💻 *www.internity.fr*

Rouen   Cybercafé, rue Percée   ☎ 02 35 95 30 58
💻 *www.cybernet76.com*
(up a little side road to the left of the tourist office)
Open Tuesdays to Saturdays 9.30am to 7pm.

Employment Agencies

The main offices of the national employment agency, ANPE, are as follows:

Dieppe	route Vallon	☎ 02 32 14 60 20
Le Havre	22 avenue du Général Archinard	☎ 02 35 19 33 00
Rouen	1 place Cauchoise rue Four	☎ 02 32 08 33 00 ☎ 02 32 81 62 10
Rouen	12 place Gare	☎ 02 35 95 93 60

Communications

France Télécom

General	Dial ☎ 1014 or ☎ 08 00 10 14 76 or go to 💻 *www.francetelecom.fr* Local France Télécom shops are listed below.
Dieppe	16 rue Victor Hugo
Le Havre	place de l'Hôtel de Ville Open Mondays to Saturdays 9.30am to 12.30pm and 2 to 7pm.
Neufchâtel	rue Chauchoise (this shop is tucked away at the back of the car park) Open Mondays to Saturdays 9am to noon and 2 to 6pm.
Rouen	6 rue Guillaume le Conquérant (north of the river) Centre Commercial St Sever (south of the river)
Rouen	26 rue des Victoires Open Tuesdays to Saturdays 9am to 12.30pm and 2 to 6.30pm Saturdays 6pm.

Internet Access

Dieppe	@rt au Bar, 19 rue de Sygogne	☎ 02 35 40 48 35

💻 *www.artaubar@wanadoo.fr*
(down a small road off the seafront at the foot of the chateau)

	High speed internet connection. Open Mondays to Thursdays 10am to 7.30pm, Fridays and Saturdays 10am to 10.30pm.	
Le Havre	Cyber-Métro, 19 cours de la République Open 9am to 2am.	☎ 02 35 25 40 34
Neufchâtel	Médiathèque, boulevard Charvet Open Tuesdays and Fridays 3 to 6pm, Wednesdays 10am to noon and 3 to 6pm, Saturdays 10am to 4pm.	☎ 02 32 97 55 90
Rouen	Cyber Net, 47 place du Vieux Marché Open 10am to 11pm every day.	☎ 02 35 07 73 02
	Place Net, 37 rue de la République Open Mondays to Saturdays 11am to midnight, Sundays and bank holidays 2pm to midnight.	☎ 02 32 76 02 22
Rouen	Cybercafé, rue Percée 🖳 *www.cybernet76.com* (up a little side road to the left of the tourist office) Tuesdays to Saturdays 9.30am to 7pm.	☎ 02 35 95 30 58

Mobile Telephones

See page 62.

Domestic Services

Clothes Alterations

Dieppe	Retouches Tous Vêtements, rue Lemoyne Clothes, curtains and leather goods.	☎ 02 35 82 33 80
Le Havre	Rapid'Couture, 285 rue Aristide Briand	☎ 02 35 53 37 28
Rouen	le Fil et l'Aiguille, 7 bis rue Edmond Labbé	☎ 02 35 96 40 18

Crèches & Nurseries

Dieppe	le Toboggan, Résidence Lemeunier, rue du 74ième RI	☎ 02 35 06 12 30

Le Havre	Baby-Sitting, Antenne du CROUS, 115 rue C. Delavigne	☎ 02 35 19 74 74
Rouen	Crèche 'Forbras' 26 rue des Capucins	☎ 02 35 70 01 36
	Baby-Sitting, CROUS, 3 rue d'Herbouville	☎ 02 35 08 50 00
Rouen	les Petits Princes, 1 rue Gustav Priès	☎ 02 35 95 17 89

Equipment & Tool Hire

Dieppe	Régis Location, avenue Normandie Sussex 🖥 www.regis-location.fr	☎ 02 35 06 16 16
Le Havre	Laho Equipement, 30 rue Mulhouse 🖥 www.laho.fr	☎ 02 35 26 60 61
Rouen	Régis Location, ZA les 2 Rivières, route de Lyon	☎ 02 35 08 46 46

Garden Services

| Le Havre | Entreprise Mabire Paysages, rue Bigne à Fosse
Garden design and maintenance, hedge cutting, fencing, planting and tree surgery. | ☎ 02 35 54 31 85 |
| Vatteville la Rue | 3 Horizons Lefebvre
(south of Yvetot, near the Seine) | ☎ 02 35 96 10 55 |

Marquee Hire

| Rouen | Bultel Location, 71 avenue du Mont Riboudet
🖥 www.bultel-location.com
Linen, china, tables and chairs also for hire. | ☎ 02 35 71 82 72 |

Septic Tank Services

Le Havre	Omin, 551 boulevard Jules Durand	☎ 02 35 24 17 93
Neufchâtel	Viam, Esclavelles	☎ 02 32 97 15 18
Rouen	Viam, 33 quai France	☎ 02 35 73 76 06

Entertainment

This section isn't intended to be a definitive guide but gives a wide range of ideas for the department. Prices and opening hours were correct at the time of writing, but it's best to check before travelling long distances.

Cinemas

Dieppe	Rex, place Nationale	☎ 02 35 84 22 74
Le Havre	Gaumont, Centre Commercial, Montivilliers (north-east of the town)	☎ 08 92 69 66 96
Neufchâtel	le Normandy, rue Poissonnière	☎ 02 32 97 16 47
Rouen	Gaumont, rue de la République 🖳 *www.cinemasgaumont.com* (in the centre of town, just north of the Pont Corneille) Recently renovated cinema with armchair seating.	☎ 08 92 69 66 96
Rouen	le Drakkar, 4 avenue du Général Leclerc	☎ 02 35 95 04 55

Festivals

There are many festivals in this department, just a small selection of which are detailed here.

March	Yvetot Foire aux Arbres et aux Végétaux For one weekend in March the horticulturists from the region gather for a large tree and plant fair that includes a cider-making competition.	☎ 02 35 95 08 40
	Each spring, there's a large balloon festival at Yvetot.	
May	Dieppe Fête des Fleurs, Flower festival on Ascension weekend.	
	Rouen Festival des Arts du Cirque	☎ 02 32 80 31 66
Rouen	le Melville, 75 rue du Général Leclerc Held at Grand Quevilly during the last two weeks of the month.	☎ 02 32 76 73 20

June	Dieppe	☎ 02 32 14 40 60

June — Dieppe ☎ 02 32 14 40 60
Festival of Music and a Horse & Harness Parade, both in the town centre.

Le Havre — Peintures sous les Arcades ☎ 02 32 74 04 04
Local amateur painters and artists meet under the arcades of rue de Paris in the centre of the town.

Le Havre — Les z'estivales ☎ 02 32 74 04 04
Every weekend the beach at Le Havre is transformed into a setting for street theatre, concerts and performers.

July — Dieppe ☎ 02 32 14 40 60
Dog show on the lawns along the seafront

August — Le Havre — Corsiflor ☎ 02 32 74 04 04
A flower procession in the form of a parade of floats decorated with flowers and groups of musicians that travel through the streets of Le Havre showering confetti on bystanders.

Pourville sur Mer — Festival des Folklores du Monde ☎ 02 35 84 71 06
Folk festival held mid-August

Autumn — Le Havre ☎ 02 32 74 04 04
Bi-annual Transat Jacques Vabre sailing race, held in 2005, 2007, etc.

September — Dieppe ☎ 02 32 14 40 60
Vintage car rally through the streets of Dieppe.

Dieppe ☎ 02 32 14 40 60
International kite festival held on the lawns along the seafront every two years; the next is 2006.

October — Le Havre — Normandy Marathon ☎ 02 32 74 04 04
A marathon from Honfleur to Le Havre via the Pont de Normandie

L'Arbalète — Journeée de la Pomme et du Cidre
Day long celebration of the apple harvest and cider production.

Libraries

Dieppe   Médiathèque, 1 quai Bérigny   ☎ 02 35 06 62 62
                      Open Tuesdays, Thursdays and Fridays 2 to 6.30pm,
                      Wednesdays 10.30am to 6.30pm, Saturdays and Sundays
                      2 to 6.30pm (July and August Tuesdays to Saturdays 2 to
                      6pm). This library has a very small selection of books in
                      English.

Le Havre   17 rue Jules Lecesne   ☎ 02 32 74 07 40
                      🖳 *www.biblio.ville-lehavre.fr*
                      Open Tuesdays and Fridays 10am to 7pm, Wednesdays
                      and Saturdays 10am to 6pm and Thursdays noon to 6pm
                      (during the summer holidays Tuesdays to Saturdays 10am
                      to 5pm, Thursdays noon to 5pm). This library has English
                      and bilingual books.

Neufchâtel   boulevard Charvet   ☎ 02 32 97 55 90
                      ✉ *mediatheque.neufchatel-en-bray@wanadoo.fr*
                      Open Tuesdays and Fridays 3 to 6pm, Wednesdays 10am
                      to noon and 3 to 6pm, Saturdays 10am to 4pm. This library
                      has a selection of English books.

Rouen   There are six public libraries in Rouen; the one listed
                      below has the longest opening hours and stocks English
                      books.

                      Espace du Palais, 1ère Etage, 8 allée Eugène
                      Delacroix   ☎ 02 35 70 61 06
                      Open Tuesdays, Thursdays and Fridays noon to 6pm,
                      Wednesdays 10am to 6pm, Saturdays 11am to 6pm.

Yvetot   9 rue Pierre de Coubertin   ☎ 02 33 95 01 13
                      Open Tuesdays, Thursdays and Fridays 2 to 7pm,
                      Wednesdays 10am to noon and 1.30 to 6pm, Saturdays
                      10am to noon and 1.30 to 5.30pm. These hours change in
                      the summer holidays.

Theatres

Fécamp   Théâtre le Passage, 54 rue Jules Ferry ☎ 02 35 29 22 81
                      🖳 *www.theatre-lepassage-fecamp.fr*

Le Havre   Théâtre de l'Hôtel de Ville, place de l'Hôtel
                      de Ville   ☎ 02 35 19 45 74

Rouen   Opéra de Rouen, 7 rue du Docteur
                      Rambert   ☎ 02 35 98 50 98
                      🖳 *www.operaderouen.com*

Théâtre Charles Dullin, allée des Arcades,
Grand Quevilly   ☎ 02 35 68 48 91

Théâtre Duchamp-Villon, 'Hanger 23',
boulevard Emile Duchemin   ☎ 02 32 18 28 28
(opposite Lapeyre)

Video & DVD Hire

See page 67.

French Teachers & Courses

Dieppe   Centre d'Activités Socials Bel Air, impasse
                des Canadiens, Neuville   ☎ 02 35 06 19 99
                (north-east of the town, just behind the ferry terminal)

Le Havre   Alliance Française, 133 boulevard
                François 1er   ☎ 02 35 21 28 78
                ✉ alliance.francaise.le.havre@wanadoo.fr
                An international organisation specialising in teaching
                French as a foreign language.

Rouen   AVF, 7 rue du Vieux Palais   ☎ 02 35 88 57 30
                French conversation classes are held on Mondays at 5pm,
                Wednesdays at 4pm and Thursdays at 10am.

                Educasia, 15 rue de l'Ancienne Prison ☎ 02 35 70 01 35
                ✉ educasia@wanadoo.fr

Leisure Activities

This section isn't intended to be a definitive guide but gives a wide range
of ideas for the department. Prices and opening hours were correct at the
time of writing, but it's best to check before travelling long distances.

Arts & Crafts

Dieppe   Peintres et Sculpteurs Dieppois, 6 rue
                des Bains   ☎ 02 35 82 63 03

Le Havre   Temps Libre, 7 rue du Perrey   ☎ 02 35 41 15 27
                Various art courses for children and adults.

Neufchâtel   Art en Bray, Office de Tourisme, 6 place
                Notre Dame   ☎ 02 35 93 22 96

Pottery and painting classes. Enquire at the tourist office for current information.

Rouen AVF, 7 rue du Vieux Palais   ☎ 02 35 88 57 30
Drawing and painting classes every other Monday at 2pm, painting on wood every Tuesday at 2pm and painting on porcelain every other Tuesday at 2pm.

Maison St Sever, 10 rue St Julien   ☎ 02 32 81 50 20
Classes for painting, drawing and painting on silk.

MJC Grieu, 3 rue de Genève   ☎ 02 35 71 94 76
Pottery classes.

Rouen Ecole d'Arts Plastiques, 7 rue
Percée   ☎ 02 35 96 36 90
Various classes for children and adults in drawing, painting, modelling and sculpture.

Bridge

Le Havre Ecole de Bridge, 14 rue Alexandre
Dictus   ☎ 02 35 45 20 26
Contact C. Couppey.

Rouen AVF, 7 rue du Vieux Palais   ☎ 02 35 88 57 30
Bridge for beginners every Tuesday at 9.30am.

Maison St Sever, 10 rue St Julien   ☎ 02 32 81 50 20

Rouen Club de Bridge d'Yvetot, Salle Pierre
& Marie Curie   ☎ 02 35 56 69 89
Meetings on Mondays at 2pm and Fridays at 8.30pm.

Children's Activity Clubs

Dieppe MCJ, 8 rue du 19 Août 1842   ☎ 02 35 84 16 92

Le Havre Association St Thomas d'Aquin, 39
rue Louis Delamare   ☎ 02 35 41 32 84
🖳 www.stthomas.fr.st

Rouen MJC Rive Gauche, place des
Faïenciers   ☎ 02 32 81 53 60

MJC Grieu, 3 rue de Genève   ☎ 02 35 71 94 76

Rouen Maison de Jeunes et Culture, 9 avenue
de Verdun   ☎ 02 35 56 89 11

Choral Singing

Dieppe	Ensemble Vocal de Dieppe	☎ 02 35 85 76 65
	Contact Philippe Gautrot.	

Neufchâtel	Harmonie Municipale	☎ 02 35 93 18 29
	Contact M. Despérez.	

Rouen   les Ecoles de Musique de Rouen, 1 ter
             rue Marie Duboccage   ☎ 02 35 72 21 54
             Five choirs including a children's choir, adult mixed choir
             and women's choir.

Circus Skills

Le Havre   Ecole de Cirque, avenue des Tréfileries,
             Vallée Béreult   ☎ 02 35 48 04 33

Rouen   MJC Rive Gauche, place des
             Faïenciers   ☎ 02 32 81 53 60

Computer Training

Le Havre   Programme Informatique, 7 rue du
             Perrey   ☎ 02 35 41 15 27
             A wide selection of courses held throughout the week
             including Mac, Works Suite, internet and complete beginner
             courses.

Rouen   Acore Formation, 9 place de la
             Cathédrale   ☎ 02 35 88 66 59

Neufchâtel   ANI Informatique   ☎ 02 32 97 04 61
             Contact M. Labro.

Dancing

Dieppe   Ecole Nationale de Musique et de Danse de la Région
             Dieppoise, 63 rue de la Barre   ☎ 02 32 14 44 50

Le Havre   Centre de Danse Anne Chetoui, 89 rue Ernest
             Renan   ☎ 02 35 21 35 38
             Introduction to dance, plus classes in rock, ballroom, jazz
             and tap.

             O Evénements, Palais des Régates, Sainte
             Adresse   ☎ 02 35 45 29 81
             (on the tip of the coast north of Le Havre)
             Tea dances every Friday and Sunday afternoon from 3pm.

Prével Swing Danse Studio, 31 bis
rue d'Après Mannevillette   ☎ 02 35 22 78 76
🖥 *www.prevelswingdanse.fr.tc*
Courses for adults and children including jazz, salsa, rock
and Latin American. The first session is free.

Neufchâtel   Association Harmony Danse, Espace Culturel
St Vincent, rue St Vincent   ☎ 02 35 90 87 54
Ballet and modern jazz for children and teenagers.

Rouen   Conservatoire National de Région, 50 avenue de la
Porte des Champs   ☎ 02 32 08 13 50
Ballet, modern and introductory classes.

Rouen   Maison de Jeunes et Culture, 9 avenue
de Verdun   ☎ 02 35 56 89 11
Various dance workshops including ballet, jazz, ballroom
and fitness.

Country Western Dance Club   ☎ 02 32 70 86 60
Contact Nathalie Karpp.

Drama

Dieppe   Théâtre en Ciel, 43 avenue Vauban   ☎ 02 35 84 72 30

Rouen   MJC Rive Gauche, place des
Faïenciers   ☎ 02 32 81 53 60
🖥 *www.rouencitejeunes.org*

Rouen   le Théâtre en Face, 25 rue Carnot   ☎ 02 35 95 65 10

Dress Making

Rouen   MJC Rive Gauche, place des
Faïenciers   ☎ 02 32 81 53 60
🖥 *www.rouencitejeunes.org*

Flower Arranging

Rouen   AVF, 7 rue du Vieux Palais   ☎ 02 35 88 57 30
This group meets one Thursday a month from 5 to 7pm.

Gardening

Dieppe   les Amis des Fleurs, 51 boulevard
de Verdun   ☎ 02 35 93 23 24
Horticultural society for Dieppe and the surrounding areas.
Contact M. Savoye.

Gym

Le Havre	Gymnastique Volontaire, Piscine du Cours, cours de la République	☎ 02 35 22 59 05

Neufchâtel — Association Club Form, l'Elan, 12 rue St Vincent   ☎ 02 35 94 77 84
A variety of classes including step and high impact.

Rouen — MJC Rive Gauche, place des Faïenciers   ☎ 02 32 81 53 60
💻 *www.rouencitejeunes.org*
A wide range of classes including those specifically for women, the overweight and seniors.

Rouen — Maison de Jeunes et Culture, 9 avenue de Verdun   ☎ 02 35 56 89 11
Various classes held including aerobic and stretching.

Gyms & Health Clubs

Neufchâtel — Association Club Form, l'Elan, 12 rue St Vincent   ☎ 02 35 94 77 84
A variety of fitness classes. Open Mondays to Saturdays 10.30am to 12.30pm and 1.30 to 4.30pm.

Rouen — Gym's New's Form's, 33 route de Darnétal   ☎ 02 35 07 04 44
💻 *www.planet-fitness.fr*

Ice Skating

Le Havre — Patinoire, 106 rue Louis Blanc   ☎ 02 35 47 02 11

Rouen — Patinoire Île Lacroix   ☎ 02 35 47 02 11
Hours vary according to school holidays.

St Martin en Campagne — Ludibulle, rue de l'Ancienne Foire   ☎ 02 35 84 84
(east of Dieppe just in from the coast)

Music

Dieppe — Ecole Nationale de Musique et de Danse de la Région Dieppoise, 63 rue de la Barre   ☎ 02 32 14 44 50

Le Havre — Ecole Nationale de Musique, de Danse et d'Art Dramatique, 70 cours de la République   ☎ 02 35 11 33 80

| Neufchâtel | Ecole de Musique et de Théâtre Boieldieu, 3 rue Faubourg des Fontaines ☎ 02 35 94 15 80 |

Neufchâtel   Ecole de Musique et de Théâtre Boieldieu,
                    3 rue Faubourg des Fontaines   ☎ 02 35 94 15 80

Rouen   Ecole de Musique F. Boitard, rue Pierre
                    de Coubertin   ☎ 02 35 95 82 72
                    Open to people of all ages for instrumental lessons or
                    vocal training.

                    les Ecoles de Musique de Rouen, 1 ter
                    rue Marie Duboccage   ☎ 02 35 72 21 54
                    A wide range of instruments taught from violin and guitar to
                    saxophone, flute and drums. There are currently seven
                    orchestras run by this music school.

                    MJC Rive Gauche, place des
                    Faïenciers   ☎ 02 32 81 53 60
                    🖳 www.rouencitejeunes.org
                    For something a bit different, here you can learn how to
                    play the didgeridoo.

                    la Musique Municipale, 37 rue
                    Lechevallier   ☎ 02 35 96 79 76
                    This is the town band, playing on drums and brass
                    instruments.

Scouts & Guides

Rouen   Guides de France, Secteur d'Yvetot et
                    Cœur de Caux   ☎ 02 35 96 99 56
                    ✉ guides.yvetot@free.fr
                    Contact Mme Lamure.

                    Scouts de France, Secteur d'Yvetot et
                    Cœur de Caux   ☎ 02 35 96 99 56
                    ✉ scouts.yvetot@free.fr
                    Contact Mme Lamure.

Social Groups

Rotary Club

Rouen   Rotary Club d'Yvetot, contact
                    M. Bichot   ☎ 02 35 95 44 43

Town Twinning

Le Havre   Hôtel de Ville, Mairie du Havre   ☎ 02 35 19 42 19
                    ✉ Annick.Faury@ville-lehavre.fr
                    Twinned with Southampton. Contact Annick Faury.

| Neufchâtel | Comité des Echanges Internationaux, Hôtel de Ville ☎ 02 35 93 62 45 |
| | Twinned with Whitchurch in England. |

Rouen   Comité de Jumelage de Rouen et Norwich,
20 avenue Jacques Chastellain   ☎ 02 35 07 19 65

Hôtel de Ville, place de l'Hôtel
de Ville   ☎ 02 32 70 44 70
Twinned with Lanark in Scotland.

Welcome Groups

General   Accueil des Villes Françaises (AVF)
🖳 *www.avf.asso.fr*
Some towns have a branch of this organisation, which is specifically to help newcomers settle into the town. The site is available in English.

Dieppe   Dieppe AVF Accueil, 16 rue Sainte
Catherine   ☎ 02 32 90 11 82

Le Havre   Le Havre AVF, 16 rue du Maréchal
Galliéni   ☎ 02 35 42 38 65
✉ *avflehavre@wanadoo.fr*

Neufchâtel   Neufchâtel Accueil   ☎ 02 35 93 88 22
Contact Mme Mols.

Rouen   AVF, 7 rue du Vieux Palais   ☎ 02 35 88 57 30
Open Mondays and Wednesdays 2.30 to 5pm, Tuesdays 2.30 to 6pm, Thursdays 9.30 to 11am and 2.30 to 5pm. Meetings once a month: *les Vikings* for under 35s the fourth Wednesday of each month in the evening, and *les Rollons* for the over 35s the third Thursday of the month at 8pm. There are coffee mornings for young mothers once a month at 2.30pm, held in various homes.

Stamp Collecting

Dieppe   Association Philatélique, Maison des
Associations, rue Notre Dame   ☎ 02 35 85 34 28

Neufchâtel   Association Philatélique   ☎ 06 88 83 23 34
Contact Mme Muster.

Rouen   Association Philatélique Yvetotaise ☎ 02 35 56 99 79
Contact M. Bianchini.

	Maison St Sever, 10 rue St Julien	☎ 02 32 81 50 20
	Normandie Philatélie, rue Jeanne d'Arc Stamp collectors' shop.	☎ 02 35 71 61 84

Yoga

Dieppe	Centre Armoni, 48 rue Montigny	☎ 02 35 06 10 81
	Group and individual sessions by appointment.	
Le Havre	ATSCAF	☎ 02 35 48 63 03
Neufchâtel	ASPTT, Dojo David Douillet, rue de la Grande Flandre	☎ 02 32 97 10 56
Rouen	MJC Rive Gauche, place des Faïenciers 🖳 *www.rouencitejeunes.org*	☎ 02 32 81 53 60
Yvetot	Maison de Jeunes et Culture, 9 avenue de Verdun	☎ 02 35 56 89 11

Medical Facilities & Emergency Services

Ambulances

See page 68.

Doctors

English-speakers may like to contact the following doctors:

Dieppe	Cabinet Médical, 2 rue de la Halle au Blé	☎ 02 35 84 15 73
	duty doctor out of hours	☎ 02 32 14 49 00
Le Havre	Dr Brasse, 21 rue Pierre Brossolette	☎ 02 35 42 14 84
	duty doctor out of hours	☎ 02 32 73 32 33
Neufchâtel	Dr Le Cornu, 12 place Marquis	☎ 02 35 93 02 29
	duty doctor out of hours	☎ 02 35 93 15 15
Rouen	Cabinet Médical des Hauts de Grieu, 20 rue Soeur Marie Ernestine	☎ 02 35 71 02 07
	duty doctor out of hours	☎ 02 35 03 03 30

| Yvetot | Dr Le Marie, 3 rue P. & M. Curie | ☎ 02 35 95 12 76 |

Gendarmeries

Dieppe	24 rue Jehan Véron	☎ 02 35 82 04 35
Le Havre	186 boulevard de Strasbourg	☎ 02 35 42 40 65
Neufchâtel	1 rue Gendarmerie	☎ 02 35 93 00 17
Rouen	39 rue Louis Ricard	☎ 02 35 07 89 50
Yvetot	rue Edmond Labbé	☎ 02 35 95 00 17

Health Authority

| General | Caisse Primaire d'Assurance Maladie, 50 avenue Bretagne, Rouen   ☎ 02 35 03 63 63 |

This is the regional office for the whole of Normandy. Other offices are listed below.

Dieppe	boulevard Georges Clémenceau	☎ 02 35 04 78 00
Le Havre	222 boulevard de Strasbourg	☎ 02 32 74 80 00
Neufchâtel	La Maison des Services, boulevard du Maréchal Joffre ☎ 02 35 15 77 60

There's a representative here every Wednesday and Friday from 9am to noon and the second and third Thursday of each month from 9am to noon.

| Yvetot | place de la Gare   ☎ 02 35 95 06 76 |

Open Mondays to Fridays from 8 to 11.45am and 1 to 4.30pm.

Hospitals

The hospitals listed below have an emergency department unless otherwise stated.

Dieppe	Centre Hospitalier, avenue Pasteur	☎ 02 32 14 76 76
Le Havre	Groupe Hospitalier du Havre, 55 bis rue Georges Flaubert	☎ 02 32 73 32 32
Neufchâtel	Centre Hospitalier, route Gaillefontaine	☎ 02 32 97 56 56

| Rouen | Centre Hospitalier Universitaire de Rouen, 1 rue de Germont ☎ 02 32 88 89 90 |

| Yvetot | Hôpital Asselin Hédelin, 14 avenue Foch ☎ 02 35 95 73 00 |

This hospital doesn't have an emergency department.

Nightlife

This section isn't intended to be a definitive guide but gives a wide range of ideas for the department. Prices and opening hours were correct at the time of writing, but it's best to check before travelling long distances.

| Dieppe | l'Abordage, 3 boulevard de Verdun ☎ 02 32 14 48 00 |

This piano bar is within the casino complex on the seafront.

Cambridge Pub, rue de l'Epée ☎ 02 32 90 17 45
Beers (including Guinness) and cocktails.

Dieppe Bowling, Centre Commercial
du Belvédère ☎ 02 32 14 00 20
(near the hospital and Auchan, directly south of the town centre)
Bowling, bar, snacks and cocktails. Open 2pm to 2am (4am at weekends).

Grand Casino, 3 boulevard de Verdun ☎ 02 32 14 48 00
🖥 www.casino-dieppe.fr
On the seafront, this casino has roulette, blackjack, gaming machines, a restaurant and a piano bar.

D'Julz, 22 rue de l'Epée ☎ 02 35 40 04 45
Café/bar open 5pm to 2am.

Au Scottish, rue St Jacques ☎ 02 35 84 13 16
Despite the name, this is an Irish pub open 4pm to 2am, 4am on Saturdays.

le Verrazane, boulevard de Verdun ☎ 02 35 84 31 31
Part of la Présidence hotel, this cocktail bar overlooks the seafront and has a wide selection of drinks, with and without alcohol. Open every day until 2am.

| Le Havre | Bowling, 47 rue François Mazeline ☎ 02 35 24 32 52 |

Bowling complex open Tuesdays to Thursdays 4pm to 1am, Fridays until 2am, Saturdays 2pm to 2am, Sundays 2 to 8pm. Karaoke on Fridays from 9.30pm. The whole complex is non-smoking.

le Camp Gourou, 163 rue Victor
Hugo   ☎ 02 35 22 00 92
Bar/club open Tuesdays to Saturdays 6pm to 2am,
Sundays 7pm to 2am.

le Duplex, Quai George V   ☎ 06 09 40 11 07
Nightclub open Tuesdays to Saturdays 11pm to 4am.
Karaoke Thursdays and Fridays.

le Fun Time, 66 rue Maréchal
Galliéni   ☎ 02 35 42 31 71
Pool, pinball machines, 3D simulators and table football.

Grain d'Sable, 18 boulevard Albert 1er   ☎ 02 35 42 68 78
A lively bar with cocktails, overlooking the sea and open
until 2am.

Lalexia, 26 rue Georges Heuillard   ☎ 02 35 21 28 70
Nightclub.

le Lucky, 51 rue Bernadin de
St Pierre   ☎ 02 35 22 70 63
Open Mondays 5pm to 2am, Tuesdays to Saturdays 6pm to
2am; happy 'hour' 7 to 9pm. Themed evenings and
concerts.

McDaid's, 97 rue Paul Doumer   ☎ 02 35 41 30 40
Irish pub with darts, pool and live music. Open every day
4pm to 2am.

le Siècle, 17 rue des Magasins
Généraux   ☎ 06 88 21 13 71
This club is open Wednesdays to Saturdays. Free entry
Wednesdays.

Fécamp   Casino de Fécamp   ☎ 02 35 28 01 06
Gaming machines, dinner dances and afternoon tea
dances.

Forges les Eaux   Casino de Forges les Eaux, 87 avenue
des Sources   ☎ 02 32 89 50 50
🖳 *www.casinoforges.com*
(south-east of Neufchâtel)
Restaurant, cocktail bar and 260 gaming machines, stud
poker, blackjack, English and French roulette. Open 10am
to 4am daily.

Rouen   Bagatelle, 124 boulevard du 11 Novembre,
Petit Quevilly   ☎ 02 33 72 03 93

This club is open Fridays, Saturdays and bank holidays 11pm to 5am.

le Boston, avenue Aristide Briand ☎ 02 35 52 42 10
Cocktail bar within the Hôtel Mercure.

Bowling du Bois Cany, 22 boulevard Pierre
Brossolette, Grand Quevilly   ☎ 02 32 11 58 58
🖥 www.valcke-bowling.com
(south of the city centre)

la Brocherie, Hameau St Thomas,
Roumare   ☎ 02 35 33 14 14
Disco to the north-west side of the city.

le Crooner, 75 avenue du Mont
Riboudet   ☎ 02 32 10 34 34
Disco.

Exo 7, 13 place de Chartreux   ☎ 02 35 03 32 30
🖥 www.exo7.net
Concert venue and disco with themed evenings: '70s, '80s,
Halloween, etc. Open from 11pm Thursdays to Sundays.

Zénith, avenue des Canadiens,
Grand Quevilly   ☎ 08 91 67 10 17
🖥 www.zenith-de-rouen.com
A major concert venue for the region.

Rouen   St Bernard Café, 1 avenue du
                 Maréchal Foch   ☎ 02 35 95 06 75
                 🖥 www.saintbernardcafe.fr.fm
                 A music bar with cocktails, tequila and drinks by the metre!

Pets

Farriers

General   Hervé Martin, 218 rue Parquet,
                 Froberville   ☎ 02 35 29 33 45
                 (based near Fécamp, on the coast)

Bully   Didier Lefebvre, 9 rue Potiers   ☎ 02 35 93 59 63
                 (just south-west of Neufchâtel)

La Bellière   Bertrand Thierre, 11 route Lavoir ☎ 02 35 09 26 71
                 (north-east of Rouen, near the border of the department)

Horse Dentists

Vets don't deal with teeth rasping and there are specialist equine dentists. You must telephone in advance to be booked onto the next circuit.

General	Bruno Lesage	☎ 06 85 40 06 30

Pet Parlours

See page 79.

SPA

Lintot	SPA de Bolbec, les Côtes	☎ 02 35 38 86 25
Dieppe	SPA de Dieppe, rue Octave Mureau, St Aubin sur Scie	☎ 02 35 84 26 17
Rouen	7 bis avenue Jacques Chastellain	☎ 02 35 70 20 36

Veterinary Clinics

See page 80.

Places to Visit

This section isn't intended to be a definitive guide but gives a wide range of ideas for the department. Prices and opening hours were correct at the time of writing, but it's best to check before travelling long distances.

Animal Parks & Aquariums

Clères   Parc de Clères, 32 avenue du Parc   ☎ 02 35 33 23 08
Zoological gardens set in a historic site with medieval ruins and Renaissance chateau. Animals include antelopes, gibbons and kangaroos with a large collection of birds, some of which are extremely rare. Open every day from March to November.

Beaches & Leisure Parks

General   There are many beaches along the coast of Seine-Maritime including (from west to east) Etretat, Fécamp, la Poterie – Cap d'Antifer, Le Tréport, Mesnil-Val, St Aubin sur Mer, St Valery en Caux, Sotteville sur Mer and Yport (see also **Dieppe** below). Note that these are mostly pebble beaches.

| Cany Barville | Base de Loisirs du Lac de Caniel, route du Lac ☎ 02 35 97 40 55 |

Cany Barville — Base de Loisirs du Lac de Caniel, route du Lac ☎ 02 35 97 40 55
💻 *www.lacdecaniel.fr*
(near the coast, north of Yvetot)
Based around a 70ha (175-acre) lake with waterskiing, pedalos, kayaking, windsurfing, water slide in the summer, skate ramps, playground, nature trails and bungee jumping.

Dieppe — At low tide there's fine sand at the western end of the beach, plus sandy beaches at Pourville only a few km to the west of Dieppe and Puys to the east.

Piscine de la Plage, boulevard du Maréchal Foch ☎ 02 35 06 05 66
Outdoor pool with paddling pools and water slides on the seafront. Open June to August.

Jumièges — Base de Plein Air et de Loisirs, Jumièges le Mesnil ☎ 02 35 37 93 84
Archery, crazy golf, mountain bike trails, sailing, windsurfing and canoeing.

Boat, Train & Wagon Rides

Boat Trips

Caudebec lès Elbeuf — Rives de Seine Croisières, 72 rue Scheurer Kestner ☎ 02 35 78 31 70
💻 *www.rives.seine.croisieres.fr*
Boat cruises on the river Seine between Rouen and Vernon.

Fécamp — Tante Fine, quai Bérigny ☎ 02 35 29 78 01
An old sailing vessel offering sea trips, cruises and discovery days.

Le Havre — Club de Loisirs Nautiques Thalassa, boulevard Clémenceau ☎ 02 35 22 71 5z
💻 *www.clnthalassa.com*
Night sailing from €12 for a three-hour evening trip to either Honfleur or Deauville plus day and weekend trips.

Rouen — Cavalier de la Salle II, quai de Boisguilbert ☎ 02 32 08 32 40
From April to October this boat departs at 2.30pm every Saturday for a one-and-a-half-hour journey on the river Seine.

Train Rides

Dieppe

Petit Train Touristique ☎ 02 35 04 56 08
This 'train' takes you around the town giving a commentary as you pass places of interest. Operates between April and September, departing from outside the tourist office for a tour of around an hour. €6 for adults, €4 for children up to ten years old.

Rouen

le Petit Train de Rouen, place de la
Cathédrale ☎ 02 32 18 40 23
This 'train' takes you on a discovery tour of the old and picturesque parts of the city. Departures every hour from 10am to 5pm, April to October.

Chateaux

Ermenouville

Château du Mesnil Geoffroy ☎ 02 35 57 12 77
🖳 www.chateau-mesnil-geoffroy.com
This 18th century chateau, privately owned by Prince and Princess Kayali, is exceptionally furnished. Outside there's a large rose garden with over 2,000 roses. A maze and the 12ha (30 acres) of park and gardens have been recently restored to the original plans. Open May to September Fridays to Sundays and bank holidays 2.30 to 6pm.

Gonfreville
l'Orcher

Château d'Orcher ☎ 02 35 45 45 91
This chateau dates back to the tenth century and has a superb view over the bay. Open July to mid-August Fridays to Wednesdays 2 to 6pm. Entry €5, under ten-year-olds free.

St Maurice
d'Etelan

Château d'Etelan ☎ 02 35 39 91 27
Once the site of a fortress, of which only the cellar, fortress wall and guard century remain, the chateau is a flamboyant gothic-style building with unique windows and statues, completed in 1494. Open mid-July to the end of August Wednesdays to Mondays 10.30am to 12.30pm and 2.30 to 6.30pm. Adults €4, under ten-year-olds free.

St Pierre de
Manneville

Manoir de Villers, 30 route de
Sahurs ☎ 02 35 32 07 02
🖳 www.manoirdevillers.com
The timbered manor house was built in the 16th century and has been in the same family since 1764. The park has a chapel and small chalet and is open from May to September Saturdays to Wednesdays 2.30 to 5.30pm and plays host to exhibitions, shows and art courses throughout the year. The manor is open April to October Saturdays 2.30 to 5.30pm, Sundays and bank holidays 3 to 6.30pm.

Adults €7 park and house, €6 park only; children €3 park and house (no reduction for park only).

Tourville sur Arques	Château de Miromesnil ☎ 02 35 85 02 80 Dating from the 15th century and rebuilt during the 17th century this turreted chateau has a beautiful park with a chapel and an unusual kitchen garden.

Miscellaneous

Ardouval

Val-Ygot V1 Site, Forêt d'Eawy
On the edge of the Eawy forest this site includes 13 concrete buildings and a section of the launch ramp for the V1 flying bombs used on London by the Germans in the Second World War. This is the only such site and there's free access all year round.

Bolleville

Trace Viking, le Clos Masure de Bolleville, Hameau de Guillerville ☎ 02 35 31 21 83
🖳 www.traceviking.fr
A reconstruction of Viking life complete with a typical village, boats and crafts. Open May to October Tuesdays to Fridays 10am to 6pm, weekends and bank holidays 10am to 7pm. Adults €8, children €6, under six-year-olds free.

Jumièges

Abbaye de Jumièges ☎ 02 35 37 24 02
This abbey was founded in 654 and pillaged during the Viking raids, regaining its splendour under the Dukes of Normandy. Confiscated during the Revolution, it was then used as a stone quarry and has stood as majestic ruins ever since. Open mid-April to mid-September every day 9.30am to 7pm; mid-September to mid-April and Easter weekend 9.30am to 1pm and 2.30 to 5.30pm. Closed 1st January, 1st May, 1st and 11th November and 25th December. Guided tours available and tour information in English. Night time illuminated tours from Easter to September.

Les Loges

Vélo-Rail, Gare des Loges ☎ 02 35 29 49 61
Pedal along the old railway line between Etretat and les Loges on specially designed platforms.

Massy

Artmazia, 25 route de Neufchâtel ☎ 02 35 93 17 12
🖳 www.artmazia.com
(just south-west of Neufchâtel)
The longest permanent natural maze in the world with 3,500 copper beech trees and over 3km (2mi) of paths, with sculptures and various attractions along the way. Open May to September Wednesdays to Mondays 2.30pm to 6.30pm. Adults €5, children €3.

| St Maclou de Folleville | Moulin de l'Arbalète ☎ 02 35 32 67 11 |

St Maclou de Folleville **Moulin de l'Arbalète** ☎ 02 35 32 67 11
This mill is still used to grind cereals, fresh bread is baked and the water mill also produces a small amount of electricity. Tours from April to 1st November on Wednesdays, weekends and bank holidays 2 to 6pm (July and August every day). Adults €3.50, children €2.

Museums, Memorials & Galleries

Dieppe **Château-Musée de Dieppe, rue de Chastes** ☎ 02 35 84 19 76
(at the top of the hill on the west side of town)
There's a collection of ancient ivory carvings, paintings by Boudin, Pissarro, Braque and other works inspired by Dieppe. Open June to September daily 10am to noon and 2 to 6pm; October to May Wednesdays to Mondays 10am to noon and 2 to 5pm. Adults €3, 12 to 17-year-olds €1.50.

Cité de la Mer, rue de l'Asile Thomas ☎ 02 35 06 93 20
🖥 www.estrancitedelamer.free.fr
Exhibits explain the history of boat building and the fishing industry along this part of the coast, with a marine biology area and a small aquarium. Guided visits with an interpreter are available by appointment. Open every day 10am to noon and 2 to 6pm (till 6.30pm in July and August).

Duclair **Musée Août 1944, Château du Taillis, Hameau St Paul** ☎ 02 35 37 95 46
This museum is a reminder of the last battles on the river Seine before the Liberation with the use of photographs, military equipment and documents. Open mid-April to 1st November Wednesdays to Sundays 10am to noon and 2 to 5pm.

Eu **Musée Traditions Verrières, rue Sémichon** ☎ 02 35 86 21 91
The history of glass and the development of glass making techniques from blowing to the semi-automatic machines used today. Open April to October Tuesdays, weekends and bank holidays 2.30 to 6pm (July to September also open Wednesdays).

Fécamp **Palais Bénédictine, 110 rue Alexandre le Grand** ☎ 02 35 10 26 10
This museum displays the art collected by the self-styled Alexandre Le Grand throughout his life and the distillery presents the history and secrets of the Benedictine liqueur with a tasting available at the end of the tour. Adults €5.20, 10 to 18-year-olds €2.60, under tens free.

Le Havre	**Musée Malraux, 2 boulevard Clémenceau** ☎ 02 35 19 62 62 Fine arts collection including Impressionist paintings and works by Boudin. Open Mondays and Wednesdays to Fridays 11am to 6pm, weekends 11am to 7pm. Adults €3.80, under 18s free.
	Musée d'Histoire Naturelle, place du Vieux Marché ☎ 02 35 41 37 28 This natural history museum includes collections of minerals and ornithology. Open Mondays, Thursdays and Fridays 2.30 to 5.30pm, Wednesdays and weekends 10 to 11.30am and 2.30 to 5.30pm. Free entry.
Martainville Epreville	**Musée d'Art Traditional, Château de Martainville** ☎ 02 35 23 44 70 This 15th century chateau has 20 rooms tracing the rural way of life in Normandy from the 15th to the 19th century with farm interiors, clothes, headdresses and a large collection of everyday items, arts, crafts and furniture. Open 10am to 12.30pm and 2 to 6pm (5pm in winter); closed Tuesdays and some bank holidays.
Notre Dame de Bondeville	**Corderie Vallois, 185 route de Dieppe** ☎ 02 35 74 35 35 (just outside Rouen) The former Vallois rope works has been carefully restored and the machinery operates once again, with demonstrations of the manufacture of twisted and braided rope. Open daily 1.30 to 6pm (closed some bank holidays).
Rouen	**Musée des Antiquités, 198 rue Beauvoisine** ☎ 02 35 98 55 10 A museum of antiques, sculptures and artefacts dating from 2000BC. Exhibitions include The Bronze Age, The Iron Age, The Gallo-Roman Period and The Vikings. Open Mondays and Wednesdays to Saturdays 10am to 12.15pm and 1.30 to 5.30pm, Sundays 2 to 6pm.
	Musée des Beaux Arts, Esplanade Marcel Duchamp ☎ 02 35 71 28 40 Various collections including Impressionism and contemporary art. Open 10am to 6pm. Adults €3, children €3.
St Nicolas d'Aliermont	**Musée de l'Horlogerie, 323 rue Edouard Cannevel** ☎ 02 35 04 53 98 A museum of clocks and time pieces. Open Thursdays 9am to noon and Fridays by appointment. Entry €2.

Parks, Gardens & Forests

Caudebec en
Caux

Forêt du Trait Maulévrier
Stretching along the banks of the river Seine this 3,000ha (7,500-acre) forest offers many paths for walkers and cyclists and has some good vantage points over the Seine valley.

Le Havre

Jardin Japonaise, quai Lamandé   ☎ 02 32 74 04 04
Japanese garden with guided tours available lasting an hour and a half, advance booking needed with the tourist office for the tours. Open to the public for guided tours only, mid-May to mid-September Sundays at 3pm. Adults €6, under 12-year-olds €4. Booking required.

Serre Tropicale, rue Pierre Mendès France (Forêt de Montgeon)
(north side of the town)
These tropical gardens are open May to October Mondays to Fridays 2 to 6.30pm, Saturdays 9am to 12.30pm and 2 to 6.30pm, Sundays and bank holidays 2 to 6.30pm; November to April until 5pm weekdays and 5.30pm weekends and bank holidays.

St Saëns

Forêt Domaniale d'Eawy
Stretching north from Saint Saëns towards the coast, this forest 7,000ha (17,500 acres) between the valleys of Varenne and Béthune and includes a beech plantation and the base where V1 rockets were launched at Ardouval during the Second World War (see **Miscellaneous** on page 337).

Regional Produce

Etretat

Fromagerie le Valaine, Manoir de Cateuil, route du Havre   ☎ 02 35 27 14 02
🖥 *www.etretat.net/le-valaine*
This is a goat farm that shows the breeding and feeding of these animals, milk processing and cheese making, with the opportunity to taste the products at the end. The shop sells the cheese as well as farmhouse cider, ice cream and chocolates. Open March to November every day 9am to 12.30pm and 2 to 7pm. Guided tours, lasting around an hour, at 11am from Easter to June and September to November on Sundays and bank holidays at 11am; July and August Saturdays to Wednesdays and bank holidays. Adults €5, 8 to17-year-olds €4, under eights free.

St Crespin

la Ferme du Manoir de Camp   ☎ 02 35 83 30 07
🖥 *www.manoirdecamp.com*

(south of Dieppe, from the N27 take the D149 towards Longueville sur Scie)
This angora goat farm is open to visitors every day from 10am to 6pm and angora/mohair products are for sale including jumpers and socks.

St Maclou la Brière
les Vergers de la Brière, route de Fauville   ☎ 02 35 27 41 09
A living museum of apples and cider with a collection of old equipment once used take make the cider of the Pays de Caux, explanations of the techniques used by the producers and a tasting of the finished product. Open July and August every day 10am to noon and 2 to 6pm (bank holidays 2 to 6pm only; closed 1st January, 1st May and 25th December).

Professional Services

The following offices have an English-speaking professional.

Accountants

Rouen   M. Lamy, 52 rampe Bouvreuil   ☎ 02 35 88 62 00

Solicitors & Notaires

Rouen   Maître Puyt, 3 rue Charles de Gaulle, Notre Dame de Bondeville   ☎ 02 32 82 85 35
(the north-west outskirts of the city)

Religion

Anglican Services in English

Rouen   All Saintes, 16 rue Duguay Trouin   ☎ 02 35 74 28 49
Contact Revd. Bernard Vignot for details of services.

Catholic Churches

Dieppe   Eglise St Jacques
Presbytère, 4 rue Sainte Catherine   ☎ 02 35 84 21 65

Le Havre   Cathédrale Notre Dame
Services on Saturdays at 6pm and Sundays at 10am.

Neufchâtel   Eglise Notre Dame
Services on Saturdays at 7pm and Sundays at 10am.

Rouen	Cathédrale Notre Dame de Rouen
	Services Tuesdays to Saturdays at 8 and 10am, Sundays at 8.30am, 10am and noon.
Yvetot	St Pierre d'Yvetot
	Services on Sundays at 9.45 and 11.15am.

Protestant Churches

Selected churches are listed below.

Dieppe	Eglise Evangélique, rue de la Providence, les Vertus, St Aubin sur Scie	☎ 02 35 40 27 45
	Eglise Réformée, 76 rue de la Barre	☎ 02 35 84 24 22
Le Havre	Eglise Protestante, 47 rue Anatole France	☎ 02 35 45 52 26
	Evangélique du Havre, 39 avenue Rouget de Lisle	☎ 02 35 48 80 70
Rouen	Eglise Réformée de Rouen, 46 rue Buffon	☎ 02 35 71 08 66
	Pasteur	☎ 02 35 71 44 30
	Eglise Evangélique Baptiste, 50 rue Albert Camus	☎ 02 35 63 38 86
	Eglise Evangélique Protestante, 17 rue Achille Flaubert	☎ 02 35 71 64 22
Yvetot	Eglise Protestante Evangélique, rue de l'Avalasse	☎ 02 35 56 51 00

Synagogues

Le Havre	38 rue Victor Hugo	☎ 02 35 21 14 59

Restaurants

See page 87.

Rubbish & Recycling

See page 88.

Shopping

When available, the opening hours of various shops have been included, but these are liable to change and so it's advisable to check before travelling long distances to any specific shop.

Architectural Antiques

Yvetot   Matériaux et Traditions, 9 rue du Vieux
                       Sainte Marie   ☎ 02 35 95 86 97
                       💻 *www.materiaux-traditions.com*
                       All types of reclaimed materials included oak beams and
                       stone.

Department Stores

Le Havre   Printemps, 32 avenue René Coty   ☎ 02 32 74 84 84
                       Open Mondays to Fridays 9.30am to 7pm, Saturdays
                       9.30am to 7.30pm.

Rouen   Galeries Lafayette, 25 rue Grand
                       Pont   ☎ 02 35 88 40 09
                       Open Mondays to Saturdays 9am to 7.30pm.

                       Printemps, 4 rue du Gros Horloge   ☎ 02 32 76 32 32
                       Open Mondays to Saturdays 9am to 7pm.

DIY

See page 95.

Frozen Food

Dieppe   Picard, 91 avenue Gambetta   ☎ 02 35 82 56 52
                       💻 *www.picard.fr*
                       Open Mondays 3 to 7.30pm, Tuesdays to Fridays 9.30am
                       to 12.30pm and 2.30 to 7.30pm, Saturdays 9am to 7.30pm.

Le Havre   Picard, 12 place des Halles   ☎ 02 35 43 67 68
                       Open Mondays 2.30 to 7.30pm, Tuesdays to Fridays 9am
                       to 12.30pm and 2.30 to 7.30pm, Saturdays 9am to 1pm
                       and 2 to 7.30pm, Sundays 10am to 12.30pm.

Rouen   Picard, 8 rue Guillaume le
                       Conquérant   ☎ 02 35 88 66 01
                       Open Mondays 3 to 7.30pm, Tuesdays to Fridays 9am to
                       12.30pm and 3 to 7.30pm, Saturdays 9am to 7.30pm.

Garden Centres

See page 95.

Hypermarkets

See **Retail Parks** on page 346.

Kitchens & Bathrooms

See page 96.

Markets

Dieppe	Tuesday and Thursday mornings by the Eglise St Jacques.
	All day Saturdays in Grande Rue.
	Wednesday mornings at avenue Boucher de Perthes, Janval.
	Thursday mornings, place Henri Dunant, Neuville.
Le Havre	There are 15 markets across the town, including the following:
	Wednesday and Friday mornings at place du Château d'Eau, Aplemont.
	Friday mornings at place du Dr Levesque, Bléville.
	Saturday mornings, avenue du 8 Mai 1945, Caucriauville.
	All day Saturdays at rue Demidoff.
	Tuesdays, Thursdays and Saturdays 8.30am to 7pm at cours de la République, by the station.
Neufchâtel	There's a fish market on Wednesday mornings and a traditional market on Saturday mornings.
Rouen	There are 21 markets across the city each week, including: Tuesday all day markets at place St Marc, place des Emmurées and place de la Calende.
	Wednesday mornings at place du Vieux Marché and Ile Lacroix.

Thursday mornings at place du Vieux Marché, St Clément and place des Emmurées.

Friday all day markets at place St Marc and place de la Calende.

Saturday all day markets at place St Marc and place des Emmurées.

Sunday mornings at place St Marc and place du Vieux Marché.

Yvetot   There's a large market on Wednesdays and a smaller market Saturday mornings. The second weekend in March there's a large horticultural market.

Music

Dieppe   la Boîte à Musique, 27 rue de la Halle
au Blé   ☎ 02 35 84 17 47

Le Havre   Music Partitions, 9 rue Paul Doumer ☎ 02 35 21 06 88

Rouen   Music Mélody, 51 rue Juifs   ☎ 02 35 89 77 48
Sale, hire and repair of musical instruments.

Yvetot   Vuylsteke Musique, 10 rue des
Victoires   ☎ 02 35 95 21 41

Organic Produce

Dieppe   l'Asticot Bio, rue d'Ecosse   ☎ 02 35 84 62 27

Le Havre   Marché Bio, 5 rue St Jacques Notre
Dame   ☎ 02 35 21 23 53
Open Tuesdays and Saturdays 10am to 7.30pm,
Wednesdays to Fridays 10am to 1pm and 3.30 to 7.30pm.

Rouen   Gourmand' Grain, 3 rue du Petit
Salut   ☎ 02 35 98 15 74
This organic shop includes a lunchtime organic and
vegetarian restaurant. Open Tuesdays to Saturdays 9am
to 7pm.

Yvetot   Biotéro, 23 rue du Vieux Sainte
Marie   ☎ 02 35 95 14 78

Retail Parks

Dieppe   Centre Belvédère   ☎ 02 32 90 52 00
🖥 *www.auchan.fr*
(on the south side of the town, off the ring road)
The Auchan hypermarket is open Mondays to Saturdays
8.30am to 10pm and the complex includes a bar, dry
cleaner's, photo booth, hairdresser's, chemist's, mobile
phone shop, jeweller's and computer games shop. The
shops in the complex are generally open shorter hours than
the hypermarket, closing at around 8pm. Main shops
include:
- Aubert – baby goods;
- Auchan – hypermarket;
- Buffalo Grill – steak house-style restaurant;
- BUT – furniture;
- Conforama – furniture and household electrical goods;
- Cuisines Schmidt – kitchens;
- Darty – electrical goods;
- Décathlon – sports goods;
- GP Decors – wallpaper and paint;
- Mr Meuble – furniture.

Le Havre   Montivilliers   ☎ 02 32 79 64 00
(on the north-west side of the town)
Main shops include:
- Auchan – hypermarket;
- Chantemur – wallpaper and paint;
- Chaussland – shoes;
- Darty – electrical goods;
- Gémo – clothes;
- Leroy Merlin – DIY superstore;
- Mondial Tissues – fabric shop;
- Picard – frozen food;
- Toys R Us – toys.

Rouen   Centre Bois Cany, Grand Quevilly   ☎ 02 35 18 34 34
🖥 *www.geant.fr*
(south of the city in the direction of Le Havre)
This hypermarket is open 9am to 9pm Mondays to
Saturdays. The complex includes a pizzeria, shoe and
clothes shops, butcher's, newsagent's, jeweller's, dry
cleaner's and a bar. Main shops include:
- Chantemur – wallpaper and paint;
- Géant – hypermarket;
- Gémo – clothes;
- Jardiland – garden centre;
- Jouetland – toys;
- Matt Sports – sports goods;
- Mr Bricolage – DIY.

Rouen   le Clos aux Antes, Tourville la
                      Rivière   ☎ 02 32 96 45 45
                      (south of the city, at junction 21 ofthe A13)
                      The hypermarket is open 9am to 9pm Mondays to
                      Saturdays (till 10pm Fridays), while the shops within the
                      complex are open Mondays to Thursdays 10am to 8pm,
                      Fridays until 9pm, Saturdays 9am to 8pm. The complex
                      includes several restaurants with a central seating area,
                      mobile phone and clothes shops, opticians', jewellers' and
                      photographic shops. Main shops include:
                      ● Animalis – pet shop;
                      ● Bébé 9 – baby goods;
                      ● BUT – furniture;
                      ● Carrefour – hypermarket;
                      ● Darty – electrical goods;
                      ● Décathlon – sports goods;
                      ● Leroy Merlin – DIY;
                      ● Maison Literie – beds;
                      ● Picard – frozen food;
                      ● Toys R Us – toys.

Second-hand Goods

See page 97.

Shopping Centres

Le Havre   Espace Coty, 22 rue Casimir Périer
                      🖳 *www.espacecoty.com*
                      A modern shopping centre with over 80 shops and
                      restaurants, open Mondays to Saturdays 9.30am to 8pm.

Wines & Spirits

See page 98.

Sports & Outdoor Activities

The following is just a selection of the activities available, the large towns
having a wide range of sports facilities. Full details are available from the
tourist office or the *mairie*.

Aerial Sports

Ballooning

Rouen   Montgolfières en Normandie, 28 rue
                      de Fontenelle   ☎ 02 35 12 08 99
                      🖳 *www.montgolfieres.fr.st*

Flights are early in the morning or late in the afternoon and, including preparation and recovery, take up to four hours with a minimum flight time of one hour. Prices include champagne and a certificate.

Flying

Boos
Héli Evénements, Aéroport de Rouen Vallée de Seine, Hangar D2, rue Maryse Bastié   ☎ 06 26 26 37 47
Introductory flights and tourist flights from €60 per person (four people) for quarter of an hour.

Dieppe
Aéro Club Dieppois   ☎ 02 35 84 86 55
(south of the town)

Aérodrome de Dieppe   ☎ 06 14 22 15 93
Sightseeing helicopter flights from €35 per person; minimum of four people.

Le Havre
Aviation Service Normandie, Aéroport du Havre-Octeville   ☎ 02 35 44 89 95
Flying school, introductory flights and tourist flights from €43 per person (three people).

Yvetot
Canu Air, Aérodrome d'Yvetot, route de Cany   ☎ 02 35 56 43 05
Flying school, trial flights from €60 and tourist flights over the region from €40 per person.

Parachuting

Dieppe
Air Libre Parachutisme   ☎ 02 35 82 38 68

Le Havre
Aéroclub du Havre Jean Maridor   ☎ 02 35 48 36 91

Archery

Le Havre
Compagnie Havraise de Tir à l'Arc, Gymnase de Rouelles, 151 rue Adèle Robert   ☎ 02 35 49 59 14

Rouen
ARC Rouen Club, Espace de la Petite Bouverie, 20 allée Pierre de Coubertin   ☎ 02 35 80 57 80

Yvetot
Les Archers du Roy d'Yvetot, Gymnase du Lycée Jean XXII   ☎ 02 35 95 09 04
Contact M. Sevestre.

Badminton

Dieppe
CO FSGT   ☎ 02 35 82 09 97

| Le Havre | ASPTT, Gymnase Jean Moulin, Mare Rouge | ☎ 02 35 44 64 12 |

| Rouen | MJC Rive Gauche, place des Faïenciers
🖳 *www.rouencitejeunes.org* | ☎ 02 32 81 53 60 |

| Yvetot | Yvetot Badminton Club
Contact M. Cardonne. | ☎ 02 35 95 47 78 |

Boules/Pétanque

| Dieppe | Club Lyonnais | ☎ 02 35 76 93 26 |

| Le Havre | Amicale Bouliste de la Commune, place de la Commune | ☎ 02 35 21 52 08 |

| Neufchâtel | Pétanque Neufchâteloise, Terrain de Boules, rue du Moulin Bleu
This club meets all year and welcome all levels. Contact M. Pridot. | ☎ 02 35 93 76 99 |

| Rouen | Rouen Sapins Pétanque
Contact M. Maurcot. | ☎ 02 35 98 35 67 |

| Yvetot | Amicale Bouliste Yvetotaise
Contact M. Thorn | ☎ 02 35 56 62 46 |

Canoeing & Kayaking

| Auffay | Canoë Nature, Moulin de la Gare
🖳 *www.canoe-nature76.asso.fr*
(directly south of Dieppe and west of Neufchâtel) | ☎ 02 35 34 33 70 |

| Le Havre | KHO, Base Hardouin, boulevard Clémenceau
Sea kayaking. Training every Sunday all year round from 9am to noon, plus Thursday evenings 9pm at Le Havre and Tuesdays at Fécamp mid-May to mid-October. November to April training indoor at the municipal swimming pool. | ☎ 02 35 44 33 29 |

| Rouen | Canoë Club Normand, Espace Jacques Anquetil, Ile Lacrois
🖳 *www.ccnrouen.org*
This canoeing club offers canoe hire in July and August. | ☎ 02 35 89 09 12 |

Climbing

| Dieppe | CO FSGT | ☎ 02 35 82 09 97 |

| Le Havre | Amis de la FSGT, Gymnase Louis Blanc, rue Louis Blanc ☎ 02 35 45 10 16 |

| Rouen | Gymnase Docteur Dévé, rue du Docteur Dévé ☎ 02 35 72 59 22 Two climbing walls for beginners to competition standard. |

Cycling

| General | avenue Verte
This is a 40km (25mi) route from Dieppe to Forges les Eaux. Following an old railway line, it's open to everyone on foot, horseback, bike and rollerskates. |

Dieppe	Cyclo Club Dieppois ☎ 02 32 80 40 52
	Club des Pingouins ☎ 02 35 04 13 Mountain biking club.
	Loca Cycles, 17 rue d'Issoire ☎ 02 35 06 07 40 Traditional and mountain bikes for hire.

| Fécamp | There's a mountain bike base at Fécamp with 100km of routes for various levels of experience. A leaflet available free from the tourist office gives details of a cycle route along the coast from Fécamp to St Valery en Caux. |
| | Maison du Tourisme de Fécamp ☎ 02 35 28 51 01 |

Le Havre	Avenir Cycliste de la Porte Océane du Havre ☎ 02 35 20 38 67 Road cycling and velodrome.
	Club Alpin Français ☎ 02 35 43 01 46 🖥 www.caf-lehavre.com Mountain biking.
	Office de Tourisme, 186 boulevard Clémenceau ☎ 02 32 74 04 04 Bike hire.
	Vélocéane, at the beach car park ☎ 06 24 66 05 94 Bike hire 10am to 6pm every day in July and August, at weekends the rest of the year.

| Neufchâtel | There are seven circuits in the surrounding area suitable for mountain biking routes from 25 to 35 km, |

with four levels of difficulty. Details available from the tourist office.

Office de Tourisme, 6 place Notre Dame ☎ 02 35 93 22 96

Le Cyclotourisme, ASPTT ☎ 02 35 93 05 43
This cycle group departs from rue Cauchoise, by the France Télécom shop, Sunday mornings at 8.30am and Tuesdays and Thursdays at 2pm. Contact Yves Prevel for more information.

Rouen   VTT Rouen, contact M. Sohier ☎ 02 35 98 57 35
✉ *vtt.rouen@wanadoo.fr*

Yvetot   The tourist office has details of three routes from 20km to 40km.

Office de Tourism, 8 place Joffre ☎ 02 35 95 08 40
💻 *www.yvetot.fr*

Roue Libre Yvetotaise ☎ 02 35 95 21 56
Contact M. Roger.

Fencing

Dieppe   Fines Lames de Dieppe ☎ 02 35 83 28 80

Le Havre   Salle d'Armes du Havre, Multisport de la Gare, rue Philippe Lebon ☎ 02 35 19 61 37
Leisure and competitive groups.

Rouen   Cercle d'Escrime de Rouen, Gymnase des Cotonniers, place des Cotonniers ☎ 02 35 03 90 46
✉ *info@cercle-escrime-rouen.com*
Dedicated fencing hall. Contact M. Fausser.

Fishing

Maps are available from fishing shops and tourist offices showing local fishing waters, prices of fishing permits and dates of the fishing season. If there's a lake locally, permits will be on sale in nearby *tabacs* and fishing shops and at the *mairie*. A 15-day holiday pass costs around €30, a daily pass €11.

General   Christophe Raimbourg ☎ 02 35 83 80 16
A fishing guide, who can accompany you on river or sea trout fishing trips.

Fédération des Associations pour la Pêche
de la Seine Maritime, 11 cours
Clémenceau, Rouen   ☎ 02 35 62 01 55

Arques la Bataille   la Gaule Arquoise, Argues Loisirs   ☎ 02 35 85 87 79
One hundred hectares (250 acres) of waterways with day,
holiday and annual permits available.

Dancourt   la Truite du Buisson, le Buisson   ☎ 02 35 93 04 09
Private fishing, open from 7.30am to noon and 2 to 6.30pm.
Half day €10, full day €18. Bar open 7.30am to 8pm.

Dieppe   Cercle de la Voile de Dieppe, quai
du Carénage   ☎ 02 35 84 32 99
⌨ *www.cvdieppe.org*
Sea fishing.

Fécamp   Bateau La Ville de Fécamp, 15
rue Vicomté   ☎ 02 35 28 99 53
Sea-fishing trips. €32 for four hours.

Rouen   Mini Club de l'Ile Lacroix   ☎ 02 35 06 02 09
Contact M. Cuvier.

Football

Le Havre   Havre Athlétique Club Football, Stade Delaune,
94 rue d'Armenonville   ☎ 02 35 54 62 62

Neufchâtel   Football Club Neufchâtelois, route
de Londinières   ☎ 02 35 93 27 32
Indoor training in bad weather with teams from under 15s to
seniors. Matches on Saturdays or Sundays depending on
the category.

Rouen   Football Club Rouen 1899, Stade Robert
Diochon, 48 avenue des Canadiens,
Petit Quevilly   ☎ 02 32 81 36 36

Yvetot   Yvetot Athlétic Club   ☎ 02 35 56 51 50
Contact M. Joignant.

Golf

Dieppe   Golf Dieppe Pourville, 51 route de
Pourville   ☎ 02 35 84 25 05
⌨ *www.golf-dieppe.com*
18 holes, 5,763m, par 70, plus five practice holes. Open all
year. Green fees €27 to €36 mid-week, €33 to €45

weekends and bank holidays. Pro shop, restaurant and bilingual reception, lessons and courses available.

Etretat

Association Sportive Golf d'Etretat, route du Havre ☎ 02 35 27 04 89
🖳 *www.golfetretat.com*
18 holes, 6,073m, par 72. Open all year except Tuesdays from September to March. 9am to 7pm April to August, 5pm the rest of the year.

Octeville sur Mer

Golf du Havre, hameau de St Supplix ☎ 02 35 46 36 50
✉ *golf.le-havre@wanadoo.fr*
18 holes, 5,995m, par 72. Open mid-March to the end of October every day 8.30am to 7pm; November to mid-March Mondays, Wednesdays to Fridays 9.30am to 4pm, weekends 9am to 5.30pm. Booking advisable for the weekends. Restaurant closed Tuesdays.

Hockey

Le Havre

Havre Athlétique Club Hockey Club, Stade des Réservoirs, rue Maurice Genevoix ☎ 02 35 48 60 33
Field hockey.

HAC Hockey sur Glace, Patinoire du Havre, 106 rue Louis Blanc ☎ 02 35 49 11 66
Ice hockey.

Havre Roller Hockey, Gymnase du Bois de Bléville, 65 rue des Ponts ☎ 02 35 21 23 73

Rouen

MJC Rive Gauche, place des Faïenciers ☎ 02 32 81 53 60
🖳 *www.rouencitejeunes.org*
Roller hockey.

Patinoire Ile Lacroix ☎ 02 35 47 02 11
Ice Hockey.

Yvetot

Hockey Club Yvetotais ☎ 02 35 96 70 27
Field hockey.

Horse Riding

Dieppe

Haras des Vertus ☎ 02 35 82 55 31

Le Havre

Centre Equestre Pony Club de Montivilliers, Rond-point de la Belle Etoile, 59 rue Fontaine la Mallet, Montivilliers ☎ 02 35 55 59 59

🖳 *www.centre-equestre.fr*
An outdoor and an Olympic size indoor riding school,
courses, stabling and introductory sessions for all ages
from two years.

Mesnières en Bray	Poney Club de Mesnières, Ferme du Bois de la Ville, le Rambure (north of Neufchâtel) Lessons and courses.	☎ 02 35 94 42 16
Rouen	Poney Club, 1215 rue Herbeuse, Bois Guillaume (north of the city) Lessons, courses and hacks.	☎ 02 35 59 97 73
Yvetot	Centre Equestre l'Etrier de Mézerville, 20 rue des Moutons Introduction to riding and hacks.	☎ 02 35 56 59 12

Judo

Dieppe	Judo Club de Dieppe	☎ 02 35 84 69 49
Le Havre	Association Sportive Georges Bernanos, 2 rue Théophile Gautier 🖳 *www.judobernanos.com* Judo, baby judo, jujitsu and similar disciplines.	☎ 02 35 44 66 37
Neufchâtel	Judo CSB Neufchâtel, Dojo David Douillet, rue de la Grande Flandre Classes for all ages from five years on Monday evenings and Saturday afternoons. Contact M. Lemaître.	☎ 06 07 79 65 76
Rouen	MJC Rive Gauche, place des Faïenciers 🖳 *www.rouencitejeunes.org*	☎ 02 32 81 53 60

Kite Flying

Dieppe	Cerf Volant Club de Dieppe	☎ 02 35 06 15 56

Motorsports

Cars

Dieppe	Dieppe Rallye, 17 rue Montigny	☎ 02 35 84 52 30
Neufchâtel	Ecurie Brayonne Automobile	☎ 02 35 84 01 87

This motor club promotes and organises car rallies through the countryside. Contact M. Petit.

Karting

Anneville
Circuit Lucien Lebret ☎ 02 35 37 04 14
(15km/10mi west of Rouen)
Standard circuit with karts for 12 to 15-year-olds and more powerful ones for adults. Prices from €12 for children/€15 for adult for ten minutes.

Dieppe
Euro Dieppe Karting, Zone Louis Delaporte, Rouxmesnil-Bouteille ☎ 02 35 06 13 13
Indoor and outdoor circuits open in the summer every day from 2pm to midnight (1am on Saturdays). From €11 for ten minutes.

Rouen
Rouen Espace Karting, 149 chemin du Croisset ☎ 02 32 12 34 05
🖥 www.rouen-espace-karting.fr
Indoor track with karts for adults.

Motorbikes

Le Havre
Moto Club du Havre ☎ 02 76 80 45 90

Londinières
le Domaine de Londinières, Terrain de Cross ☎ 02 35 94 45 34
🖥 www.ledomainedelondinieres.com
This is a large site for motocross with individual instruction for €30 per hour or three-hour group sessions for €30 per person. Quad and bike hire by the quarter hour.

Quad Bikes

Auffay
Quad Nature, Moulin de la Gare ☎ 02 35 34 33 70
🖥 www.quad-nature76.asso.fr
(directly south of Dieppe and west of Neufchâtel)
Open every day by appointment for quad rides across the countryside.

Dieppe
Quad Dieppois 76, Rocade d'Arques la Bataille ☎ 02 35 85 64 37
Trips out in the countryside or on tracks for children and adults. Open Fridays and Saturdays 2 to 7pm, Sundays and bank holidays 10am to 7pm (longer hours plus Thursdays and Mondays in July and August). One hour trip €30 per person; ten minutes on the track from €5 for a child, €10 for an adult.

Paintball

Fécamp | d'Arbre en Arbre, le Parc du Val aux Clercs, avenue du Maréchal de Lattre de Tassigny ☎ 02 35 10 84 83
Adventure centre with paintball and tree top adventure circuits.

Sotteville sous le Val | Toro Distribution SARL, 62 rue Armand Barbès ☎ 02 35 03 08 82
🖳 *www.toro-distribution.com*
Everything to do with paintballing: grounds, competitions, beginners' sessions and all the equipment needed for sale or hire.

Potholing

Le Havre | Spéléo Club du Roule ☎ 02 35 20 16 73
✉ *scroule@tele2.fr*

Rouen | Club Alpin Français ☎ 02 35 95 51 11
Contact M. Thepaut.

Rollerskating

General | avenue Verte
This is a 40km (25mi) route from Dieppe to Forges les Eaux, following an old railway line. Open to everyone on foot, horseback, bike and rollerskates.

Dieppe | Rando Rollers.
From April to September roller groups depart from the Fontaine du Quai Henri IV at 8.30pm on the last Friday of the month.

There's a skate park on the seafront off the boulevard de Verdun, and the smooth tarmac promenade is ideal for rollerskating.

Le Havre | Rondes Rollers Havraises, Sport Maximum, 122 boulevard Clémenceau ☎ 02 35 21 09 05
The last Sunday of each month there's a group skating session departing from the beach at 10am and the second Friday of each month there's a night time trip departing from the beach at 9pm.

Rouen | Piste Louis Jouvet, rue Albert Dupuis ☎ 02 35 60 13 02
A 200m skating circuit for training and competitions.

There's a skate park at 1 rue Malétra.

Yvetot	There's a skate park at rue Robert Lemonnier, near the Leclerc supermarket.	

Shooting

Dieppe	Tir Club, Rouxmesnil	☎ 02 35 06 04 74
Le Havre	Union Rouellaise de Tir, Stand de Tir, 151 rue Adèle Robert	☎ 02 35 49 23 87
Yvetot	Société de Tir, l'Union, rue du Champ de Courses	☎ 02 35 95 56 40

Swimming

Dieppe	Piscine de la Plage, boulevard Maréchal Foch Outdoor pool with paddling pools and water slides.	☎ 02 35 06 05 66
Le Havre	There are four swimming pools in Le Havre (listed below). Opening hours vary according to the school holidays.	
	Caucriauville, 181 rue Edouard Vaillant	☎ 02 35 47 14 41
	Cours de la République, 37 cours de la République	☎ 02 35 25 20 93
	Mare Rouge, 105 rue Florimont Laurent	☎ 02 35 46 37 87
	Edouard Thomas, rue Pierre Ternon	☎ 02 35 26 57 18
Neufchâtel	Piscine, route de Londinières Indoor pool with aqua gym and swimming classes available.	☎ 02 35 93 06 61
Rouen	There are four swimming pools in Rouen (listed below). Opening hours vary according to the school holidays.	
	Piscine Ile Lacroix Indoor and outdoor pools	☎ 02 35 07 94 70
	Piscine Diderot, 114 boulevard de l'Europe	☎ 02 35 63 59 14

Piscine du Boulingrin, 37 boulevard
de Verdun   ☎ 02 35 98 10 11

Piscine François Salomon, rue François
Couperin   ☎ 02 35 60 10 71

Yvetot   Piscine, rue de l'Etang   ☎ 02 35 95 03 22
Indoor pool, open every day except in July and August,
when it's closed on Mondays. Hours vary according to
school holidays.

Tennis

Dieppe   Dieppe Tennis, Gymnase Delaune, chemin
des Vertus   ☎ 02 35 84 00 04

Le Havre   Tennis, 24 rue Louis Leprevost ☎ 02 35 46 08 68

Neufchâtel   ASPTT, Salle Jaques Anquetil, route
de Rocade   ☎ 02 32 97 10 56
Indoor tennis Tuesdays and Thursdays at 9pm,
Wednesdays at 8pm.
Courses for children and adults.

rue du Bihorel   ☎ 02 35 93 27 92
Outdoor courts.

Rouen   Espace de la Petite Bouverie, 20 allée
Pierre de Coubertin   ☎ 02 35 59 62 01
Eight indoor courts and six outdoor courts.

Yvetot   Yvetot Tennis Club, rue Pierre de
Coubertin   ☎ 02 35 56 51 61
The courts are available to hire by the hour.

Tree Climbing

Fécamp   d'Arbre en Arbre, le Parc du Val aux Clercs, avenue
du Maréchal de Lattre de Tassigny ☎ 02 35 10 84 83
Adventure circuits up in the tree canopy with a network of
bridges, ladders and obstacles. Full safety equipment
provided for children and adults.

Les Loges   Etretat Aventures, Château du Bois des Loges,
1132 route de Gonneville   ☎ 06 60 67 86 11
💻 *www.etretat-aventures.fr*
Adventure courses up in the trees with a selection of routes
for different skills and ages. Full safety equipment provided.
Adults €20, children €10.

| Préaux | Arb'en Ciel, impasse de la Folletière | ☎ 02 35 02 10 00 |

www.arbreenciel-aventure.com
(just north-east of Rouen)
Tree top adventure with giant swings, suspended nets,
monkey bridges, rope ladders and many aerial runways.
Four courses of varying levels of difficulty, including one for
children. Full safety equipment provided. People over 1m
50 €18, people under 1m 50 €8.

Watersports

Jetskiing

| Le Tréport | Sun Jet Passion, Mairie du Tréport | ☎ 06 81 25 94 53 |

An introduction to jet skiing.

| Sotteville sous le Val | Circuit de l'Europe, rue du Village, les Bocquets | ☎ 02 35 78 72 17 |

www.circuit-europe.com
Jet skis for hire.

Rowing

| Dieppe | Club Nautique Dieppoise | ☎ 02 35 84 27 55 |

| Le Havre | Société Havraise de l'Aviron | ☎ 02 35 47 62 21 |

Rowing on the sea, Bassin de la Barre and Canal de
Tancarville. Five day courses available, three hours per day
Mondays to Fridays, plus courses in school holidays for
everyone over 11-years-old as long as they can swim.

| Rouen | Club Nautique et Athlétique de Rouen Aviron, 20 rue de l'Industrie, Ile Lacroix | ☎ 02 35 71 41 79 |

www.cnar.free.fr
An active club with its own fitness room specifically for
rowers.

Sailing

| Dieppe | Cercle de Voile, quai du Carénage | ☎ 02 35 84 32 99 |

Weekend and week long course for beginners to
professionals.

| Etretat | Voiles et Galets d'Etretat, 5 rue Dorus | ☎ 06 10 56 69 67 |

Boat hire, courses and sailing lessons.

| Le Havre | Base Nautique Gérard Hardouin, boulevard Clémenceau | ☎ 02 35 21 27 85 |

✉ *cnph@wanadoo.fr*
Competitions and courses from September to June.

Scuba Diving

Dieppe	Club des Sports Sous-marins Dieppois	☎ 02 35 82 77 40

Le Havre	Océan'eaux 76, Piscine de Montivilliers	☎ 02 35 41 10 18

There's also diving at the Base Nautique Gérard Hardouin and the Bassin du Commerce.

Rouen	Piscine Boulingrin, 37 boulevard de Verdun	☎ 02 35 71 41 82

Contact M. Boidart-Laurent.

Waterpolo

Le Havre	Club Nautique Havrais, Piscine du Cours, Cours de la République	☎ 02 35 25 20 93

🖥 *www.cnlehavre.net*
Training on Mondays, Wednesdays and Fridays dependent on age group.

Waterskiing

Cany Barville	Base de Loisirs du Lac de Caniel, route du Lac	☎ 02 35 97 40 55

🖥 *www.lacdecaniel.fr*
(near the coast, north of Yvetot)

Windsurfing

Cany Barville	Base de Loisirs du Lac de Caniel, route du Lac	☎ 02 35 97 40 55

🖥 *www.lacdecaniel.fr*
(near the coast, north of Yvetot)

Le Havre	Base Nautique Gérard Hardouin, boulevard Clémenceau	☎ 02 35 21 27 85

Courses and introductions, open all year.

Walking

General	Comité Départemental de la Randonnée Pédestre, 1 rue Danielle Casanova, Sotteville lès Rouen	☎ 02 35 62 02 49

avenue Verte
This is a 40km (25mi) walking route that runs from Dieppe to Forges les Eaux, following an old railway line.

It's open to everyone on foot, horseback, bike and rollerskates.

| Dieppe | MCJ, 8 rue du 19 Août 1942 | ☎ 02 35 84 16 92 |

Regular walks.

| Le Havre | Rand'Océan Le Havre | ☎ 02 35 55 57 90 |

💻 *www.randoceane.free.fr*
Walks in Upper and Lower Normandy, mountains and other locations.

| Neufchâtel | l'Escargot Brayon | ☎ 02 35 93 22 96 |

Walks organised all year.

| Rouen | AVF, 7 rue du Vieux Palais | ☎ 02 35 88 57 30 |

A walk lasting around two hours is organised every other Tuesday, departing at 2pm.

MJC Grieu, 3 rue de Genève   ☎ 02 35 71 94 76
Regular walks.

| Yvetot | Association des Randonneurs du Pays de Caux | ☎ 02 35 95 45 66 |

Contact M. Masselis for details of forthcoming walks.

Tourist Offices

| General | Comité Régional du Tourisme de Seine Maritime, 6 rue Couronné, Bihorel | ☎ 02 35 12 10 10 |

💻 *www.seine-maritime-tourisme.com*

| Dieppe | Quai du Carénage | ☎ 02 32 14 40 60 |

💻 *www.dieppetourisme.com*
Open Mondays to Saturdays 9am to noon and 2 to 6pm.

| Le Havre | 186 boulevard Clémenceau | ☎ 02 32 74 04 07 |

💻 *www.lehavretourisme.com*
(on the seafront near the beach)
Winter opening times: Mondays to Fridays 9am to 6pm, Saturdays 9am to 12.30pm and 2 to 6.30pm, Sundays and bank holidays 10am to 1pm. Summer: Mondays to Saturdays 9am to 7pm, Sundays and bank holidays 10am to 12.30pm and 2.30 to 6pm.

| Neufchâtel | 6 place Notre Dame | ☎ 02 35 93 22 96 |

✉ *otsi.neufchatel-en-bray@wanadoo.fr*
Open Tuesdays, Thursdays and Fridays 9am to 12.30pm and 1.30 to 5.30pm (till 5pm Tuesdays), Saturdays 9am to

noon and 2 to 5pm; hours may increase in the summer months.

Rouen	25 place de la Cathédrale	☎ 02 32 08 32 40

💻 *www.rouentourisme.com*
(in the city centre, right by the cathedral)
This tourist office has a back room full of free leaflets.
Winter opening: Mondays to Saturdays 9am to 12.30pm
and 1.30 to 5.30pm. Summer: Mondays to Saturdays 9am
to 7pm, Sundays 9am to 1.15pm and 2 to 7pm.

Yvetot	8 place Joffre	☎ 02 35 95 08 40

💻 *www.yvetot.fr*
Open October to March Tuesdays to Saturdays 10am to noon
and 2 to 5.30pm; April to September Mondays 2 to 6.30pm,
Tuesdays to Saturdays 10am to 12.30pm and 2 to 6.30pm.

Tradesmen

Architects & Project Managers

Yvetot	PH Cornillot, 12 rue du Château
Architect.	☎ 02 35 95 38 16

Builders

Dieppe	Rénovation Dieppoise, avenue des Canadiens	☎ 02 32 90 97 76
Le Havre	FPR, 107 quai Southampton
New houses and renovation.	☎ 02 35 22 49 41
Neufchâtel	Daniel Buat, 29 rue du Général de Gaulle	☎ 02 35 93 01 13
Rouen	BTCE, 12 rue St Gervais
General building including roofing, electrics and plumbing.	☎ 02 35 70 41 60
Yvetot	Tradi-Caux, rue Percée	☎ 02 35 56 46 76

These companies specialise in new construction.

Neufchâtel	Habitat Concept, 36 bis Grande Rue St Jacques	☎ 02 32 97 46 26
Yvetot	Pierres et Traditions Normandes, rue Pasteur	☎ 02 35 95 41 41

Carpenters

Many carpentry firms that make wooden windows and doors also work in aluminium.

Dieppe	Menuiserie Blondel, 32 rue St Rémy	☎ 02 35 40 26 43
Le Havre	Entreprise Fleury, 6 rue des Castors, Montivilliers	☎ 02 35 30 13 70
Neufchâtel	G. Depoix, rue du Maréchal Foch Gates, shutters, fences and doors.	☎ 02 35 94 09 20
Rouen	Delaunay Père et Fils, 28 rue Sapins 🖥 *www.membres.lycos.fr/menuiseriedelaunay*	☎ 02 35 70 48 69
Yvetot	Charpente Callais, la Mare des Villes, 1 route des Tots, Autretot General carpentry including new and renovation work.	☎ 02 35 95 63 44

Chimney Sweeps

Dieppe	Frank Leloup, 3 rue Paul Bazin, Neuville lès Dieppe	☎ 02 35 06 27 76
Le Havre	Delta T, 15 rue de la Commune, Montivilliers	☎ 02 35 20 20 93
Neufchâtel	René Desanglois, 33 boulevard Maréchal Joffre	☎ 02 35 93 20 46
Rouen	l'Ardoisier, 645 route de Gournay, St Jacques Parnetal Chimney sweep and roofer.	☎ 02 35 23 28 32
Yvetot	Picard, route de la Linerie, Baons le Comte	☎ 02 35 95 22 64

Electricians

Dieppe	Prosper Mohr, ZA Grèges, Grèges	☎ 02 35 04 40 35
Le Havre	Sté Telam, 29 rue Paul Doumer	☎ 02 35 41 33 87
Neufchâtel	Didier Lebon, 18 Hameau d'Autrecourt, Mesnières en Bray (just north of the town) Electrics and heating.	☎ 02 35 93 24 84

| Rouen | Euro'Elec, 14 route de Havre | ☎ 02 35 15 01 81 |

General electrics, alarms, heating and electric gates.

| Yvetot | GBB, 31 rue du Vieux Sainte Marie | ☎ 02 35 95 01 68 |

Electrics, plumbing and heating.

Loft Conversions

| Rouen | Afa Semi, 4 bis rue Eugène Boudin | ☎ 02 35 70 33 99 |

Painters & Decorators

Le Havre	GHP Peinture, 82 rue Stendhal	☎ 02 35 48 48 28
Neufchâtel	Picard Frères, rue Jossier	☎ 02 35 93 25 57
Rouen	Lecoq Peinture, 258 rue de Paris, Sotteville lès Rouen	☎ 02 35 03 21 57
Yvetot	Peinture Roussel, 7 avenue de l'Industrie, Sainte Marie des Champs	☎ 02 35 95 14 86

Plumbers

| Dieppe | Herpin, 7 avenue Normandie Sussex | ☎ 02 35 84 32 06 |

Plumbing, roofing, bathrooms and central heating.

| Le Havre | ETEC, 153 rue Verdun | ☎ 02 35 21 25 59 |

Plumbing, electrics and heating.

| Neufchâtel | Ph. Berdeaux, rue du Marous | ☎ 02 35 93 02 07 |

Plumbing and heating.

| Rouen | Saillard, 5 rue Ernemont | ☎ 02 35 71 39 40 |

Plumbing, heating and roofing.

| Yvetot | Caux-Thermic, rue Edmond Labbé | ☎ 02 32 70 11 00 |

Utilities

Electricity & Gas

| General | EDF/GDF Services Normandie Rouen, le Mesnil Roux, Barentin | ☎ 08 10 07 60 76 |

🖳 www.edf.fr
🖳 www.gazdefrance.com

EDF/GDF local offices are listed below. (These offices don't have direct telephone numbers.)

Barentin	Le Mesnil Roux
Dieppe	route du Vallon, Val Druel
Le Havre	624 rue Maréchal Joffre, Bolbec
Rouen	46 avenue de Bretagne

Heating Oil

Dieppe	Auchan Fioul, Centre Belvédère	☎ 02 32 90 52 00
Le Havre	Worex SNC, 6 impasse du Port V	☎ 0 810 62 17 17
Quincampoix	Cottard Fioul, 48 place Mairie (just north-east of Rouen)	☎ 02 35 34 72 87
Yvetot	Hoye-Gabriel, 17 rue du Clos des Parts	☎ 02 35 95 10 97

Water

The main water supply companies are listed below. If you aren't covered by one of these, your *mairie* will have details of your water supplier.

General	Communauté de l'Agglomération Havraise, place Hôtel de Ville, Le Havre	☎ 02 35 19 45 45
	Générale des Eaux *emergencies* route Escarpe, Dieppe 101 route Valmont, Fécamp 2 avenue Léon Blum, Grand Couronne 6 rue d'Alembert, Petit Quevilly, Rouen rue Edmond Labbé	☎ 08 10 33 31 11 ☎ 0 8 11 90 08 00
	Lyonnaise des Eaux *emergencies* 1 rue Jules Ferry, Bolbec 10 rue Gustave Nicole, Fécamp 37 rue Raymond Duflo, Maromme 67 rue St Vincent, Neufchâtel	☎ 08 10 88 48 84 ☎ 0 8 10 38 43 84 ☎ 0 8 10 38 43 84 ☎ 02 32 82 75 00 ☎ 02 35 93 05 53
	Sade (Service des Eaux), 1027 boulevard Normandie, Barentin	☎ 02 35 91 02 03

| | Société des Eaux de Picardie, 12 avenue Stade, Eu | ☎ 02 35 50 57 50 |

Wood

Le Tilleul	Pascal Goupil, route du Havre (north of Le Havre)	☎ 02 35 27 21 19
Montville	Bois et Paysage, 354 rue au Sel Ham du Bois Isambert (north of Rouen)	☎ 02 35 33 57 23
Rouen	Bruno Henry, 147 boulevard Jean Jaurès	☎ 02 35 07 64 66
Touffreville la Corbeline	Caux-Bois, route Val au Cesne (south of Yvetot)	☎ 02 35 95 15 79

INDEX

D

E

N

O

P

R

S

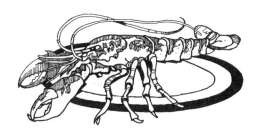

SURVIVAL BOOKS ON FRANCE

Buying a Home in France is essential reading for anyone planning to purchase property in France and is designed to guide you through the property jungle and make it a pleasant and enjoyable experience. Most importantly, it's packed with vital information to help you **avoid the sort of disasters that can turn your dream home into a nightmare!**

Living and Working in France is essential reading for anyone planning to live or work in France, including retirees, visitors, business people, migrants and students. It's packed with important and useful information designed to help you **avoid costly mistakes and save both time and money.**

The Alien's Guide to France provides an 'alternative' look at life in the 'Hexagon' and will help you to appreciate the peculiarities (in both senses) of its inhabitants.

The Best Places to Buy a Home in France is the most comprehensive and up-to-date homebuying guide to France, containing detailed regional guides to help you choose the ideal location for your home.

Lifelines books are essential guides to specific regions of France, containing everything you need to know about local life. Titles in the series currently include Dordogne/Lot, and Poitou-Charentes.

Renovating & Maintaining Your French Home is the ultimate guide to renovating and maintaining your dream home in France, including practical advice and time- and money-saving tips.

Foreigners in France: Triumphs & Disasters is a collection of real-life experiences of people who have emigrated to France, providing a 'warts and all' picture of everyday life in all parts of the country.

Order your copies today by phone, fax, mail or e-mail from: Survival Books, PO Box 146, Wetherby, West Yorks. LS23 6XZ, United Kingdom (☎/🖳 +44 (0)1937-843523, ✉ orders@ survivalbooks.net, 🖳 www.survivalbooks.net).

		Price (incl. p&p)			Total
Qty.	Title	UK	Europe	World	
	The Alien's Guide to Britain	£6.95	£8.95	£12.45	
	The Alien's Guide to France	£6.95	£8.95	£12.45	
	The Best Places to Buy a Home in France	£13.95	£15.95	£19.45	
	The Best Places to Buy a Home in Spain	£13.95	£15.95	£19.45	
	Buying a Home Abroad	£13.95	£15.95	£19.45	
	Buying a Home in Cyprus	£13.95	£15.95	£19.45	
	Buying a Home in Florida	£13.95	£15.95	£19.45	
	Buying a Home in France	£13.95	£15.95	£19.45	
	Buying a Home in Greece	£13.95	£15.95	£19.45	
	Buying a Home in Ireland	£11.95	£13.95	£17.45	
	Buying a Home in Italy	£13.95	£15.95	£19.45	
	Buying a Home in Portugal	£13.95	£15.95	£19.45	
	Buying a Home in South Africa	£13.95	£15.95	£19.45	
	Buying a Home in Spain	£13.95	£15.95	£19.45	
	Buying, Letting & Selling Property	£11.95	£13.95	£17.45	
	Foreigners in France: Triumphs & Disasters	£11.95	£13.95	£17.45	
	Foreigners in Spain: Triumphs & Disasters	£11.95	£13.95	£17.45	
	Costa Blanca Lifeline	£11.95	£13.95	£17.45	
	Costa del Sol Lifeline	£11.95	£13.95	£17.45	
	Dordogne/Lot Lifeline	£11.95	£13.95	£17.45	
	Poitou-Charentes Lifeline	£11.95	£13.95	£17.45	
	Living & Working Abroad	£14.95	£16.95	£20.45	
	Living & Working in America	£14.95	£16.95	£20.45	
	Living & Working in Australia	£14.95	£16.95	£20.45	
	Living & Working in Britain	£14.95	£16.95	£20.45	
	Living & Working in Canada	£16.95	£18.95	£22.45	
	Living & Working in the European Union	£16.95	£18.95	£22.45	
	Living & Working in the Far East	£16.95	£18.95	£22.45	
	Living & Working in France	£14.95	£16.95	£20.45	
Total carried forward (see over)					

ORDER FORM

Qty.	Title	Price (incl. p&p) UK	Europe	World	Total Total brought forward
	Living & Working in Germany	£16.95	£18.95	£22.45	
	L&W in the Gulf States & Saudi Arabia	£16.95	£18.95	£22.45	
	L&W in Holland, Belgium & Luxembourg	£14.95	£16.95	£20.45	
	Living & Working in Ireland	£14.95	£16.95	£20.45	
	Living & Working in Italy	£16.95	£18.95	£22.45	
	Living & Working in London	£13.95	£15.95	£19.45	
	Living & Working in New Zealand	£14.95	£16.95	£20.45	
	Living & Working in Spain	£14.95	£16.95	£20.45	
	Living & Working in Switzerland	£16.95	£18.95	£22.45	
	Making a Living in Spain	£13.95	£15.95	£19.45	
	Normandy Lifeline	£11.95	£13.95	£17.45	
	Renovating & Maintaining Your French Home	£16.95	£18.95	£22.45	
	Retiring Abroad	£14.95	£16.95	£20.45	
	Grand Total				

Order your copies today by phone, fax, post or email from: Survival Books, PO Box 3780, YEOVIL, BA21 5WX, United Kingdom (☎/▤ +44 (0)1935-700060, ✉ sales@ survivalbooks.net, 🖳 www.survivalbooks.net). If you aren't entirely satisfied, simply return them to us within 14 days for a full and unconditional refund.

I enclose a cheque for the grand total/Please charge my Amex/Delta/Maestro (Switch)/MasterCard/Visa card as follows. (delete as applicable)

Card No. _ _ _ _   _ _ _ _   _ _ _ _   _ _ _ _   Security Code* _ _ _

Expiry date _____   Issue number (Maestro/Switch only) _____

Signature _____   Tel. No. _____

NAME _____

ADDRESS _____

_____

_____

* The security code is the last three digits on the signature strip.